GLOBAL ECONOMIC STUDIES

CONDITIONS FOR FOREIGN INVESTMENTS IN INDIA

GLOBAL ECONOMIC STUDIES

Additional books in this series can be found on Nova's website at:

https://www.novapublishers.com/catalog/index.php?cPath=23_29&seriesp=
Global+Economic+Studies

Additional E-books in this series can be found on Nova's website at:

https://www.novapublishers.com/catalog/index.php?cPath=23_29&seriespe=
Global+Economic+Studies

GLOBAL ECONOMIC STUDIES

CONDITIONS FOR FOREIGN INVESTMENTS IN INDIA

BRENT M. CARDENAS
AND
ZACKARY R. BERG
EDITORS

Nova Science Publishers, Inc.

New York

For permission to use material from this book please contact us:
Telephone 631-231-7269; Fax 631-231-8175
Web Site: http://www.novapublishers.com

LIBRARY OF CONGRESS CATALOGING-IN-PUBLICATION DATA

Available upon request.
ISBN: 978-1-60456-862-2

Published by Nova Science Publishers, Inc. † New York

CONTENTS

Preface		**vii**
Chapter 1	Challenges to Sustained Economic Growth in India *Jim Saxton*	**1**
Chapter 2	Competitive Conditions for Foreign Direct Investment in India *Office of Industries, U.S. International Trade Commission*	**9**
Chapter 3	The Environment for Agricultural and Agribusiness Investment in India *Maurice Landes*	**121**
Chapter 4	Openness to Foreign Investment - 2009 Investment Climate Statement - India *Bureau of Economic, Energy and Business Affairs*	**163**
Index		**183**

PREFACE

Net foreign direct investment (FDI) flows into India reached $15.7 billion in India's 2006-07 fiscal year, more than triple the $4.7 billion recorded during 2005-06, with the largest share of FDI flows from Mauritius, followed by the United States and the United Kingdom. This book examines FDI in India, in the context of the Indian economic and regulatory environment. Presented are FDI trends in India, by country and by industry, using official government data from India, the United States, and international organizations. Additionally, this book discusses specific investment activities of multinational companies in India, representing a wide range of countries and industries. This book consists of public documents which have been located, gathered, combined, reformatted, and enhanced with a subject index, selectively edited and bound to provide easy access.

Chapter 1 - After India initiated comprehensive reforms in 1991, economic growth accelerated. In 2006, India's real GDP grew by 9.2 percent.

This research report (1) reviews India's economic reforms; (2) compares India's economy with a peer group of large developing economies in Asia – the People's Republic of China, Indonesia, Malaysia, the Philippines, and Thailand – that compete with India both in export markets and for inward foreign direct investment; and (3) assesses the challenges that India must overcome to sustain rapid economic growth and reduce poverty over the long term. If India meets these challenges, it will become a far more important trade and investment partner for the United States.

Chapter 2 - Net foreign direct investment (FDI) flows into India reached $15.7 billion in India's 2006–07 fiscal year, more than triple the $4.7 billion recorded during 2005–06, with the largest share of FDI flows from Mauritius, followed by the United States and the United Kingdom. This study examines FDI in India, in the context of the Indian economic and regulatory environment. We present FDI trends in India, by country and by industry, using official government data from India, the United States, and international organizations. To supplement the official data, the study also discusses specific investment activities of multinational companies in India, representing a wide range of countries and industries. To illustrate the driving forces behind these trends, the study also discusses the investment climate in India, Indian government incentives to foreign investors, particularly Special Economic Zones, the Indian regulatory environment as it affects investment, and the effect of India's global, regional, and bilateral trade agreements on investment from the United States and other countries. Finally, the study presents two case studies. The first examines global

FDI in India's automobile industry. The second analyzes the effects of India's 2005 Patent Law on FDI in the pharmaceutical industry.

Chapter 3 - Despite strong overall economic growth and strengthening food demand, investment in Indian agriculture and agribusiness has remained sluggish, and growth in farm output has slowed, since the early 1990s. An array of policies and regulations affecting agricultural production, marketing, and food processing—along with weak infrastructure and a lack of market services—have discouraged private investment by farmers and large, vertically integrated agribusinesses. The policy environment has grown more investor friendly since the late 1990s and private investment appears to be responding, but significant barriers remain and the pace of future reforms remains uncertain.

Chapter 4 - India continues controlling foreign investment with limits on equity and voting rights, mandatory government approvals, and capital controls. Since 1991, as it has slowly implemented a program of economic reform, the GOI has gradually relaxed many of these constraints. Nonetheless, a complex array of restrictions remains, along with an undercurrent of resentment towards foreign investment from some quarters. Foreign direct investment (FDI) is still prohibited in some sectors or sub-sectors.

In: Conditions for Foreign Direct Investment in India
Ed: Brent M. Cardenas and Zackary R. Berg

ISBN: 978-1-60456-862-2

Chapter 1

CHALLENGES TO SUSTAINED ECONOMIC GROWTH IN INDIA*

Jim Saxton
Joint Economic Committee

After India initiated comprehensive reforms in 1991, economic growth accelerated. In 2006, India's real GDP grew by 9.2 percent.

This research report (1) reviews India's economic reforms; (2) compares India's economy with a peer group of large developing economies in Asia – the People's Republic of China, Indonesia, Malaysia, the Philippines, and Thailand – that compete with India both in export markets and for inward foreign direct investment; and (3) assesses the challenges that India must overcome to sustain rapid economic growth and reduce poverty over the long term. If India meets these challenges, it will become a far more important trade and investment partner for the United States.

ECONOMIC REFORM

From 1947 to 1984, India had a development policy of import substitution industrialization. This policy promoted domestic manufacturing by discouraging imports through international trade and investment barriers, domestic regulations, and subsidies. To implement this policy, India instituted Soviet-style central planning, established many government-owned enterprises (GOEs), and granted monopolies to GOEs in energy, telecommunications, and transportation.

Unlike China, India retained a significant private sector. To enforce compliance with its five- year economic plans, India instituted comprehensive controls, known as the *license raj* (regime). Under the license raj, both private firms and GOEs needed government approval to (1) establish new facilities, (2) expand production capacity, (3) launch new products, or (4)

* This is an edited, reformatted and augmented version of a U. S. Congress publication dated May 2007.

close or relocate existing facilities. India also limited the manufacturing of certain goods to small firms.

This policy produced anemic economic growth. In 1984, Prime Minister Rajiv Gandhi began economic reform by abolishing the licensing system for twenty-five industries and substantially liberalizing it for others.

An economic crisis prompted Prime Minister Narasimha Rao to initiate sweeping reforms in 1991. India progressively abolished licensing for all industries except atomic energy, defense equipment, alcoholic beverages, and tobacco. India slashed its average applied import tariff rate from 79.2 percent in 1991 to 16.0 percent in 2005, phased-out quantitative restrictions on almost all imports by 2001, and eased restrictions on foreign investment.

Since 1991, the leaders of India's two major parties, the Bharatiya Janata Party (BJP) and the Congress Party, have supported further liberalization. Given India's fractious multiparty parliamentary system, opposition from minor parties has forced both BJP- and Congress-led governments to delay or weaken proposed reforms during the last fifteen years. While the direction of economic policy is clear, the liberalization has been slower than many policymakers would like.

Bifurcated Economy

India is the world's second most populous country. In contrast to China, India's working age population (ages 15 to 64) is projected to grow by 53.9 percent from 691 million in 2005 to 1.064 billion in 2050.

India favored developing internationally competitive colleges, universities, and technical institutes for a limited number of students. Because of India's linguistic diversity, English remained the preferred language of instruction. Hence, India developed a large pool of educated, highly skilled, English-speaking managerial, professional, and technical workers compared with the peer group.

In contrast, competing Asian economies favored expanding the availability of primary education to all children. Consequently, India's adult literacy rate of 61.0 percent compares unfavorably with literacy rates of the peer group.

During the last two decades, the peer group followed a development strategy of export promotion industrialization that encouraged export- oriented labor-intensive manufacturing of apparel, footwear, sporting goods, and toys as well as final assembly of consumer electronics.

In contrast, India encouraged knowledge- intensive business services and software industries and capital-intensive manufacturing of capital goods and high-tech goods to exploit its comparative advantage in educated, highly skilled, English-speaking workers. This strategy created a developed sector of India's economy that supports 190 million Indians in middle-class lifestyles.

Another sector of India's economy is underdeveloped. In the peer group, the economic importance of agriculture declined as workers left the countryside and took more productive, better paying jobs in labor-intensive manufacturing and final assembly in cities. This transition has been slow in India.

Agriculture still accounted for 18.4 percent of India's GDP in 2006 and 54.2 percent of India's total employment in 2004, both higher than competing Asian economies.

Manufacturing accounted for only 15.4 percent of India's GDP in 2006, lower than competing Asian economies.

As a result, India suffers from far more extreme poverty than the peer group. In 2003, 340 million Indians or 30.7 percent of India's population each lived on less than $1 per day.

CHALLENGES TO LONG-TERM GROWTH

India must create millions of new jobs for unskilled and semi-skilled workers that are currently unemployed or underemployed in subsistence agriculture. Although employment in India's knowledge-intensive and capital-intensive industries is soaring, these jobs generally require a higher education or specialized skills. In competing Asian economies, export-oriented labor-intensive manufacturing and final assembly created the first urban jobs for unskilled and semi-skilled workers moving from farms to the cities. A number of policies have contributed to the relatively slow growth of labor-intensive manufacturing and final assembly in India.

(A) Inadequate infrastructure

(1) Electricity

Three central GOEs generate most of India's electricity, while state electricity boards (SEBs) distribute electricity. State policymakers require these boards to provide electricity selectively to some farms and lower caste households for free or at subsidized prices. This encourages other households to steal up to 50 percent of the electricity generated through illegal connections to the grid.

Subsidized or stolen electricity costs state governments the equivalent of 2.5 percent of India's GDP a year. To offset these losses, state electricity boards overcharge industrial firms. On average, Indian manufacturers pay 60 percent more for electricity than their Southeast Asian competitors and 100 percent more than their U.S. competitors. The central government has recently required SEBs to reduce their subsidies to agricultural and household customers gradually and limit the maximum rate differential among various customers to no more than 20 percent by 2011.

Electricity demand exceeds supply by 7 percent on average and by 12 percent at peak usage. Chronic shortages cause frequent outages. Manufacturers lose power about once every two days, seven times more frequently than in China. Outages reduce the output of Indian manufacturers by 8.4 percent, four times the output loss rate in China.

The Investment Commission of India (ICI) estimated that India must spend $200 billion (equal to 25.7 percent of 2005 GDP) over the next seven years to build 90 gigawatts of generating capacity. India needs foreign direct investment (FDI) to supplement central government plans to increase generating capacity by 67 gigawatts. The inability of cash-strapped SEBs to guarantee payments to private generators and the bitter controversy over FDI by three U.S. firms in a large generation project near Dabhol during the 1990s discouraged large-scale FDI in electricity.

(2) Transportation

India's airports, ports, railways, and roads are grossly inadequate.

Inefficient ports slow turnaround time to 3.5 days.[1] Manufacturers pay about 35 percent more to ship an identical cargo to the United States from India than from China. The ICI reported that India must spend $19 billion (equal to 2.5 percent of 2005 GDP) over the next nine years on port facilities to increase efficiency.

The ICI estimated that India must spend $15 billion (equal to 2.1 percent of 2005 GDP) over the next five years on civil aviation to alleviate congestion. After years of delay, India has finally begun the expansion of the existing airports in

Delhi and Mumbai and the construction of new airports in Hyderabad and Bangalore in 2005.

Policymakers require a central GOE, Indian Railways, to charge substantially below market fares for passengers. To recoup these losses, Indian Railways charges firms above market freight rates. Extremely high rail costs have caused manufacturers to shift the bulk of their domestic freight to trucks. Unfortunately, India's road system cannot accommodate this demand.

The ICI estimated that India must spend $60 billion (equal to 8.2 percent of 2005 GDP) over the next five years to improve its roadways. India is currently building two major multi-lane highway projects, the 5,864 km Golden Quadrilateral project and the 7,300 km North-South and East-West corridor project. However, India's expenditures on rail and road transportation compare unfavorably with the peer group.

(B) Workforce Quality

Soaring demand for English-speaking managerial, professional, and technical workers from India's booming knowledge-intensive and capital-intensive industries is now outstripping its previously plentiful supply. Skilled labor shortages have ignited a bidding war. Some firms are recruiting from the United States, while others are outsourcing jobs to subsidiaries or contractors in the United States.

Widespread adult illiteracy prevents many Indian workers from securing jobs in knowledge- intensive and capital-intensive industries. India is expanding the access of its children to primary education. As a result, the literacy rate among Indians ages 15 to 24 has increased to 76.7 percent in 2004. Nevertheless, India's primary school enrollment and young adult literacy rates still compare unfavorably with the peer group.

(C) Incomplete Economic Reforms

(1) Remnants of license Raj

In 2006, the World Bank found that India ranked 134th of 175 economies as an overall place to do business. Among the peer group, only Indonesia fared worse. India's ranking in opening new facilities, paying taxes, trading across borders, enforcing contracts, and closing a bankrupt business were lower than the peer group.

(2) Rigid labor market

India's rigid labor laws are a major impediment to labor-intensive manufacturing. These laws slow the transition of the 93.6 percent of Indian workers who are employed in agriculture or the informal urban sector into generally higher productivity jobs in the formal urban sector.[2]

India's labor laws apply to employers with ten or more workers, become more stringent as the number of employees increase, encourage unionization, and generally favor workers over employers. Any seven workers can form a union and bargain collectively with their employer. Government officials may intervene in collective bargaining on the behalf of "general economic interests." Firms with 100 or more employees need state government permission, which is almost never given, to fire or lay-off permanent employees.

To gain flexibility, firms engage in avoidance and evasion behaviors that are inefficient and reduce the potential size of India's economy. For example, small firms avoid labor regulation by limiting their output and hiring nine or fewer workers. An estimated 57 percent of medium-size firms with ten to ninety-nine workers do not register to evade labor laws. Firms invest in costly laborsaving equipment and use temporary workers whenever possible to avoid hiring permanent workers. As a result, the share of temporary workers increased from 12 percent of all manufacturing employment in 1990 to 23 percent in 2002.

(3) Inefficient government-dominated financial system

India's central government-controlled financial system is highly inefficient in channeling India's saving into productive investment. India has an impressive saving rate of 32.5 percent of GDP, but only one-half of household saving is channeled through banks and other financial institutions. One-third of household saving is invested in housing, and most of the remainder is invested in 44 million low-productivity micro-enterprises.

Indians bought $10 billion of gold in 2005. Over time, Indians have accumulated over 15,000 tons of gold that are worth $272 billion. Because banks cannot lend gold bars and jewelry, a large portion of Indian savings cannot be intermediated into economically productive investments through banks and other financial institutions. This reduces the potential size of India's economy.

Government-owned banks control more than 74 percent of India's banking assets. India limits foreign direct investment to 74 percent in private banks, 20 percent in government-owned banks, and 26 percent in insurers.

India strictly regulates asset allocation. Because of these policies, the central and state governments and their government-owned enterprises absorb 70 percent of all credit from banks and other financial institutions.

Excessive regulations have stunted India's corporate debt and equity markets as external financing sources for large private Indian firms. Consequently, these firms must rely on bank loans to a larger extent than similar firms elsewhere, crowding out small- and medium-size firms.

The McKinsey Global Institute reported that reforming India's financial system would increase the current size of India's economy by $47.3 billion and would boost India's potential real GDP growth rate to 9.4 percent a year over the next decade.

(4) International trade and investment liberalization

In 2007, India reduced its peak import tariff rate on most non-agricultural goods to 10 percent. Nevertheless, import tariff rates on agricultural goods remain extremely high. India also retains significant non-tariff trade barriers including cumbersome customs procedures and weak enforcement of copyright protection for recordings and software.

India's international trade flows do not compare favorably with competing Asian economies. India's two-way goods trade as a percent of GDP was only 32.0 percent in 2005, lowest among the peer group. Despite its size, India accounted for only 1.3 percent of world goods exports and 1.6 percent of world goods imports in 2005.

Likewise, India trailed competing Asian economies in attracting foreign direct investment. From 1991 to 2005, India's average annual FDI inflows were equivalent to 0.7 percent of GDP. During the same period, China's average annual FDI inflows were equivalent to 3.6 percent of GDP. As a result, India accumulated a stock of FDI equivalent to 5.8 percent of GDP in 2005, the lowest among the peer group.

(D) Corruption

India ranked 70th of 163 countries in the *2006 Corruption Perceptions Index* compiled by Transparency International, tied with China. In *The World Bank Investment Climate Survey*, 38.1 percent of Indian firms cited corruption as a major obstacle to economic growth.

(E) Chronic Large Fiscal Deficits

In fiscal year 2006-07, the consolidated deficit for both the central and state governments was 6.3 percent of GDP. The relatively high fiscal deficits compared with the peer group limit the ability of central and state policymakers to fund education and necessary investments in infrastructure. High fiscal deficits may also deter some central policymakers from deregulating financial services.

Conclusion

Although its economy is booming, India must confront a number of challenges to sustain rapid economic growth over the long term. India's knowledge-intensive and capital-intensive industries cannot provide the millions of jobs that India's rapidly growing workforce will need in the future. India should encourage labor-intensive manufacturing to create jobs for these workers.

India must overcome a number of challenges to foster labor-intensive manufacturing and broaden economic prosperity. India's electricity supply is costly and undependable, and its transportation system is woefully inadequate. High adult illiteracy prevents many workers from benefiting from India's boom. Government-dominated banks and financial institutions are inefficient and allocate too much of India's saving based on political criteria. While India has liberalized its international trade and investment regime since 1991, India's economy is still too insulated from international competition. Corruption remains widespread.

Since 1991, the Indian people have supported an economic transformation from socialism toward capitalism through their democratic institutions. If central and state policymakers exercise leadership and address these remaining challenges, India will become a far more important trade and investment partner to the United States in the future than India has been in past decades.

End Notes

[1] Turnaround time is less than 6 hours in both Hong Kong and Singapore.

[2] Workers in the formal urban sector receive higher real wages than workers in the rural and informal urban sectors. Moreover, workers in the formal urban sector have old-age pension and health insurance benefits that are unavailable to workers in the rural and informal urban sectors.

In: Conditions for Foreign Direct Investment in India
Ed: Brent M. Cardenas and Zackary R. Berg
ISBN: 978-1-60456-862-2

Chapter 2

COMPETITIVE CONDITIONS FOR FOREIGN DIRECT INVESTMENT IN INDIA*

U.S. International Trade Commission

ABSTRACT

Net foreign direct investment (FDI) flows into India reached $15.7 billion in India's 2006–07 fiscal year, more than triple the $4.7 billion recorded during 2005–06, with the largest share of FDI flows from Mauritius, followed by the United States and the United Kingdom. This study examines FDI in India, in the context of the Indian economic and regulatory environment. We present FDI trends in India, by country and by industry, using official government data from India, the United States, and international organizations. To supplement the official data, the study also discusses specific investment activities of multinational companies in India, representing a wide range of countries and industries. To illustrate the driving forces behind these trends, the study also discusses the investment climate in India, Indian government incentives to foreign investors, particularly Special Economic Zones, the Indian regulatory environment as it affects investment, and the effect of India's global, regional, and bilateral trade agreements on investment from the United States and other countries. Finally, the study presents two case studies. The first examines global FDI in India's automobile industry. The second analyzes the effects of India's 2005 Patent Law on FDI in the pharmaceutical industry.

EXECUTIVE SUMMARY

India's recent liberalization of its foreign investment regulations has generated strong interest by foreign investors, turning India into one of the fastest growing destinations for global foreign direct investment (FDI) inflows. Foreign firms are setting up joint ventures and

* This is an edited, reformatted and augmented version of a U. S. International Trade Commission publication dated July 2007.

wholly owned enterprises in services such as computer software, telecommunications, financial services, and tourism, and manufactured goods including transportation equipment, chemicals, pharmaceuticals, and food processing. This study examines FDI flows into India, by country and by industry, supplemented by a discussion of major foreign acquisitions of Indian companies, and greenfield FDI by foreign firms. The study also examines India's investment environment, special economic zones, investment-related regulations and international agreements. Two chapters present case studies of FDI in India's automotive industry, and the effect of the 2005 Patent Law changes on FDI in the pharmaceutical industry. Principal findings regarding FDI in India include:

- Net FDI in India was valued at $4.7 billion in the 2005–06 Indian fiscal year, and more than tripled, to $15.7 billion, in the 2006–07 fiscal year. Almost one-half of all FDI is invested in the Mumbai and New Delhi regions.
- By country, the largest investors in India are Mauritius, the United States, and the United Kingdom. Investors based in many countries have taken advantage of the India-Mauritius bilateral tax treaty to set up holding companies in Mauritius which subsequently invest in India, thus reducing their tax obligations. By industry, the largest destinations for FDI are electrical equipment (including computer software and electronics), services, telecommunications, and transportation.
- India offers both positive and negative incentives for foreign investors. Positives include strong economic growth leading to increased buying power by the middle class, low wages compared to OECD countries, and an educated work force. Negatives include inadequate infrastructure, rising salaries for key jobs, and bureaucratic delays in obtaining necessary permits and licenses.
- India's Special Economic Zones (SEZs) attract foreign investment by providing tax incentives, assistance with bureaucratic and administrative problems, and access to reliable infrastructure. Investment-related regulations outside the SEZs have been increasingly liberalized since 1991, with important improvements in intellectual property regulation.
- U.S., European, and Japanese automakers and auto component manufacturers all have significant investments in India. Most FDI in the automotive industry has been focused on sales to the domestic market, but more foreign investors are now producing autos and components in India for export.
- India's 2005 changes to its Patent Law have motivated substantial new FDI in the pharmaceutical industry, but global pharmaceutical firms are waiting to see how the new law is interpreted before further expanding product patenting and commercialization activities in India.

1. INTRODUCTION

Purpose and Scope

India is the second largest country in the world, with a population of over 1 billion people. As a developing country, India's economy is characterized by wage rates that are significantly lower than those in most developed countries. These two traits combine to make India a natural destination for foreign direct investment (FDI). Until recently, however, India has attracted only a small share of global FDI, primarily due to government restrictions on foreign involvement in the economy. But beginning in 1991 and accelerating rapidly since 2000, India has liberalized its investment regulations and actively encouraged new foreign investment, a sharp reversal from decades of discouraging economic integration with the global economy.

Global investors have responded with enthusiasm. Total net foreign investment inflows were $17.2 billion in 2005–06, of which net FDI was valued at $4.7 billion in 2005–06.[1] Net FDI inflows for the 2006–07 fiscal year weremore than tripled to $15.7 billion.[2] India received cumulative net FDI inflows of $48.2 billion between August 1991 and December 2006.[3]

The remainder of this chapter gives an overview of FDI activity in India, particularly in the service sector (the largest target for FDI in India to date), and discusses the data used in the study. The study then closely examines trends related to FDI in India, including the principal country sources and industry destinations of this capital, and the regional destinations of FDI within the country. We also look at major multinational corporations invested in India today, and the role of U.S. investors. The study goes on to examine India's economic climate for FDI, its regulatory environment, the incentives available to foreign investors through Special Economic Zones (SEZs), and the effect of India's international economic agreements on inbound FDI trends. We present two case studies of industries that hold special interest for foreign investors. The first examines FDI in India's passenger vehicle and components industry, illustrating global investors' active involvement in India's manufacturing sector. The second analyzes the effects of India's 2005 Patent Law on FDI in the Indian pharmaceuticals industry.

Overview of FDI Activity in India

Country Sources of FBI

Foreign investors have begun to take a more active role in the Indian economy in recent years. By country, the largest direct investor in India is Mauritius, largely because of the India-Mauritius double-taxation treaty.[4] Firms based in Mauritius invested $16.0 billion in India between 1991 and 2006, equal to 39 percent of total FDI inflows. The second largest investor in India is the United States, with total capital flows of $5.6 billion during the 1991–2006 period, followed by the United Kingdom, the Netherlands, and Japan.[5] Between 1991 and 2005, the United States ranked first in terms of total FDI approvals, which amounted to $67.8 billion (24 percent of total FDI approvals).[6] The largest shares of U.S. investment are directed to the fuels, telecommunications, electrical equipment, food processing, and services sectors.[7]

The warming of the political and economic relationship between the United States and India is likely to further encourage U.S. investment there. An important example of the closer relationship is the U.S.-India Civil Nuclear Cooperation Initiative, passed into U.S. law in December 2006.[8] The United States has also reduced the use of export controls on exports to India. As of February 2007, only 1 percent of U.S. exports to India required a license, down from 24 percent in 1999 and 90 percent in previous years. In recognition of the improved relationship, the U.S. Department of Commerce is in the process of establishing its new "Trusted Customer" program, set to begin in 2007 with India as the first partner country. The program is expected to encourage repeat exports of U.S. goods to India.[9] This will promote additional FDI by U.S. firms in India, as the Trusted Customer program will make it easier for U.S.-based multinational corporations (MNCs) to ship goods to their affiliates in India for manufacturing or additional processing.

FBI in India's Service Sector

The service sector has been the primary destination of FDI in India since 1991. As identified by India's Ministry of Commerce & Industry, the service sector accounted for 17 percent of total FDI inflows to India between August 1991 and December 2006. Another 17 percent of FDI inflows is invested in the telecommunications and transportation industries, which generally involve both equipment and services.[10] From the mid-1990s, India has been an important destination for investment in offshoring services such as software, call centers, and other business process outsourcing (BPO).[11] According to one recent estimate, India's information technology (IT) offshoring market will be valued in excess of $200 billion by 2008, with more than one-fourth of the world IT offshoring market centered in India. Revenue from offshore services is predicted to equal 7 percent of India's GDP by 2008, and account for one-third of foreign exchange flows into the country.[12] This flow of capital relies on India's well-educated, English-speaking, and relatively low-paid workers.[13] India has offered substantial incentives to attract FDI in IT and BPO-related services offshoring, up to an estimated $6,000 per full-time equivalent worker (FTE) in the IT services area, and $2,000 per FTE in the BPO area.[14]

According to some reports, however, increasing competition is making it more difficult for Indian firms to attract and keep BPO employees with the necessary skills, leading to increasing wages. IBM, for example, increased its Indian staff by 36 percent in 2006, to 53,000 workers, and has plans to invest a further $6 billion in India over the next 3 years, for an expected total of 120,000 employees in the country by 2008.[15] Hiring difficulties are among the factors that have encouraged some India-based BPO firms to engage in outbound FDI by establishing facilities outside of India. Infosys Technologies, for instance, reportedly has plans to employ 6,000 workers in China, and Satyam Computer Services has 500 people based in China, with more to come, along with 2,500 workers each in Malaysia, Egypt, and Saudi Arabia.[16]

Most Indian industries have been fully opened to FDI, with foreigners permitted to own up to 100 percent of equity in Indian companies. However, India continues to limit FDI in a number of industries by enforcing overall caps on total foreign-owned equity shares, with the caps changing as India's liberalization process continues. Permitted equity limits for foreign investors vary for different industries. The level of FDI activity following each change in regulations testifies to foreign investors' interest in the Indian market, particularly in key service sectors. Equity limits for foreign investment in most types of telecommunications companies were raised from 49 percent to 74 percent in November 2005, resulting in a wave of new FDI primarily focused on India's cellular telecommunications industry. Cumulative FDI inflows in telecommunications from August 1991 to December 2006 were $3.9 billion, and annual inflows jumped from $588 million in 2004–05 to $3.0 billion in 2005–06.[17] The value of reported mergers and acquisitions (M&A) in telecommunications rose from $105 million in 2003 to $1.2 billion in 2004, $4.1 billion in 2006, and $11.4 billion in just the first 3 months of 2007, primarily on the strength of Vodafone Group's $11.1 billion acquisition of Hutchison Essar Telecom, which was approved in April 2007.[18]

India's stock exchanges have also been recently opened to foreign investment, with a 26 percent foreign equity cap, limited to 5 percent for any single foreign investor. Foreign investors reached the 26 percent cap in the National Stock Exchange of India in March 2007. As of the same date, the Singapore Exchange and Deutsche Borse each controlled 5 percent of the Bombay Stock Exchange.[19]

Other industries which maintain significant barriers to FDI include the insurance sector and newspaper publishing, where foreign equity is limited to 26 percent, and the retail sector, where foreign firms are permitted to invest up to 51 percent equity, but only in single-brand distribution outlets.[20] Foreign investors have also expressed interest in investing in these sectors, as India's government debates whether to lift the limits. In the retail sector, Wal-Mart announced a joint venture with India-based Bharti in November 2006, under which Bharti would invest $2.5 billion in a new chain of retail stores that would be 100 percent owned by the Indian firm. Wal-Mart would provide logistics and wholesale supply services through a 50:50 joint venture with Bharti. The deal is widely seen as a way for Wal-Mart to enter the growing Indian retail market despite the FDI restrictions.[21]

In the insurance industry, foreign investment was first permitted in 2000, with the lifting of the Indian state-owned insurance company's monopoly, allowing competition from both domestic and foreign-owned private firms. During the 2000–01 fiscal year, 16 privately owned firms entered the Indian market, most as 26 percent joint ventures between globally competitive foreign insurers and Indian firms.[22] Amid expectations that the government would raise the foreign equity limit to 49 percent, at least six insurance joint ventures concluded agreements that would allow the foreign partner to raise its share to that level once government regulations have changed, but as of April 2007, the equity limit for foreign insurance investors remains at 26 percent.[23]

Data

The data for this study were drawn from a variety of sources. Data for FDI stocks and flows into India come primarily from official Indian government sources, and reflect actual FDI from cross-border equity flows, where available. These data are supplemented by U.S. data where additional detail on U.S.-India FDI flows is required. Official data are compiled on a balance of payments (BOP) basis, and reflects the amount of capital that crosses borders during a given calendar or fiscal year.[24] These data are the most comprehensive available, but they specifically exclude details on individual company transactions to safeguard the confidentiality of the reporting companies. Unless otherwise specified, data are presented for the 5 year time period from 2002 through 2006.

To supplement the official equity flows data, the study uses information from separate commercial databases reflecting M&A and greenfield FDI,[25] and occasionally uses Indian government data on FDI approvals. These data lend additional insight into the industry and country sources of FDI into India. The databases are compiled from press reports. Thus, while they cover the majority of M&A or greenfield FDI transactions, it is not possible to be sure that data on all transactions have been included, or that transactions have not been included more than once. In particular, many reported transactions do not include data for the value of the transaction. In addition, data compiled from the databases are not directly comparable to the official FDI data. Reported transaction values in the databases do not account for how much of the capital is transferred in a given calendar year or fiscal year, or for noncash transactions such as equity swaps that may not appear in official BOP statistics. For these reasons, data compiled from these databases should be considered illustrative, rather than comprehensive. Similarly, FDI approvals are only an indicator of companies' intentions. Many approved projects are never realized, or are significantly modified between approval and implementation.

Information is also drawn from publicly available reports from international financial institutions, country governments, commercial sources, press reports, and interviews with industry representatives.

2. FDI in India

Overview of FDI Flows

Foreign direct investment (FDI) capital flows into India have increased dramatically since 1991, when India's opened it economy to FDI, and inflows have accelerated since 2000. FDI inflows to India reached $11.1 billion in calendar year 2006 (figure 2-1), almost double the 2005 figure, and are expected to continue increasing in 2007. The Indian government has announced a target of $25 billion in new FDI inflows for the 2007–08 fiscal year.[26] Global FDI has experienced a corresponding resurgence since 2004, recording year-on-year increases of 29 percent in 2005 and 27 percent in 2004, after declining for several years in the early 2000s.[27] Consistent with the global pattern, FDI inflows into India declined between 2001 and 2003, before experiencing a resurgence that surpassed average global growth, with year-on-year increases of 45 and 72 percent, respectively, in fiscal years 2004–05 and 2005–06.[28]

Preliminary data for inward FDI[29] for the 2006–07 fiscal year show FDI inflows of $15.7 billion, representing an increase of 184 percent, in rupee terms, over the preceding fiscal year.[30] While the percentage increase is large compared to the global average, the value of inward FDI flows to India relative to all developing countries remains small (figure 2-2). However, FDI inflows to India surpassed inflows to South Korea in 2006, making India the fourth largest destination for FDI in Asia, behind China, Hong Kong,and Singapore.[31]

New equity capital flows take one of two forms: M&A and greenfield investment. In a merger or acquisition, one firm acquires an equity stake in an existing foreign firm. Greenfield FDI takes place as the establishment of a new overseas affiliate by a parent company. India does not provide FDI statistics that break out M&A vs. greenfield FDI. For most developing countries, however, the greenfield route is more prominent, as there are fewer existing companies available to acquire, as compared with developed countries. As noted in chapter 1, this study uses private databases to illustrate the trends related to FDI through both routes, but data obtained from those databases is not consistent with official FDI inflows data. In fact, the figures reported for total investment through greenfield FDI and M&A investment are considerably larger than the values for total FDI inflows reported by the government of India for FDI through the two routes combined. For greenfield FDI, OCO Consulting reports a total of $55.5 billion invested in India in 2006, while Bureau van Dijk reports M&A transactions of $2.8 billion.[32] Together, these are far above India's total reported FDI inflows of $11.1 billion.

There are several possible reasons for the disparities in these data. First, the greenfield projects listed are approved or announced by companies, but some of them are never realized. Second, many greenfield and M&A projects take more than one year to complete. Official FDI statistics include only the actual amount of capital invested in each year, rather than the project total. Finally, many of the projects listed in the commercial databases are not fully funded by the overseas investor. For joint ventures between Indian and foreign firms, for example, the databases list the entire value of the project, even if a share of the capital comes from an Indian entity and would thus not be included as FDI inflows. The official FDI figures contain only the amount of capital invested from abroad, while the greenfield and M&A data include the total value of the project.

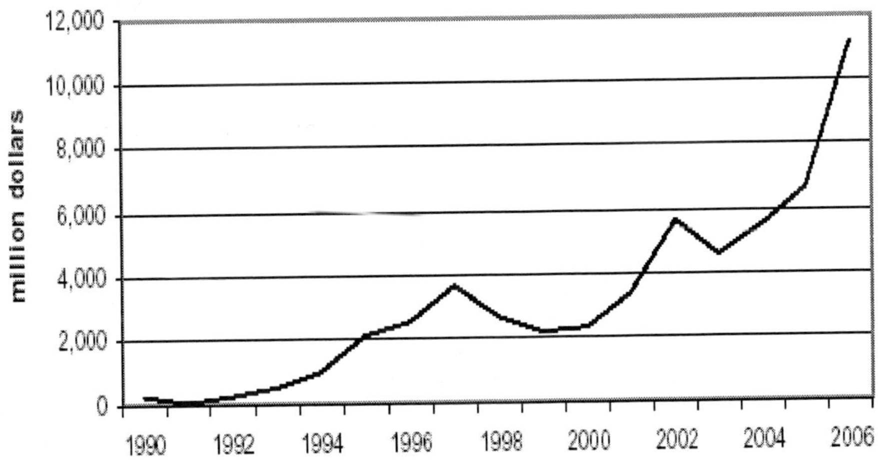

Source: UNCTAD, Country Fact Sheet, UNCTAD online database and Government of India, Ministry of Commerce & Industry, Department of Industrial Policy and Promotion, FDI Statistics 2006.

Figure 2-1. FDI inflows to India, 1990–2006

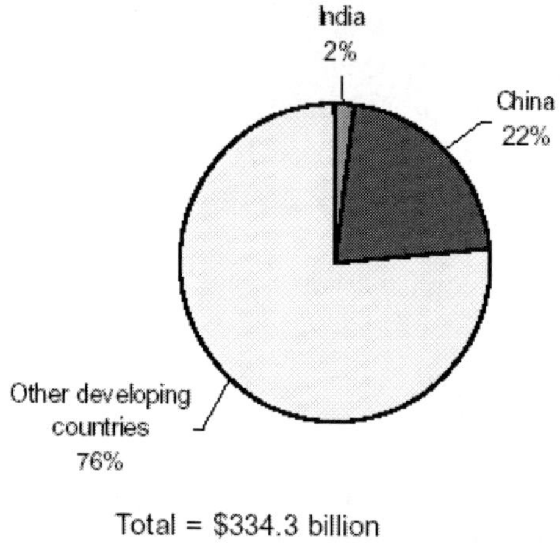

Source: UNCTAD, Country Fact Sheet.

Figure 2-2. FDI inflows to developing countries, 2005

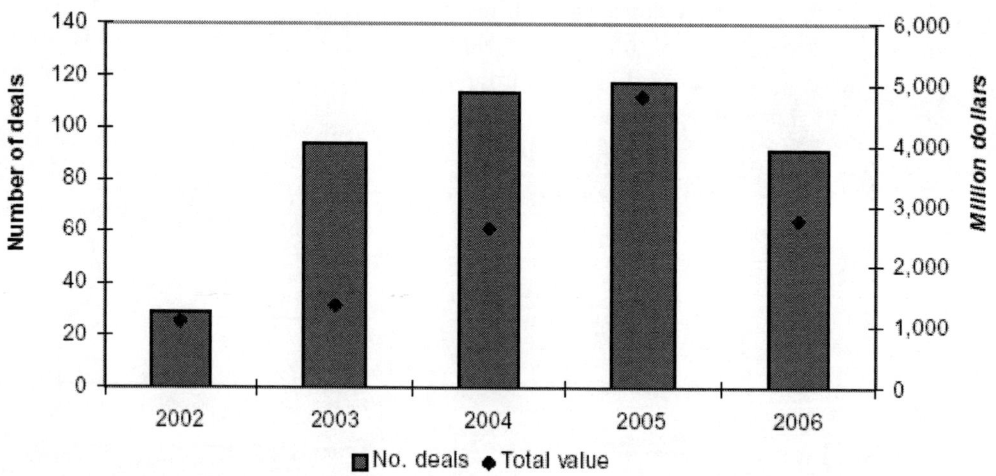

Source: Bureau van Dijk, Zephyr Mergers and Acquistions database.

Figure 2-3. M&A in India, by number of projects and value, 2000–06

Mergers and acquisitions

Figure 2-3 shows the trend of known completed M&A deals and their value, between 2002 and 2006. The bars on the figure indicate a sharp increase in the number of acquisitions completed in recent years.[33] The data illustrate that overall deal value increased through 2005, and fell more sharply than the number of deals in 2006.[34] The top 15 acquisitions by foreign firms in India during the same time period, by value, are presented in table 2-1. They are split almost evenly between services and manufacturing, with 8 service sector transactions, 6 manufacturing deals, and 1 utility acquisition. U.S. firms were the acquirers in 8 of the deals, with the remainder split among a number of countries.

Table 2-1. Top 15 acquisitions in India, by value, 2002–06

Acquirer	Target	Deal value (million dollars)	Industry of target	Date of completion	Acquirer country
Aegis Group plc	Percept Out Of Home	1000.0	Advertising	1/11/05	United Kingdom
Holcim Ltd	Ambuja Cement India	604.1	Cement manufacturing	4/7/05	Switzerland
CLP Power International Ltd	Gujarat Powergen Energy Corp.	594.0	Utilities	2/21/02	British Virgin Islands
Oracle Corp.	I-Flex Solutions	563.0	Computer software services	11/24/05	United States
Mylan Laboratories	Matrix Laboratories	548.2	Pharmaceuticals	1/8/07	United States
Merrill Lynch	DSP Merrill Lynch	499.3	Investment banking services	3/23/06	United States
Holderind Investments Ltd	Gujarat Ambuja Cements Ltd	476.4	Cement manufacturing	1/30/06	Mauritius
Electronic Data Systems Corp.	Mphasis BFL Ltd	368.9	Business process outsourcing services	6/9/06	United States
ADC Telecommunications	Krone Communications Ltd	350.0	Electronics manufacturing	5/22/04	United States
Hewlett-Packard Co.	Digital GlobalSoft	325.0	Computer software services	4/1/04	United States
Prudential plc	ICICI Prudential Life Insurance Company	280.1	Insurance	11/24/04	United Kingdom
WM Wrigley Jr Co.	Joyco India Pvt Ltd	264.5	Food processing	4/1/04	United States
Flextronics International	Hughes Software (India)	226.5	Computer software services	10/19/04	United States
Holcim Ltd	Ambuja Cement India Ltd	204.7	Cement manufacturing	4/7/2005	Switzerland
P&O Steam Navigation Co.	Mundra International Container Terminal	195.0	Port Services	6/5/03	United Kingdom

Source: Bureau van Dijk, *Zephyr Mergers and Acquisitions database*.

Table 2-2. Largest 15 greenfield FDI projects in India, 2002–06

Source country	Investing Company	Destination state	Capital (million dollars)	Technology/Product	Key business function
Canada	Royal Indian Rag International	Karnataka	9,000	Residential development	Construction
Luxembourg	Arcelor-Mittal	Bihar	8,940	Steel Products	Manufacturing
Netherlands	Ispat Industries	Maharashtra	4,458	Steel Cold Rolling/Forming	Manufacturing
Singapore	Flextronics	Andhra Pradesh	3,000	Wafers	Manufacturing
USA	Advanced Micro Devices (AMD)	Andhra Pradesh	3,000	Microprocessor	Manufacturing
South Korea	Pohang Iron & Steel (POSCO)	Orissa	3,000	Steel products	Manufacturing
Netherlands	EuropeanAeronautic Defence and Space	Karnataka	2,600	Aircraft	R & D
UK	Vedanta Resources	Orissa	2,100	Aluminum Products	Manufacturing
Netherlands	Ispat Industries	Karnataka	2,000	Steel products	Manufacturing
Canada	Niko Resources	Andhra Pradesh	2,000	Natural gas exploration	Extraction
Venezuela	Petroleos de Venezuela	Rajasthan	2,000	Petroleum exploration	Extraction
Japan	Nissan	Orissa	1,500	Passenger Cars	Manufacturing
UAE	Emaar Properties	Haryana	1,500	Property developer/	Construction
				management	
USA	AES India	Chattisgarh	1,200	Electricity/gas utilities	Electricity
Germany	SAP	Haryana	1,000	Enterprise application software	R&D

Source: *LocoMonitor FDI database; and The Financial Express*, "EADS to Open Technology Centre in Bangalore."

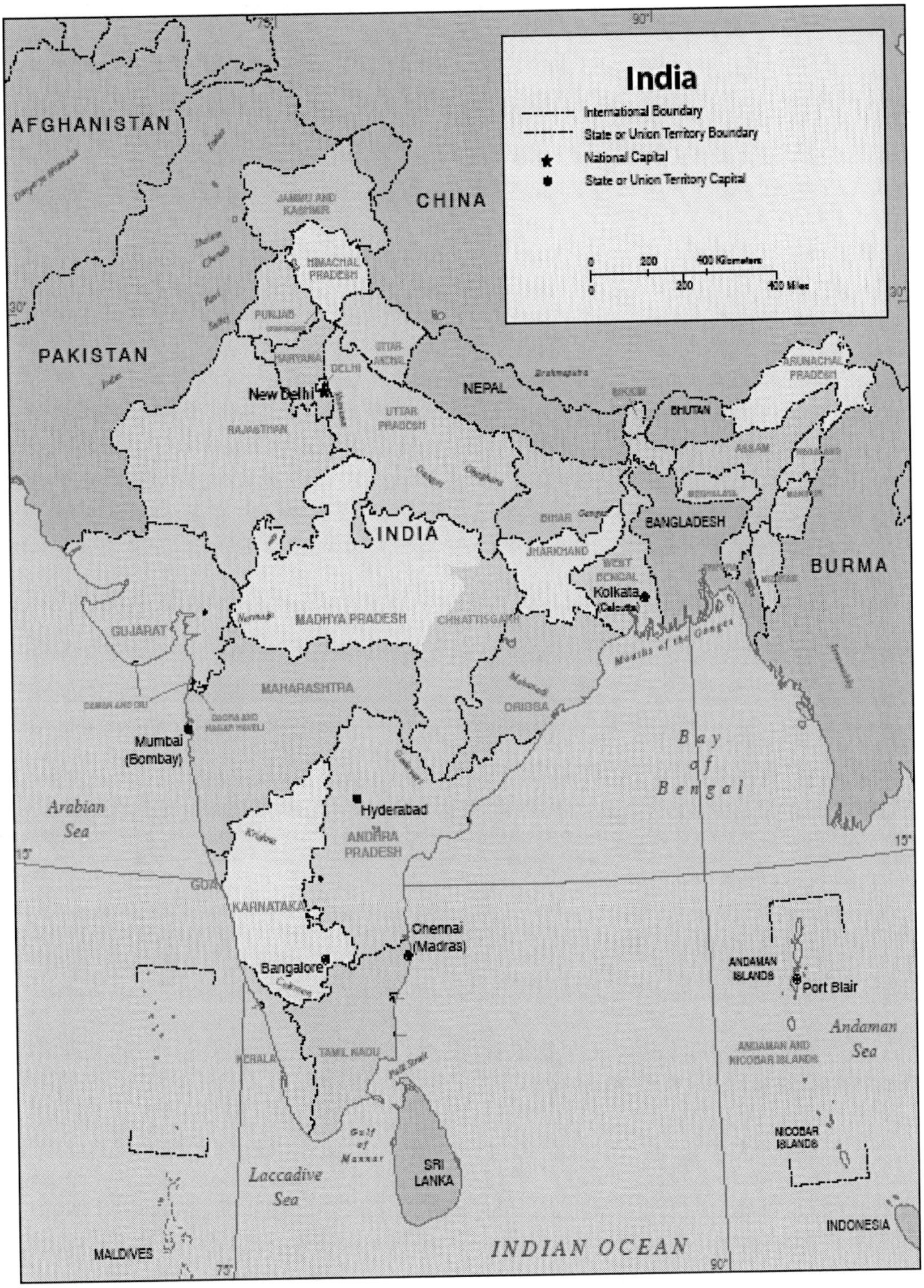

Source: Copyright 2006 Map Resources

Figure 2-4. Map of India

Greenfield FBI in India

India has also become a more attractive destination for greenfield FDI in recent years. Available data show that the number of greenfield FDI projects in India rose from 247 to 980 between 2002 and 2006, increasing at an average annual rate of 41 percent. Although these data do not capture the value of all greenfield projects (numerous projects are reported without the accompanying investment value), reported greenfield project values increased from $4.2 billion in 2002 to $55.5 billion in 2006.[35]

Between 2002 and 2006, 15 of the 300 projects that reported investment values were worth at least $1 billion each (table 2-2). These projects were concentrated in heavy industry;[36] property, tourism, and leisure;[37] and electronics,[38] from a diverse range of source countries.[39] All but one of these projects are new facilities. By business function, the projects are spread among manufacturing, construction, resource extraction, and R&D.

The bulk of greenfield FDI in India is destined for new facilities rather than expansions of existing ones. The share of expansion projects has been declining steadily over the period from 22 percent of reported projects in 2002 to 11 percent in 2006. Expansion projects accounted for 16 percent of total greenfield FDI during the period, with almost one-half of projects in the information and communication technology (ICT) sector.[40]

Table 2-3. FDI Equity Inflows, January 2000–December 2006, by region

Rank	RBI - Regional Office	State/UT*	FDI Inflows-millions USD	Share of Total (%)
1	Mumbai	Maharashtra, Dadra & Haveli, Daman & Diu*	7,486.6	24.9
2	New Delhi	Delhi, Uttar Pradesh, Haryana	7,045.0	23.4
3	Chennai	Tamil Nadu, Puducherry	2,295.1	7.6
4	Bangalore	Karnataka	2,052.4	6.8
5	Hyderabad	Andra Pradesh	1,572.2	3.9
6	Ahmedabad	Gujarat	970.3	3.7
	All Other		8,999.6	30.1
Total			32,152.2	

Source: Government of India, Ministry of Commerce & Industry, Department of Industrial Policy and Promotion, FDI Statistics 2006.

Note: Because of rounding, figures may not add up to the totals shown.

Distribution of FDI within India

FDI inflows within India are heavily concentrated around two major cities, Mumbai and New Delhi, with Chennai, Bangalore, Hyderabad and Ahmedabad also drawing significant shares of FDI inflows (figure 2-4). For statistical purposes, India's Department of Industrial Policy and Promotion (DIPP) divides the country into 16 regional offices. As illustrated in table 2-3, the top 6 regions account for two-thirds of all FDI inflows to India between 2000 and 2006, with the Mumbai and New Delhi regions together accounting for just under one-half of the total.[41] This is consistent with greenfield FDI data, which shows that the 5 Indian states that received the largest number of greenfield FDI projects in 2006, based on the total number of projects reported, were Maharashtra (20 percent, includes the city of Mumbai), Karnataka (15 percent, includes the city of Bangalore), Tamil Nadu (13 percent, includes the city of Chennai), Delhi (9 percent, includes the city of New Delhi), and Andhra Pradesh (8 percent, includes the city of Hyderabad).

The key industries attracting FDI to the Maharashtra region are energy, transportation, services, telecommunications, and electrical equipment.[42] Maharashtra's transportation industry holds a particular concentration of MNC affiliates in auto components manufacturing. Prominent examples include INR Spicer India, owned by U.S.-based Dana Corp.; Kalyani Lemmerz Ltd., owned by U.S.-based Hayes Lemmerz International; Schrader Duncan, an affiliate of British-based Tomkins plc; and Fiat India, an auto parts subsidiary of the Italian auto manufacturer.[43] In the services area, leading firms include Standard Chartered Bank, an affiliate of the British-based bank; I-Flex Solutions, owned by U.S.- based Oracle Corp.; Citicorp Finance and E-Serve International, both affiliates of U.S.-based Citigroup; and South East Asia Marine Engineering and Construction, owned by Technip Offshore International, based in France.[44]

The key sectors attracting FDI inflows to Delhi are similar: telecommunications, transportation, electrical equipment (including software), and services.[45] Delhi ranks second in total FDI inflows behind Maharashtra. U.S.-owned IBM is not only the largest computer services company in India, but is also the MNC with the largest number of employees in India (approximately 53,000), second only to IBM's work force in the United States.[46] In addition to Delhi, IBM also has facilities in Bangalore, Chennai, Kolkata, Pune, Gurgaon, and Hyderabad. Goodyear, one of the largest global tire manufacturers, has built two manufacturing facilities near Delhi, entering into a joint venture with Indian company Ceat Ltd. and acquiring India-based South Asia Tyres.[47] Goodyear has made an initial investment of $12.3 million to redesign 300 retail outlets to better adapt to Indian consumer preferences.[48]

The states of Uttar Pradesh and Haryana are also contained in the New Delhi region, as identified by India's statistical agencies. The geographic proximity of both states to New Delhi helps them to attract FDI. Due to its abundance of natural resources, Uttar Pradesh attracts FDI in chemicals, pharmaceuticals, and mining and minerals.[49] Haryana attracts FDI in the electrical equipment, transportation, and food processing sectors.[50] Japan-based Honda Motor Co. has a large presence throughout India, including Honda's joint venture with Hero Cycles, which has grown into the world's largest motorcycle company since its inception in 1984. The company's presence in Haryana includes an R&D center that supports two manufacturing facilities which together produce over 3 million motorcycles annually. U.S-based Dow Corning and U.K.-based GlaxoSmithKline have invested in the state's chemical and pharmaceutical industries, respectively.

Automotive and auto components are the largest sectors attracting FDI into Tamil Nadu. Ford, Hyundai, and Mitsubushi all have multi-million dollar investments in Tamil Nadu. The state capital, Chennai, is sometimes called the "Detroit of India."[51] Other sectors attracting FDI include port infrastructure, ICT, and electronics.[52] The bulk of projects in Andhra Pradesh, which includes the city of Hyderabad, are associated with software and, to a lesser extent, hardware for computers and telecommunications. The same is true of projects in Karnataka, where Bangalore is located; Karnataka also has a large number of projects in the automotive sector (34).

India's more rural areas have attracted a smaller number of high-value projects. Large greenfield FDI projects in Orissa include bauxite mining and associated aluminum smelting operations as well as steel and automotive facilities. Pohang Iron and Steel Co.'s (POSCO -

Korea) planned steel mill in Orissa is expected to be the largest FDI project in India, and will ultimately involve $12 billion in total FDI on 4000 acres, with an annual steel making capacity of 12 million tons by 2020.[53] As of May 2007, however, the POSCO project was generating intense local opposition by farmers worried about the loss of thier land, and its future was uncertain. Luxembourg-based Arcelor-Mittal, the world's largest steel maker, has also signed a memorandum of understanding with the Orissa state goverment to build an $8.7 billion steel mill, but faces similar opposition to its plans.[54] Other companies investing in greenfield metals production and auto projects in Orissa include Russian Aluminum, Vedanta Resources (United Kingdom), Dubai Aluminum, and Nissan (Japan).[55] The state of Orissa accounted for 15 and 30 percent, respectively, of the total value of greenfield FDI reported in 2004 and 2005. As of April 2007, Arcelor-Mittal was also considering investing in a second large steel mill in India, in the state of Jharkhand.[56]

FDI Flows to India by Source Country

Mauritius is the largest country investor in India, followed by the United States and the United Kingdom. Table 2-4 shows the top 10 country sources of FDI flows to India between 1991 and 2006.

The United States and the European Union are the largest acquirers of Indian companies, measured by both value and number of deals (figure 2-5). For the number of M&A deals with a reported value, the U.S. and the EU together accounted for over $8 billion, or roughly 67 percent of the total value in the Indian M&A market between 2000 and 2006. Indian government statistics do not present information on the industry distribution of FDI inflows from each source country. However, an analysis of M&A and greenfield FDI project data sheds light on the industry destinations for the major countries (table 2-5).

Table 2-4. Top Country Investors in India, 2006

Country	FDI Inflows, April–December, 2006-07	FDI Inflows, August 1991–December 2006	Share of FDI inflows, August 1991– December 2006
	(Million dollars)		(percent)
Mauritius	4,215	16,000	33
United States	607	5,645	12
United Kingdom	1,682	3,662	8
Netherlands	488	2,482	5
Japan	52	2,176	5
Singapore	533	1,583	3
Germany	70	1,652	3
France	80	858	2
South Korea	62	814	2
Switzerland	47	683	1
All other	1,434	12,617	26
Total	9,270	48,172	

Source: Government of India, Ministry of Commerce & Industry, Department of Industrial Policy and Promotion, Fact Sheet on Foreign Direct Investment.

Note: Share of total inflows may not sum to 100 due to rounding. Shares are calculated in U.S. dollars and may not match shares calculated in Indian rupees.

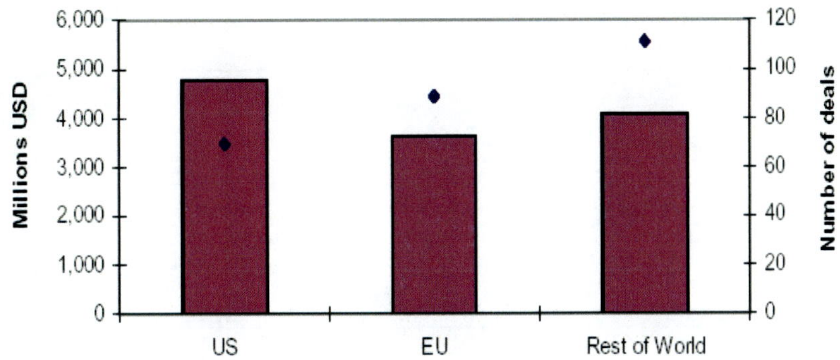

Source: Compiled from Bureau van Dijk, Zephyr Mergers and Acquisitions datebase.

Figure 2-5. India M&A number of deals with known value, 2000–06

Table 2-5. India, M&A deals by acquirer country and industry of the target company, 2000–06

Acquirer Countries	Manufacturing	Information	Financial Services	Professional, Scientific, and Technical Services	Other	Total
United States	39	55	13	56	43	206
European Union	93	22	12	33	18	178
Singapore	11	10	0	11	5	37
Japan	12	2	3	4	6	27
Mauritius	10	1	3	3	5	22
Australia	2	5	1	6	4	18
Switzerland	9	0	0	0	0	9
Korea	4	2	0	2	0	8
Rest of World	35	11	7	14	15	82
Total	215	108	39	129	66	557

Source: Compiled from Bureau van Dijk, *Zephyr Mergers and Acquisitions database*.

Notes: Due to rounding and multiple target company industry classifications, numbers may not add to total. Industry groups reflect the North American Industry Classification System (NAICS) also used in official U.S. Government statistics.

Manufacturing is the leading industry destination, followed by information (including telecommunications services) and professional, scientific, and technical services (including business services such as data processing and telephone call centers). Figure 2-6 shows the leading countries in terms of greenfield FDI from 2002 through 2006.

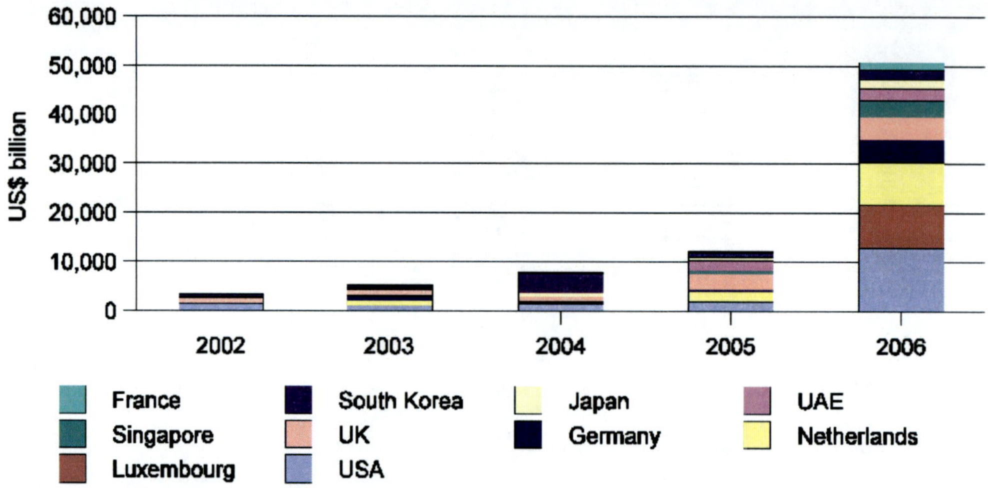

Source: OCO Consulting Ltd. *LocoMonitor FDI database*

Figure 2-6. Total reported greenfield FDI by selected Countries2002-08

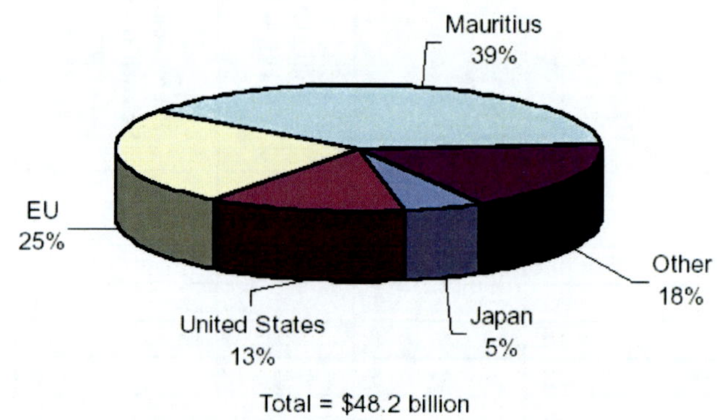

Source: Compiled from Department of Industrial Policy and Promotion, Fact Sheet on Foreign Direct Investment.

Note: Shares are calculated in Indian rupees, and may not match shares calculated in U.S.

Figure 2-7. Share of top investing countries, cumulative FDI equity inflows, August 1991–December 2006

Mauritius

According to Indian government statistics, Mauritius accounts for the largest share of cumulative FDI inflows to India from 1991 to 2006, nearly 40 percent (figure 2-7). It is[57] unlikely, given the small size of the Mauritian economy, that much of the capital destined for India originated in Mauritius. According to LocoMonitor data, only four greenfield FDI projects (all from 2002) list Mauritius as the source country. Many companies based[58] outside of India utilize Mauritian holding companies to take advantage of the India- Mauritius Double Taxation Avoidance Agreement (DTAA). The DTAA allows foreign firms to bypass Indian capital gains taxes, and may allow some India-based firms to avoid paying certain taxes through a process known as "round tripping."[59]

The extent of round tripping by Indian companies through Mauritius is unknown. However, the Indian government is concerned enough about this problem to have asked the government of Mauritius to set up a joint monitoring mechanism to study these investment flows.[60] The potential loss of tax revenue is of particular concern to the Indian government. The existence of the treaty makes it difficult to clearly understand the pattern of FDI flows,[61] and likely leads to reduced tax revenues collected by the Indian government. Chapter 5 presents a more complete discussion of the DTAA.

United States

The United States is the second largest source of FDI in India (13 percent of the total), valued at $5.6 billion in cumulative inflows between August 1991 and December 2006. According to the Indian government, the top sectors attracting FDI from the United States to India during 1991–2004 (latest available) are fuel (36 percent), telecommunications (11 percent), electrical equipment (10 percent), food processing (9 percent), and services (8 percent).[62]

According to the available M&A data, the two top sectors attracting FDI inflows from the United States are computer systems design and programming and manufacturing. These data roughly correspond to the overall FDI sectoral breakdown with the exception of fuel (including power generation and oil refineries). Given India's general lack of existing power infrastructure, operations involved with power generation and oil refineries may be better suited to greenfield investments. U.S. companies that are actively pursuing or have recently completed M&A deals in the Indian telecommunications, electrical equipment, and service sectors include Oracle, Intel, IBM, HP, and Electronic Data Systems (EDS). Ford, Parker-Hannifin, Sara Lee, SC Johnson, and Caterpillar have been actively investing in the manufacturing sector.[63]

According to Indian government statistics, FDI inflows from the United States accounted for 13 percent of total FDI inflows between August 1991 and December 2006. According to LocoMonitor data for 2002–06, U.S. greenfield investment has averaged 44 percent of the total number of projects listed and 18 percent of the total reported value for projects. The industry receiving the largest share of U.S. greenfield FDI has been followed by electronics and business services (figure 2-8). Among the announced ICT projects that have value data reported, Google's $1 billion investment in internet infrastructure in Andhra Pradesh is the largest. The internet search engine company intends to open a "server farm" (a collection of computer servers) to enhance its internet and data storage services in Asia.[64] Most of the other U.S.-funded ICT projects are for software development.[65]

Reported greenfield FDI projects by U.S. companies have been generally smaller by value (about one-third the size, on average) than projects financed by non-U.S. companies. Some of this disparity in size may be explained by the much greater emphasis on R&D activities, including software development, by U.S. firms than by non-U.S. firms investing in India. Over one-half of all listed R&D projects were funded by U.S. companies, and research facilities tend to require considerably less capital than manufacturing facilities. Since 2002, many of the major U.S. software and computer brands, such as Microsoft, Honeywell, Cisco Systems, Adobe Systems, McAfee, and Intel have established R&D operations in India, primarily in Hyderabad or Bangalore.

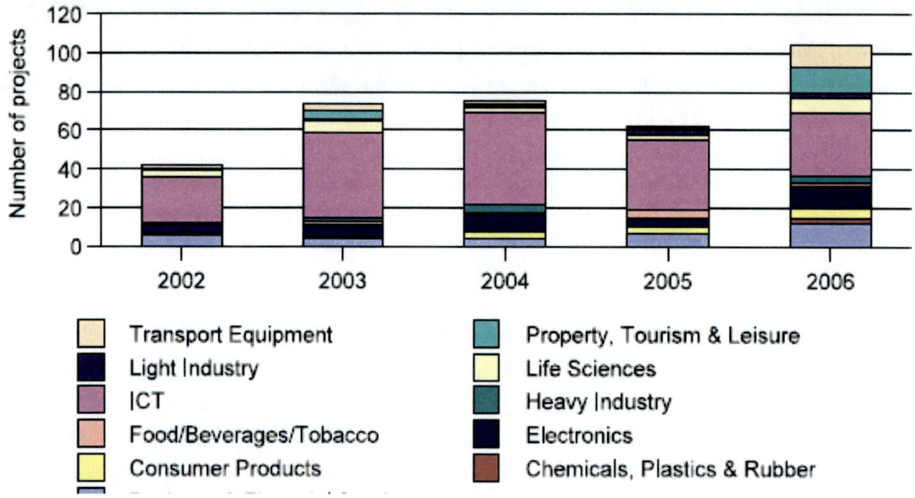

Source: OCO Consulting Ltd., *LocoMonitor FDI database*

Figure 2-8. US reported Greenfield FDI projects in India, by cluster 2002-06

The majority of U.S. electronics companies that have announced greenfield projects in India are concentrated in the semiconductor sector. By far the largest such project is AMD's chip manufacturing facility in Hyderabad, Andhra Pradesh. This $3 billion site will produce about 30,000 wafers per month, with each wafer containing between 100 and 1,000 chips. Intel plans to invest close to $1 billion in India, primarily expanding the company's R&D center in Bangalore, over a multi-year period.[66]

Official data on FDI flows and stocks is compiled on a balance of payments (BOP) basis, and reflects the total capital that crosses borders. These data are one indicator of the level of FDI in a given country, and generally the indicator that is most widely available. An alternate indicator of FDI activity is the extent of operations by foreign-owned affiliates in a given economy. These data are not available for all countries. For the United States, however, there is a substantial amount of available information, including data on sales and assets of U.S.-owned affiliates in India, employment by those affiliates, and R&D performed by U.S.-owned firms in India.

assets of U.S.-owned affiliates in India, employment by those affiliates, and R&D performed by U.S.-owned firms in India.

In 2004 (latest available), there were 577 affiliates of U.S. firms in India, of which 198 were majority-owned by U.S. firms (table 2-6). U.S. majority-owned affiliates (MOFAs)[67] employed a total of 165,600 workers in India. The largest share (36 percent) was found in the manufacturing sector, most prominently in the machinery, chemicals, and transportation equipment manufacturing segments. Other important categories of employment are professional, scientific, and technical services; and wholesale trade, with 29 percent and 18 percent of U.S. affiliate employment, respectively. While manufacturing remains the largest sector for U.S. employment, the latter two sectors have accounted for an increasing share of employment by U.S.-owned affiliates in recent years (figure 2-9). U.S.-owned manufacturing affiliates also reported larger assets than affiliates in other sectors in 2004, followed by finance and insurance, and utilities affiliates (figure 2-10).

Table 2-6. Selected data for U.S. majority-owned affiliates in India, 2004

	All industries	Manufacturing	Wholesale trade	Professional, scientific, and technical services	Information	Financial services
Number of affiliates (units)	198	N/A	N/A	N/A	N/A	N/A
Employment (thousands)	166	60	30	48	11	3
Million dollars						
Assets	20,188	6,453	2,146	1,520	2,277	3,344
Sales	13,100	6,569	3,620	1,293	745	243
Value-added	3,937	1,689	931	812	346	30
Net income	637	235	158	171	89	11

Source: USDOC, BEA International Economic Accounts, "Operations of Multinational Companies".

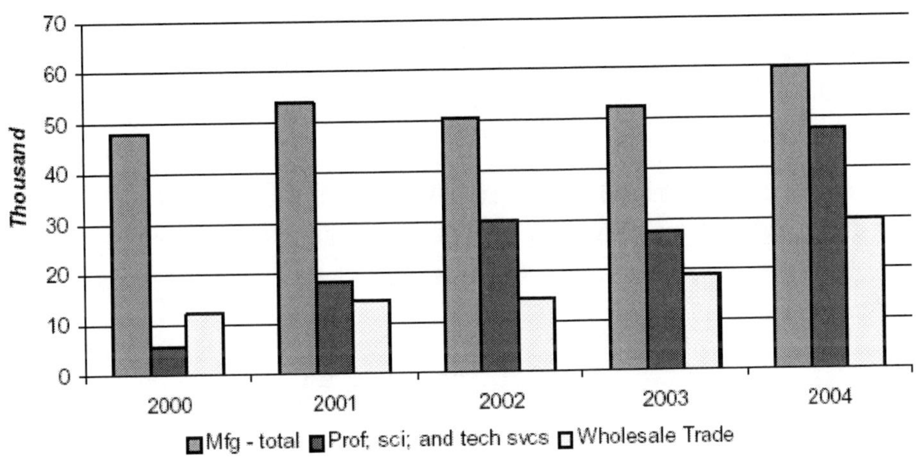

Source: Bureau van Dijk, *Zephyr Mergers and Acquisitions database*

Figure 2-9. Employment, MOFAs, India, 2000–04

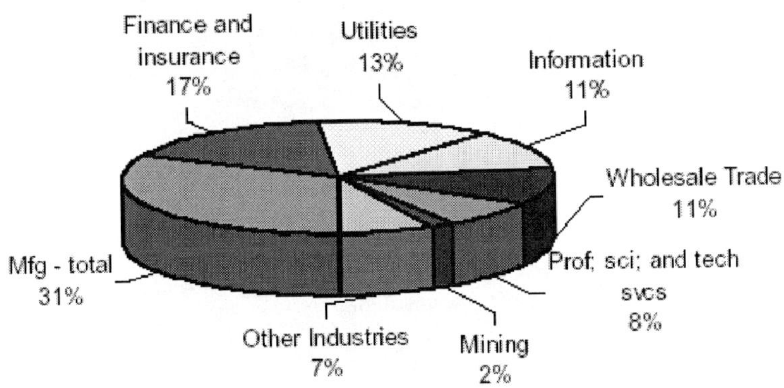

Source: USDOC, BEA, International Economic Accounts, "Operations of Multinational Companies".

Figure 2-10. MOFA Assets, 2004

The top four sectors in terms of value-added by U.S.-owned affiliates in India were, respectively, manufacturing; wholesale trade; professional, scientific, and technical services; and information services (primarily telecommunications, most likely).[68] Within the manufacturing sector, the largest industries were chemicals and machinery manufacturing. In 2003, U.S. MOFAs reported R&D-related expenditures of $81 million in India. Of this total, 43 percent was in the manufacturing sector, with most of the remainder likely in the area of professional, scientific, and technical services.[69] Given the sharp increase in overall FDI in India since 2003, and the individual projects noted above, R&D-related expenditures by U.S. MOFAs have also likely increased.

European union

Within the European Union, the largest country investors were the United Kingdom and the Netherlands, with $3.7 billion and $2.5 billion, respectively, of cumulative FDI inflows between 1991 and 2006. The United Kingdom, the Netherlands, and Germany together accounted for almost 75 percent of all FDI flows from the EU to India (figure 2-11). All EU countries together accounted for approximately 25 percent of all FDI inflows to India between August 1991 and December 2006. FDI from the EU to India is primarily concentrated in the power/energy, telecommunications, and transportation sectors.[70]

The available M&A data shows that the top sectors attracting FDI from the European Union are similar to FDI from the United States. Manufacturing; information services; and professional, scientific, and technical services have attracted the largest shares of FDI inflows from the EU to India since 2000. Unilever, Reuters Group, P&O Ports Ltd, Vodafone, and Barclays are examples of EU companies investing in India by means of mergers and acquisitions.

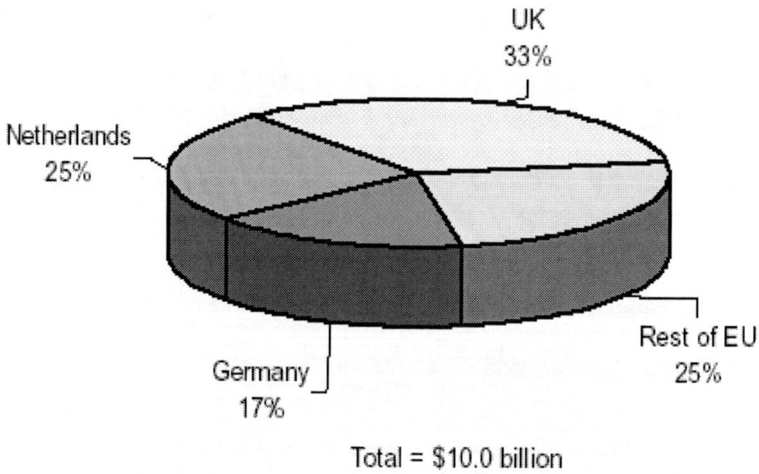

Source: Compiled from *Department of Industrial Policy and Promotion, FDI Statistics 2006* .

Figure 2-11. EU share of FDI stock in India, 1991–2006

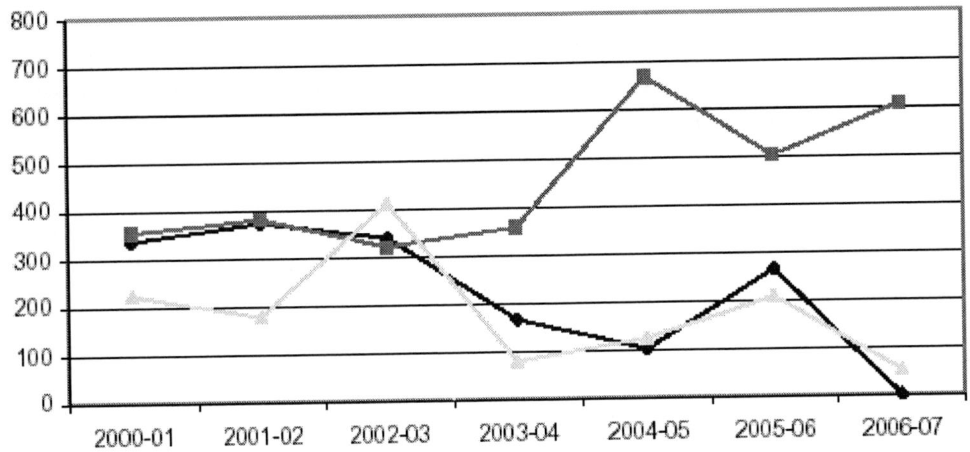

Source: Compiled from Government of India, Ministry of Commerce & Industry, Department of Industrial Policy and Promotion, *FDI Statistics*.

Note: Data for 2006-07 reflect April through December only.

Figure 2-12. FDI inflows, selected countries, 2000–06

European companies accounted for 31 percent of the total number and 43 percent of the total value for all reported greenfield FDI projects. The number of EU greenfield projects was distributed among four major clusters: ICT (17 percent), heavy industry (16 percent), business and financial services (15 percent), and transport (11 percent). However, the heavy industry cluster accounted for the majority (68 percent) of the total value of these projects.[71]

Japan

Japan was the fourth largest source of cumulative FDI inflows in India between 1991 and 2006, but the recent trend of FDI inflows from Japan differs from those of other source countries. FDI inflows to India from most other principal source countries have steadily increased since 2000, but inflows from Japan to India have decreased during this time period (figure 2-12).[72] There does not appear to be a single factor that explains the recent decline in FDI inflows from Japan to India. India is, however, one of the largest recipients of Japanese Official Development Assistance (ODA), through which Japan has assisted India in building infrastructure, including electricity generation, transportation, and water supply. It is possible that this Japanese government assistance may crowd out some private sector Japanese investment.

The top sectors attracting FDI inflows from Japan to India (January 2000 to November 2006) are transportation (54 percent), electrical equipment (7 percent), telecommunications, and services (3 percent).[73] The available M&A data corresponds with the overall FDI trends in sectors attracting inflows from Japan to India. Companies dealing in the transportation industry, specifically automobiles, and the auto component/peripheral industries dominate M&A activity from Japan to India, including Yamaha Motors, Toyota, Kirloskar Auto Parts Ltd., and Mitsubishi Heavy Industries Ltd. Japanese companies have also invested in an estimated 148 greenfield FDI projects valued at least at $3.7 billion between 2002 and 2006.[74]

Japanese companies accounted for a relatively small share of greenfield FDI in India: 5 percent of the projects and 4 percent of the value. The transport equipment cluster received the largest share (34 percent) of Japanese greenfield FDI projects and 79 percent of Japanese greenfield FDI value. The largest project in the cluster is Nissan's $1.5 billion, export-oriented passenger car plant in Manesar, Orissa.[75] The ICT and electronics clusters each garnered 17 percent of the projects, but only small amounts of value. The only other cluster to receive more than a 10 percent share of Japanese capital was the chemical, plastics, and rubber industry. In one prominent example, Mitsubishi Chemical is investing $368 million to expand its existing basic organic chemicals production in Haldia, West Bengal.[76]

In April 2007, Japanese and Indian officials announced a major new collaboration between the two countries to build a new Delhi-Mumbai industrial corridor, to be funded through a public-private partnership and private-sector FDI, primarily from Japanese companies. The project is expected to begin in January 2008 with initial investment of $2 billion from the two countries. The corridor will cross 6 states and extend for 1,483 km, in an area inhabited by 180 million people. At completion in 2015, the corridor is expected to include total FDI of $45–50 billion. A large share of that total is destined for infrastructure, including a 4,000 MW power plant, 3 ports, and 6 airports, along with additional connections to existing ports. Private investment is expected to fund 10-12 new industrial zones, upgrade 5–6 existing airports, and set up 10 logistics parks. The Indian government expects that by 2020, the industrial corridor will contribute to employment growth of 15 percent in the region, 28 percent growth in industrial output, and 38 percent growth in exports.[77]

United Arab Emirates (UAE)

The UAE ranked fourteenth in FDI stock in India in 2006, but the two countries are in the process of signing several economic and political cooperation agreements which will likely lead to increased UAE investment in India. The March 2007 visit to India by officials from Dubai has already produced commitments for cross border investments of over $30 billion over the next two years.[78]

Sectors attracting interest from the UAE include ports, infrastructure, and hotel construction. One notable recent agreement involves a 50:50 joint venture between Dubai-based Nakheel and Indian real estate developer DLF. The company plans to develop 40,000 acres for housing with an initial investment of $10 billion. Greenfield FDI projects in India from UAE-based investors are valued at more than $2 billion in each of the last two years, many of which are aimed at infrastructure and real estate development.[79]

The three clusters with the largest number of UAE-funded greenfield FDI projects during 2002–06 are light industry; property, tourism, and leisure; and logistics. The light industry projects, concentrated in textiles and building materials, are typically less capital intensive. Conversely, heavy industry had only one UAE-funded greenfield FDI project, but it was valued at $1.1 billion: Dubai Aluminum is setting up a mine, refinery, and smelter in Orissa.[80] Dubai Ports World has been the most active UAE investor in India's logistics cluster, with plans to establish container port operations in numerous Indian ports. The extensive network is, in fact, leading to questions about whether the company is gaining too large a share of the market with its control of 50 percent of India's container shipping traffic.[81]

UAE investors claim that one reason for their increased interest in India is related to the U.S. response to the September 11, 2001 terrorist attacks on the United States. The U.S.

market is perceived to be less welcoming to foreign ownership, particularly from the Gulf states, so investors are looking for other markets to absorb their investment dollars.[82]

FDI Flows to India by Industry

The sectors receiving the largest shares of total FDI inflows between August 1991 and December 2006 were the electrical equipment sector and the services sector, each accounting for 17 percent. These were followed by the telecommunications, transportation, fuels, and chemicals sectors (table 2-7).[83] The top sectors attracting FDI into India via M&A activity were manufacturing; information; and professional, scientific, and technical services.[84] These sectors correspond closely with the sectors identified by the Indian government as attracting the largest shares of FDI inflows overall.

ICT and electronics have been the largest industry recipients of greenfield FDI into India in recent years, but have seen the number of new greenfield projects plateau since 2004. These data do not signify that greenfield investment in these sectors has stagnated. Rather, the size of the projects in these industries has increased substantially. For example, global semiconductor manufacturers Advanced Micro Devices (AMD - United States) and Flextronics (Singapore) have entered into separate joint ventures with SemIndia to build semiconductor manufacturing facilities in Hyderabad. The $3 billion AMD-SemIndia joint venture will produce semiconductor chips which can then be used to manufacture electronic products in the Flextronics-SemIndia $3 billion joint venture. The chip fabrication facility will manufacture chips for cell phones, set-top boxes, personal computers, and similar products.[85] SemIndia is attempting to capitalize on India's domestic demand for semiconductors, predicted to grow from $3.3 billion in 2006 to $40 billion in 2016.[86]

The heavy industry and transport equipment sectors together attracted over $30 billion in greenfield FDI projects in 2006. The cluster with the highest reported value during 2002–06 is heavy industry. Projects in this sector tend to be highly capital intensive, with single projects frequently requiring upwards of $6 billion in startup investment costs. The largest recent examples include the POSCO and Arcelor-Mittal Steel projects noted above, and Vedanta Resources' (United Kingdom) aluminum smelter project, all planned for the state of Orissa.[87] Reported greenfield FDI in the transport equipment sector exceeded $11 billion in 2006.[88]

Another major recipient sector was property, tourism and leisure, with over $6.1 billion in 2006. This level of investment was well above the annual average for this sector, although still below the high of $9.2 billion in 2004. The Asian tsunami on December 26, 2004, may have dampened enthusiasm for such investment, as investment plunged to just over $100 million in 2005 before rebounding to $6.1 billion in 2006. The industry is expected to continue to attract substantial FDI. At least 50 non-Indian hotel chains planned to enter the market as of April 2007, targeting India's low level of hotel penetration around the country.[89] In particular, Royal Indian Raj International Corp. has signed a contract with Choice Hotels to build 15,000 hotel rooms around the country, with an estimated FDI value of $6 billion.[90]

Figure 2-13 shows that greenfield FDI projects have become more widely distributed across industries over time. In 2002, FDI projects were concentrated in the ICT industry, followed by business and financial services; and electronics. By 2006, the distribution of the projects among the clusters was more uniform, although the ICT cluster still was the largest. Figure 2-14 shows how greenfield FDI capital has been distributed among the various sectors. Note that the two "pies" are not the same size–the total amount invested in 2006 ($55.5 billion) is more than 13 times the total in 2002 ($4.2 billion). Even if an industry's share of the total pie decreased between 2002 and 2006, that industry may still have significantly increased its total greenfield FDI. The ICT sector is a case in point, down 12 percent by relative share from 2002 to 2006, but recording increased FDI of more than $4.1 billion.

Table 2-7. India, FDI by Sector, Selected Years

Sector	2006–07 (April–December)	Cumulative Inflows (August 1991–December 2006)	Share of total inflows
	(Million dollars)		(percent)
Electrical equipment	1,429	6,923	17.0
Services	3,820	6,911	17.0
Telecommunications	490	3,861	9.3
Transportation	368	3,548	8.4
Fuels (power and oil refinery)	192	2,773	6.7
Chemicals	147	2,290	5.2
Pharmaceuticals	157	1,165	2.8
Food processing	49	1,227	2.8
Cement and gypsum	210	956	2.4
Metallurgical industries	148	803	2.0

Source: Government of India, Ministry of Commerce & Industry, Department of Industrial Policy and Promotion, *FDI Statistics 2006*.

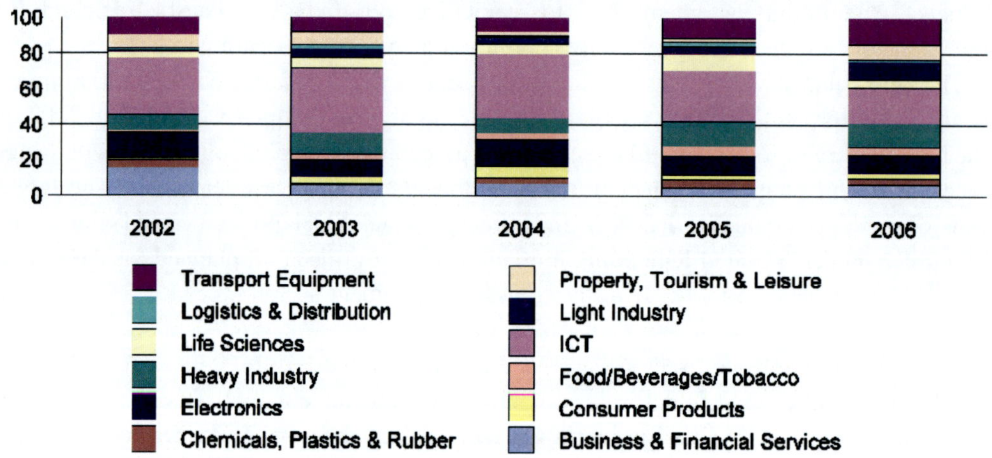

Source: OCO consulting Ltd., *Locomonitor FDI database.*

Figure 2-13. Cluster shares of total project, annually, 2002-06

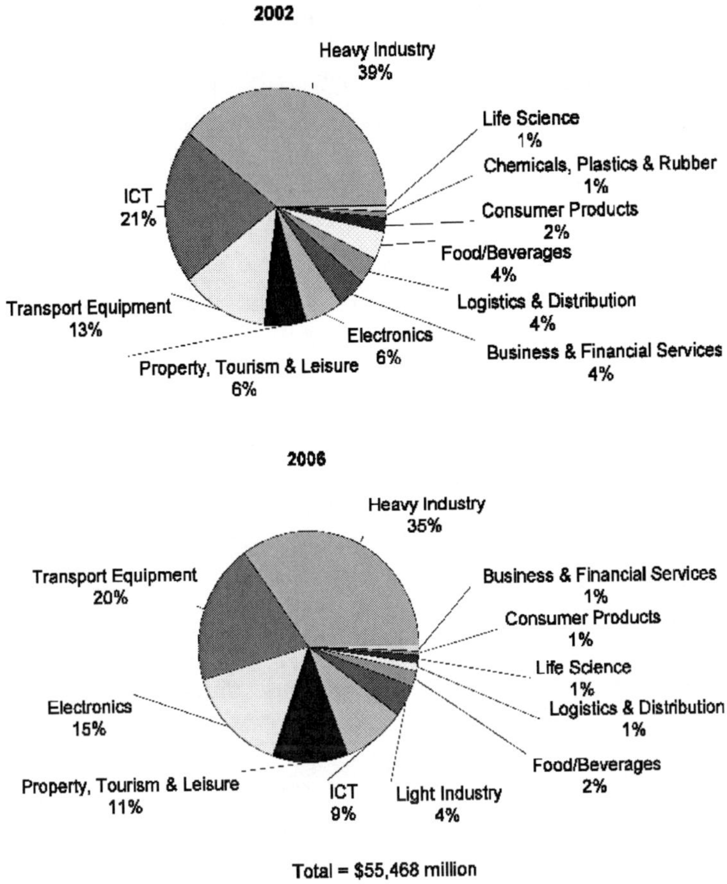

Source: OCO consulting Ltd., LocoMonitor FDI database.

Figure 2-14. Cluster shares of reported greenfield FDI in India, 2002 and 2006

3. India's FDI Environment

Introduction

In recent years, India has emerged as a desirable location for FDI by investors from the United States and many other countries. Its rapidly growing economy, low wages, and educated work force have attracted FDI in the services and manufacturing sectors to serve both the Indian market and third country markets. Foreign investors' enthusiasm for India, however, has been tempered by widespread poverty, rigidity in the labor market, rising salaries and high employee turnover in some industries, an antiquated infrastructure, weaknesses in the overall educational system, and excessive bureaucracy and corruption.

Surveys of international competitiveness and investor confidence support this mixed picture with respect to India's attractions for FDI. In the Global Competitiveness Index for 2006, India ranked 43 out of 125 countries, ahead of China, Indonesia, Mexico, and Brazil, but behind Taiwan, Korea, and Malaysia. India ranked relatively higher in several attributes, including institutions, market efficiency, business sophistication, and innovation, but relatively lower in infrastructure, macroeconomy, health and primary education, higher education and training, and technological readiness.[91] In A.T. Kearney's Foreign Direct Investment Confidence Index for 2005, India trailed only China as the most desirable location for FDI.[92] The World Bank's Doing Business Report 2007, however, ranked India only 134 out of 175 countries, a slight improvement over its 2005 ranking of 138 out of 175. By comparison, China ranked 93 out of 175 in 2006. Other rankings on the same survey included Brazil (121), Korea (23), Malaysia (25), Mexico (43), and Taiwan (47).[93]

Actual FDI into India in the past 4 years reflects these mixed perceptions with respect to the business climate in India relative to other countries. Although FDI into India increased irregularly between 2002 and 2005, from $5.6 billion to $6.6 billion, it was orders of magnitude smaller than that into China, Brazil, and Mexico (table 3-1). During the past 4 years, FDI into China, its most comparable competitor in terms of population, has been ten times that of investment into India. FDI into Brazil and Mexico during the period has been roughly three times that of India. FDI into Poland in the past 2 years surpassed that into India. A closer examination of the factors that influence FDI, such as economic growth, wage levels, infrastructure, and educational level of the work force, suggests that India is a country with vast potential that has yet to be fully realized.[94]

Table 3-1. Inward FDI Flows for Selected Countries, 2002–05, (Millions of U.S. Dollars)

Country	2002	2003	2004	2005
India	5,627	4,585	5,474	6,598
Brazil	16,590	10,144	18,146	15,066
China	52,743	53,505	60,630	72,406
Hungary	2,994	2,137	4,654	6,699
Malaysia	3,203	2,473	4,624	3,967
Mexico	18,275	14,184	18,674	18,055
Poland	4,131	4,589	12,873	7,724
Russia	3,461	7,958	15,444	14,600

Source: United Nations Conference on Trade and Development, *World Investment Report 2006.*

Economy

Strong economic growth

Few countries have experienced the economic dynamism that India has enjoyed during the past decade. This positive economic environment has attracted FDI by firms anxious to take advantage of higher Indian living standards and increased demand for goods. The Indian economy has grown, on average, more than 7 percent annually since 1994,[95] and is forecast to grow at a comparable rate in 2006. By 2004, India had become the tenth largest economy in the world and the fourth largest in purchasing-power parity terms.[96] With per capita income having more than doubled since the mid-1980s, the Indian middle class has expanded and its purchasing power has increased significantly (box 3-1).[97] Economic growth has not been accompanied by high inflation—annual inflation in India has remained close to 4 percent since 2000.[98] Increased FDI has stimulated both imports and exports, contributing to rising levels of international trade. India's imports almost tripled between 2001 and 2005, from $50.1 billion to $138.4 billion, while exports more than doubled, from $43.3 billion to $99.7 billion.[99]

Box 3-1. Foreign Investors Attracted by Strong Indian Economy

Foreign investors have noted the favorable conditions in the Indian economy and the importance of India to their global operations. Nokia, a Finnish producer of cell phones, in an announcement concerning its choice of Chennai, India as a new global network solutions center site, noted the robust nature of the Indian market and its importance to the firm's global expansion.[a] Samsung Electronics Co., Ltd., a Korean producer of cell phones and telecom systems, in an announcement involving the start-up of a mobile phone plant in Haryana State, India, stated that the Indian economy is growing by more than 7 percent a year and the cell phone market growth potential is unlimited.[b] Caterpillar Inc., a large U.S.-based producer of construction and mining equipment, recently increased its investment in India to serve growing Indian demand for its products as well as increased demand from other Asian countries.[c]

[a] Nokia, "Nokia Taps Chennai as New Nokia Global Networks Solutions Center Site."
[b] Samsung Electronics Co., Ltd., "Samsung Dedicates a Mobile Phone Plant in India."
[c] Caterpillar Inc., "Caterpillar Completes Purchase of Former Joint Venture Engine Business in India."

Poverty

Even with its strong economic growth in recent years, India remains a developing country, with many of its people enjoying little benefit from the country's economic growth. An estimated 25 percent of the population lives below the poverty line,[100] and the GNP per capita was only $620 in 2004.[101] Seventy percent of the Indian population lives in rural areas, which are often difficult to access because of poor roads.[102] This poverty and poor infrastructure make it harder for foreign firms to establish and expand their presence in much of the Indian market (box 3-2).

Labor Issues

Low wages

Foreign investors have been drawn to India not only by economic growth but also by low labor costs. Indian salaries are considerably lower than those in the United States and other industrialized countries. The average annual salary for all Indian employees in the manufacturing sector was approximately $1,080 in 2000–01; by 2003–04 (latest data available), the average annual salary had risen to approximately $1,270.[103] Annual salaries for skilled workers in India are much higher than these averages, but still substantially below salaries in the United States and other developed countries. Starting salaries offered by large

Indian firms for new engineering graduates range from $4,300 to $8,000 a year. Annual salaries for managers range from $30,000 to $51,000 and division heads earn up to $76,000.[104] Annual salaries for other occupations in India include human resource managers ($15,100), project managers ($10,000), financial analysts ($8,400), and customer service assistants ($1,600).[105]

BOX 3-2. HINDUSTAN LEVER LTD. SUCCEEDS IN THE INDIAN MARKET

Despite the difficulties presented by the Indian market, some foreign companies have succeeded there. Hindustan Lever Ltd. (HLL), a subsidiary of Unilever, is a large Indian producer of consumer products such as foods (primarily tea, coffee, and ice cream) and home and personal care products (soaps, deodorants, detergents, shampoos, and toothpaste). Formed from a merger of three Indian subsidiaries of Unilever in 1956, HLL has successfully penetrated the Indian market by establishing an extensive manufacturing, distribution, and R&D presence in India. HLL manufactures its products in approximately 80 factories located throughout India and has large R&D centers to develop new products for the Indian market. HLL's distribution network consists of about 7,000 redistribution stockists, which cover all major urban areas in India as well as approximately 250 million rural consumers. HLL has developed numerous brand names for its products, which are well recognized by urban and rural Indian consumers.

HLL has expanded its presence in India through a variety of methods. Hindustan Lever Network, the direct selling arm of HLL, consists of 350,000 sales consultants, located in 1,500 towns, selling HLL products out of their homes. These sales consultants cover 80 percent of India's urban population. Hindustan Lever Network plans to increase the number of its sales consultants to 1 million by 2008. To increase brand awareness and sales in rural areas, HLL (1) sells affordable value packs of its products, accompanied by educational brochures and audio-visual demonstrations, to millions of Indians in thousands of villages; (2) advertises via wall paintings and cinema vans; (3) advertises and gives product demonstrations at weekly markets and festivals, which draw large numbers of Indians from many isolated areas; (4) utilizes a vast distribution network (involving trucks, autos, cycles, scooters, and bullock carts) developed over the years encompassing 50,000 villages and 250 million people; and (5) is developing a home-based selling program for its products in rural areas, similar to that in urban areas, which provides poor women in small villages an opportunity to increase their income. Currently, the program involves thousands of women in 50,000 villages in 12 states.[a]

[a] Hindustan Lever Limited Web site.

Rigidity in the labor market

India's labor market is immense. The labor force totaled 427 million in 2004, an increase of 31 million since 2000, with women accounting for 28 percent of the labor force.[106] The organized, or formal, sector of the work force, however, accounts for less than 10 percent of the total.[107] Despite India's strong economic growth in recent years, the increase in employment in the organized sector of the economy has not kept pace with the growth of the labor force. This has generated national concern that the benefits of India's economic development have not been spread widely enough.

The inability of the Indian economy to generate sufficient jobs in the organized sector is due, at least in part, to cumbersome and bureaucratic labor policies at the federal and state levels.[108] Both the Indian federal and state governments have the authority to make and enforce labor laws. There are numerous federal and state laws covering labor issues, leading to administrative overlap and excessive bureaucracy. Federal and state labor agencies also generally focus their enforcement activities on the organized sector, even though this sector accounts for only a small percentage of the total Indian work force.

One of the biggest difficulties for employers in India is their inability to lay off workers. The Industrial Disputes Act of 1947 and subsequent amendments govern the layoffs of workers and the closure of plants. Firms with 100 or more employees must obtain approval from the government to shut down plants and lay off workers. Approval is typically difficult to obtain, although firms on occasion are able to reduce the number of employees by offering voluntary severance and retirement packages. Nonetheless, in the past few years, as the Indian economy has experienced greater trade liberalization, the Indian federal and state governments appear to have reduced their enforcement of the Industrial Disputes Act with respect to layoffs and plant closures, apparently in an attempt to increase the flexibility and competitiveness of Indian firms.[109] For example, one leading Indian executive has noted his firm's ability to lay off workers as long as proper procedures are followed.[110]

Rising salaries and high turnover in some industries

Strong demand for skilled workers in India has led to rising salaries and high turnover. To expand their operations in India, large multinational computer firms, automotive firms, and electronics firms have offered to double or triple the salaries of workers employed by Indian firms and have aggressively recruited graduates from top Indian universities and technical schools.[111] Scientists and engineers in Indian government research laboratories have left to pursue opportunities and higher salaries in the private sector. Indian companies have also experienced rapid turnover as their skilled workers leave and go to work for other employers. In the software services industry, one of the cornerstones of FDI in India, turnover recently has been between 15 and 30 percent annually.[112] Nevertheless, a recent survey of salaries of skilled workers in 42 occupations in India and China found that salaries in India remain below those in China. The salary differentials tended to be greater in those occupations paying higher salaries.[113]

Infrastructure

Antiquated infrastructure

The poor condition of India's infrastructure reduces both enthusiam for FDI on the part of foreign investors and India's overall economic growth. Insufficient power, rudimentary roads, antiquated ports, and an overburdened rail system make it difficult for many firms to produce and deliver goods and services in a timely and efficient fashion. India's national and state governments have achieved some success in expanding and modernizing infrastructure but a significantly higher level of investment will be necessary to maintain an infrastructure commensurate with the size of the Indian economy. The Indian government estimates that the infrastructure sector will need approximately $320 billion in investment during the next 5 years.[114]

India's capacity to produce electricity has fallen behind demand in recent years,[115] and electricity demand currently exceeds supply by 30 percent, causing frequent shortages and blackouts.[116] Numerous surveys of companies in India attest to the difficulties and added costs to production caused by an unreliable power sector. In one survey of Indian firms, respondents noted that it took 68 days to obtain an electrical connection and indicated that electrical outages caused production downtime equivalent to 8 percent of their annual sales.[117] In another survey of Indian firms, 29 percent of the managers ranked electricity as a major business constraint.[118] In a survey of private investors in India, respondents indicated that the average business in India experiences a power outage almost every other day. In response, most businesses have purchased generators to supply emergency electrical power.[119]

India's transport system has also lagged behind the country's rapid growth. Most Indian roads are narrow, congested, and poorly maintained. Only 41 percent of them are paved, and of these, only 34 percent are 2-lane roads and 1 percent are 4-lane roads. Forty percent of the rural population does not have access to all-weather roads and thus is isolated during periods of bad weather, particularly the monsoon season. Urban areas suffer from severe congestion, with rapid growth in automobile ownership compounding the problem of inadequate roads. Insufficient funds for road maintenance leads to further deterioration of the roads.[120]

The capacity of the railway system, particularly in the highly-traveled urban areas, has also lagged the growth in demand for its services. Indian seaports have experienced dramatic increases in container cargo but have not expanded cargo handling capacity commensurately. A similar situation has occurred at Indian airports, particularly at the major international airports, where annual growth in air traffic of more than 15 percent in recent years has led to congestion and delays.[121]

Insufficient infrastructure may continue to plague the Indian economy in the years ahead. It has been estimated that India needs to invest at least 8 percent of its gross domestic product annually (approximately $62 billion) in infrastructure to maintain its high rate of economic growth. Actual investment in infrastructure, though, probably has been only 3–4 percent of gross domestic product during the past decade. In addition, infrastructure projects are frequently plagued by long delays and large cost overruns. Projects are often started but not completed, or completed and not sufficiently maintained in the ensuing years. As infrastructure lags the economy, the effects are felt throughout the country, particularly in the manufacturing sector, where flexibility in production, low costs, and speed to market are particularly hampered by clogged roads and ports and power outages.[122]

Increased opportunities for private sector participation in infrastructure projects

To help alleviate the strains on the infrastructure, large government projects have been initiated, including (1) a National Highway Development Program to modernize roads connecting India's four largest cities, Delhi, Mumbai, Chennai, and Kolkata (the Golden Quadrilateral); (2) a rural roads program to better integrate rural areas into India's transportation network; (3) a National Railway Development Program to expand rail capacity between major cities and provide better connectivity to Indian seaports; (4) a National Maritime Development Program to expand freight handling capacity in India's large seaports; and (5) a program to increase capacity at the New Delhi and Mumbai airports, which handle about 50 percent of the country's air traffic.[123] Indian federal and state governments have also allowed more private sector participation in infrastructure projects, which has provided opportunities for foreign firms to benefit from Indian economic activity.

Traditionally, Indian federal and state governments have financed and built most infrastructure projects in India. In recent years, however, the Indian government has turned to the private sector, both domestic and foreign, for funding, expertise, and faster completion of projects in management, design, and construction. To attract FDI in the construction, maintenance, and operation of roads, the government has provided a number of incentives to private firms, including (1) government financing of project feasibility studies, land purchases, movement of utilities, and clearing of the land; (2) government approval of up to 100 percent foreign investment in a project; (3) government subsidies of up to 40 percent of the cost; (4) 100 percent tax exemption for 10 years out of 20 years after the start of the project; and (5) duty-free importation of road construction equipment. Private firms can recoup their investment in these road projects by charging tolls or by receiving an annual annuity from the government. Numerous foreign engineering and construction firms (and private Indian firms) have taken advantage of these road project opportunities. To date, 34 road projects have been completed by private firms, and another 34 projects are ongoing.[124] Indian state governments have also invited foreign engineering and construction firms to participate in road projects, patterning such private sector involvement after that of the national government.[125]

Opportunities for FDI in other areas of Indian infrastructure, including seaports and airports, have also increased. The Indian Ministry of Surface Transport, which operates India's seaports, would like to attract private investment of $1.9 billion to increase port capacity. India's Ministry of Civil Aviation, which operates India's airports, would like to attract $164 million in private sector investment to expand airport capacity.[126] Investment in airports is accorded favorable tax treatment—profits are exempt from taxation for the first 5 years after the start of the project; for the next 5 years, 30 percent of profits are exempt from taxation.[127] With respect to the power sector, the government of India is working with Indian state governments to reform their utilities by moving away from direct operational control, reducing subsidies, pushing for greater financial viability, and allowing greater private sector involvement in power distribution.[128]

Education

Educated work force

India's educational system is vast, educates millions, and turns out thousands of well-trained and skilled workers. India has an extensive system of schools, including primary and upper primary schools, high schools, colleges for general education, colleges for professional education (engineering, technology, medical, and teacher education), and universities/institutes.[129] In 2003–04, there were approximately 9,400 colleges for general education, 2,750 colleges for professional education, and 300 universities/institutes.[130] India has the third largest number of students in higher education in the world, trailing only the United States and China. English is the primary language of instruction in these schools, which means that most educated Indian workers speak at least some English.[131] In India, there are more than 200,000 engineering graduates annually, more than 300,000 post graduates from non-engineering colleges, 2.1 million other graduates, and about 9,000 PhDs.

Many foreign investors have established R&D centers in India and have made it an important location for software development. Indeed, 20 percent of the Fortune 500 companies have R&D facilities in India, drawn in large part by this vast pool of scientific and technical expertise (box 3-3).[132]

Box 3-3. Large U.S. Firms Tap Educated Indian Work Force

Three major U.S. companies are among the many to set up R&D facilities in India. Motorola, a U.S. provider of mobile telecommunications devices, has rapidly expanded its presence in India in recent years to take advantage of Indian engineers and software writers. In 1991, Motorola established its first R&D center in India. The firm now has six R&D centers engaged in research involving telecom switching technologies, embedded computing, converged networks, autonomic networking, and enterprise applications. India has also become a major source for software development and software solutions for Motorola, including much of the software used in Motorola cell phones sold worldwide. The firm's investment in technology and R&D in India increased from $50 million in 2002 to $85 million in 2005. Investment is projected to grow by 10-15 percent each year into the future. Employing over 2,800 Indian engineers, Motorola considers India to be an important hub for R&D and software development, as well as a center for designing and manufacturing products for regional markets.[a]

Microsoft has also turned to India for its technical expertise. Begun in 1998 with 20 employees, the Microsoft India Development Center has expanded to more than 900 employees and become the second largest Microsoft Development Center outside of corporate headquarters in Richmond, Washington. The Center works on software development for more than 35 products.[b]

Attracted by India's engineering knowledge and skills, General Electric opened the John F. Welch Technology Centre in Bangalore, India, in September 2000. This center, along with GE's three other R&D facilities in Schenectady, New York, Munich, Germany, and Shanghai, China, comprises GE's Global Research team, which conducts R&D and engineering activities for all GE businesses. The center in Bangalore conducts R&D in a number of areas, including mechanical engineering, electronic and electrical system technology, ceramics and metallurgy, chemical engineering, and polymer science and synthetic materials.[c]

[a] Motorola.
[b] Microsoft.
[c] General Electric.

Weaknesses in the educational system

For all the strengths of the Indian educational system, it is also plagued by a number of problems. Only 60 percent of the adult population is literate, so a large portion of the population lacks the skills increasingly necessary to prosper in the Indian economy. The percentage of young Indians in higher education (10 percent) is much less than that of industrialized countries (more than 50 percent) and of China (15 percent). India has many colleges and universities, but only a few are world class in terms of research and quality of teacher instruction. For the most part, funding for classrooms, libraries, laboratories, and information technology in Indian colleges and universities is inadequate. There are severe faculty shortages, teacher morale is low, bureaucracy hampers teacher accountability, and decision making is often influenced by politics. In addition, many Indian technology graduates pursue graduate study abroad and generally do not return to India. The majority of those who travel abroad for undergraduate study do not return to India after graduation. All of these deficiencies raise real questions as to the ability of the Indian educational system to continue to turn out sufficient numbers of well-trained graduates to enable India to maintain its competitiveness in the global economy.[133]

Access to Capital

The Indian financial sector has experienced significant reforms in recent years. Government control and regulation have been reduced, interest rates have been allowed to fluctuate with the market, restrictions on capital inflows have been loosened, and private firms have been encouraged to participate.[134] Although the Indian government is still the dominant actor in the financial sector, foreign firms in India can access capital through bank loans, equity markets, and international financial institutions.

India has a large banking system comprised of state-owned banks, private (Indian-owned) banks, and foreign-owned banks. The state-owned banks account for more than 70 percent of all deposits and loans. The respective percentages for private and foreign banks are 17 percent and 13 percent. The presence of foreign banks and private (Indian-owned) banks has led to increased competition in the banking sector. By providing better customer service through more bank branches, ATM machines, electronic and telephone banking, and longer hours, these banks have taken market share from the state-owned banks and forced them to become more responsive to customer needs. Some of the state-owned banks have restructured and government ownership has been reduced.[135]

State-owned banks and private (Indian-owned) banks concentrate on lending to the rural and agricultural sectors of the Indian economy and to Indian-owned companies.[136] Several dozen large foreign banks have established operations in India in recent years, including Citibank, HSBC, Deutsche Bank, Mizuho Financial Group, Abu Dhabi Commercial Bank Ltd., and American Express Bank Ltd. Among other activities, the foreign banks typically offer a full range of banking services, including loans, to the Indian operations of foreign firms.[137]

India has 23 stock exchanges with approximately 9,000 listed companies. Only two of these stock exchanges, however, the National Stock Exchange and the Bombay Stock Exchange, are true national exchanges, and they account for virtually all of the stock trading that occurs in the country. Foreign firms doing substantial business in India can raise equity capital in the Indian capital markets through the issuance of Indian Depository Receipts. A number of foreign firms are listed on the National Stock Exchange and/or the Bombay Stock Exchange, including Gillette Ind., Glaxosmith, Nestle Ltd., Novartis Ind., Siemens Ltd., and

SKF India. Unlike the active equity markets, the Indian debt market is small, with very little trading of notes and bonds, effectively precluding debt instruments as a way to raise capital.[138] The lending activities of non-Indian government agencies and international financial institutions provide another source of capital for foreign firms in the Indian market. The U.S.

Overseas Private Investment Corporation (OPIC) assists U.S. companies investing in developing countries by providing loans, guarantees, and political risk insurance. OPIC chooses projects that can strengthen a country's economy and enhance its long-term economic growth. In the past several years, OPIC has been involved in three projects in India. In 2004, it provided $360,000 in political risk insurance for modular home manufacturing; in 2005, OPIC provided $4.8 million in financing to expand a food manufacturing plant in India; and in 2006, OPIC provided $2.8 million in financing for the purchase of equipment and for marketing and distribution activities.[139]

The Asian Development Bank (ADB) assists developing countries by providing loans, technical assistance, grants, guarantees, and equity investments. In a typical year, the ADB lends about $6 billion to countries in the Asia-Pacific region and gives $180 million in technical assistance. India is one of the largest recipients of ADB assistance. In 2005, the ADB approved more than $1 billion in loans for India, $106 million in grants and technical assistance, and $21 million in equity investments and guarantees. ADB assistance for India has been concentrated in infrastructure, with loans and technical assistance for projects involving water supply, sanitation, waste management, roads, agriculture and natural resources, energy, and finance.[140] Such assistance from the ADB has generated opportunities for foreign investment by private firms. For example, many of the road projects involved both foreign and Indian engineering and construction firms.[141]

Two of the World Bank's agencies, the International Bank for Reconstruction and Development (IBRD) and the International Development Association (IDA), assist economic development in developing countries by providing low interest loans, interest free loans, and grants for projects involving infrastructure, education, health, energy, and other related purposes. India is the largest recipient of assistance from the World Bank. A sizeable part of this assistance involves the transport sector in India. The World Bank has made a number of loans totaling nearly $5 billion to expand the capacity of the rail system, assist in the construction and maintenance of national and state highways and rural roads, and to improve the system of public transportation in Mumbai.[142] These loans have provided opportunities for investment; foreign engineering and construction firms are participating in many of the road projects.[143]

The International Finance Corporation (IFC), another World Bank agency, promotes economic growth in developing countries by assisting private companies through loans, equity investments, guarantees, and technical and financial advice. The IFC has been active in India since 1956. India is the third largest recipient of IFC assistance; as of July 2006, the IFC's current assistance totaled $1.3 billion. IFC activities in India are focused on helping manufacturing firms improve their international competitiveness, increasing private sector involvement in infrastructure development, and supporting private firms in the areas of financial services, information technology, and oil and gas exploration and production. Although IFC's assistance in many instances has been directed toward Indian companies, foreign firms with operations in India have also benefitted from IFC financial aid.[144]

Bureaucracy and Corruption

Excessive bureaucracy and corruption discourage FDI by distorting the efficient allocation of resources, increasing the cost of doing business, and breeding mistrust of government officials. Although India has taken steps in recent years to open up more sectors of its economy to FDI and to streamline the investment process, FDI into the country remains hindered by government bureaucracy and corruption. Foreign businesses report instances where investment decisions and approval by Indian government ministries drag on for lengthy periods of time for no apparent reason.[145] The Indian government procurement system for certain areas of business has been plagued by instances of corruption; a number of government officials have been convicted under Indian anti-corruption laws in the past several years.[146] Recently, the World bank suspended funding for some health care projects in India due to allegations of fraud and corruption in the procurement of medicines.[147]

In a survey of business executives, respondents indicated that inefficient government bureaucracy and corruption were the second and fourth most problematic factors, respectively, for doing business in India.[148] See chapter 5 for a discussion of bureaucratic concerns related to the Indian court system.

4. Special Economic Zones

Introduction

India, like many countries, offers incentives to attract foreign investors, many of which are concentrated into special economic zones (SEZs). These zones allow the Indian government to package a number of incentives in a simplified manner and in a centralized location. SEZs offer privileged trading terms and other inducements to foreign investment. As of November 2006, 41 SEZs were operational in India, and approvals for more than 237 had been granted.[149] SEZs are growing in number, size, and production output and as a result are becoming more vital to the success of the Indian economy. Indian exports from SEZs increased by 114 percent between the 2000 and 2004 fiscal years and are expected to grow at an even faster rate in coming years. Exports from SEZs were valued at $5.1 billion for the 2005 fiscal year and are projected to reach $15 billion in the 2007 fiscal year, a 195 percent increase.[150] Electronics (half of which is software development) and gems and jewelry made up more than 75 percent of the exports from SEZs during 2002 (latest available data). Total investment in India's SEZs increased by almost 75 percent between 1998 and 2003, with the proportion of foreign investment rising 7 percent, to 25 percent of total.[151]

Incentives to Invest in SEZs

SEZs provide three types of incentives for enterprises to locate their business operations in India. First, the SEZs provide tax, tariff, and financial incentives, by defining SEZs as free trade enclaves. Second, the zones improve on the general bureaucratic and administrative situation that many businesses face when establishing in India. Third, SEZs provide reliable infrastructure that is not always available elsewhere in India. All of these incentives are applied equally to both Indian and foreign firms.

Tax and financial incentives for potential investors include substantial income tax deductions for the first 10 years of operations. For the first five years after operations begin, firms pay no income tax at all. For the next two years they receive a tax reduction of 50 percent. During years 8-10, the firm can debit up to 50 percent of its profits from the previous year to a "Special Economic Zone Re-investment Allowance Reserve Account." This value can then be used within three years of when the account was established for future reinvestments in the business, such as machinery and plant improvements. Outside of the SEZs, India's average tariff rates are still among the highest in the world.[152] This makes India a much less attractive destination for export-oriented firms that depend on imported inputs. However, tariff incentives exempt firms in SEZs from all customs duties on imported goods, so long as they are re-exported, which creates a beneficial environment for export oriented firms who need inexpensive and easy access to manufacturing inputs. Other financial incentives include the reimbursement of duties paid on furnace oil and exemptions from state and central sales taxes paid on domestic purchases. SEZ units can also borrow up to $500 million per year through recognized banking channels without maturity restrictions. Profits are allowed to be freely repatriated.[153]

SEZs allow investors to avoid many bureaucratic and administrative barriers as well. First, the limits on foreign equity ownership that apply to certain sectors in India are eliminated in SEZs. Second, all investments in SEZs are administered through the automatic route, which empowers the Reserve Bank of India (RBI) to automatically approve the investment within a period of two weeks.[154] Third, firms operating in SEZs do not need a license to import goods. Unlike in India's previous generation of Export Processing Zones (EPZs), customs inspections are kept to a minimum in order to eliminate delays in product availability. These factors provide incentives for investment by improving manufacturer's ability to access production inputs. Other administrative barriers have been eliminated as well. In general, separate documentation is no longer required for customs and the administration of the Export-Import Policy. Firms in SEZs also have an exemption from industrial licensing requirements that is normally only provided to small scale industries and sectors.[155] The clarification of these administrative procedures makes the investment process much simpler in SEZs compared to other areas of India.[156]

One of the most important incentives that SEZs provide is reliable infrastructure. The US- India CEO Forum, composed of 20 chief executives representing a broad spectrum of industrial sectors from both countries, has identified India's poor infrastructure as a key area of needed economic cooperation and a major impediment to new U.S. investment. The Forum recognized that "India's infrastructure needs exceed its domestic funding capacity" and one of its recommendations was to continue setting up large scale SEZs that comprise world-class infrastructure with integrated real estate, power, and transportation facilities.[157] Outside of the SEZs, with a population of just over 1 billion, India spends just $35 billion a year on infrastructure,[158] and investors frequently encounter difficulties related to infrastructure.[159]

Adequate infrastructure is a prerequisite for an area to be approved as an SEZ. All of India's SEZs have uninterrupted water and power supplies, guaranteed by state governments; power is distributed through sub-stations that are dedicated to distributing power only to a specific SEZ. Additional infrastructure facilities include developed plots, built-up space, and telecommunication lines, as well as supportive services, such as in-house customs facilities, post offices, banks, canteens, courier services, travel agents, medical services, shopping, food services, and worker housing. Most importantly, however, the SEZs provide reliable access to trade opportunities through well integrated transportation facilities. The majority of the zones are within 25 km of a major metropolitan area that provide ports and airports, and other transportation services essential to international merchandise trade. Even though ports and airport facilities are often not available within or directly adjacent to the zone, each SEZ provides access to these facilities through both railways and highways. Many Indian highways are narrow and congested, with poor surface quality and the rail system also faces severe capacity constraints with very high rail freight costs.[160] By contrast, most SEZs have newly built, high quality rail and highway systems that reduce congestion and transportation costs.[161] See chapter 3 for additional information on India's infrastructure concerns outside of the SEZs.

Establishment and Licensing of SEZs

In India, an SEZ is a specifically delineated, duty-free enclave that is deemed to be foreign territory for the purposes of trade operations, including tariff treatments.[162] Goods transiting into the SEZ areas from the rest of India are considered Indian exports. Goods coming from the SEZ areas into the Indian economy are treated as Indian imports. The laws, regulations, and incentives that apply to these zones are separate from those that apply to the rest of the country.[163]

In March 2000, India's new Special Economic Zone Policy modified the country's existing policy on EPZs to establish SEZs that would provide an environment to facilitate the production of goods intended for export. SEZs can be set up by the public sector, by private firms, or as joint cooperative efforts between the two sectors.[164]

The change to SEZs was meant to solve several problems with the existing EPZ policy. One significant issue was the lack of a single window application facility,[165] both within the zone and at the national level. Without such a "single window," establishing both EPZs and the individual firm units within them, required a firm to acquire individual clearances from several separate departments within the government and the EPZ administrative body. Within the EPZ, separate departments were in charge of approving and allocating land allotments, water and power supplies, and building and environmental clearances. The establishment process has been greatly simplified in the current SEZs. In addition, conditions for approval have been relaxed, customs rules have been simplified, and additional oversight responsibilities have been given directly to the Development Commissioners Office in order to maintain consistency.[166]

In the SEZ Act of 2005, the Indian government clarified and simplified the procedures for establishing an SEZ. The Act established specific minimum size requirements for different types of SEZs. There are exceptions to some regulations in order to promote certain industries or in regions of the country that are considered to be land restricted (table 4-1). Other criteria for approval reinforce that the units within the SEZ must abide by local laws and regulations as well as develop necessary infrastructure. For example, SEZs must abide by local laws in regard to area planning, sewage disposal, pollution control, as well as all other industrial and labor laws. Also, at least 35 percent of the land area must be used for the core manufacturing processes, and directly associated storage and distribution facilities. The remaining land area can be used for non-core production facilities such as hospitals, housing developments, shopping, and other commercial development.[167]

Table 4-1. India: Types of special Economic Zones

Type of SEZ	Description	Minimum size requirements	Other
		Hectares	
New multi-product SEZs	Zones with general production in a wide variety of product types and industries	1,000	
Sector specific SEZs	Zones for use on production in specific industries	100	Approved on a case by case basis
Service sector SEZs	Zones that provide only services without manufacturing capability	100	
Converted Export Processing zones	Converted from a previous EPZ	None	
Port-based SEZs	Zones based at ports or airports	None	Approved on a case by case basis
Sector specific SEZs in areas of Indian competitive advantage	Specifically applies to gems and jewelry, information technology, and bio-technology	10	Approved on a case by case basis
Multi-product SEZs in land restricted states	Land restricted in particular states[a]	200	
Sector specific SEZs in land restricted states	Land restricted in particular statesa	50	

Source: Government of India, Ministry of Commerce & Industry, "Special Economic Zones in India," http://www.sezindia.nic.in/ (accessed November 2006).

[a] Land restricted states include Assam, Arunachal Pradesh, Nagaland, Manipur, Mizoram, Tripura, Sikkim, Goa, Meghalaya, Himachal Pradesh, Jammu, Kashmir, Uttaranchal, and the Union Territories.

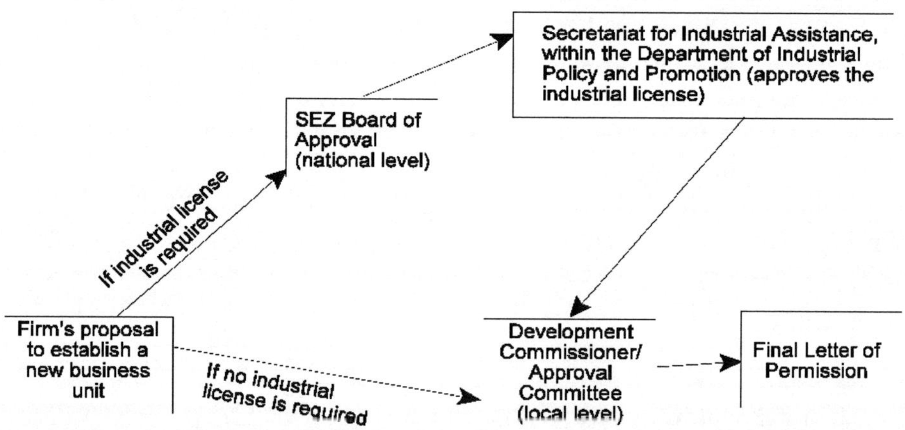

Source: Government of India, Ministry of commerce & Industry, *Special Economic Zones in India-How to Apply.*

Figure 4-1. Application process for firms establishing a business unit within an SEZ

The approval process for the development of a new SEZ is shared by the federal and state governments. Proposals for establishing an SEZ are first routed through the concerned state government, which has 45 days from the date of receipt to render a decision. The state forwards the application, along with its recommendation, to the Board of Approval, part of India's federal Department of Commerce.[168]

An individual firm's proposal to set up a new business unit within an SEZ must be approved by the Approval Committee for each Zone (figure 4-1). The Committee consists of the Development Commissioner, the Customs Authorities, and representatives of the relevant state government. The Development Commissioner is the de facto chairman of the Approval Committee and head of the SEZ. All clearances for importer-exporter code number, change in the name of the company or implementing agency, land allotments, and development plans are given through a single window facility by the Development Commissioner, generally within 15 days.[169] If approved, firms receive a letter of permission from the Commissioner, which specifies the items of manufacture or service activity, annual capacity, projected annual exports for the first years in dollar terms, net foreign exchange earnings, and any limitations regarding the sale of finished goods and their by-products in the domestic tariff area.[170]

An industrial license is required for business unit proposals involving industries retained under compulsory licensing, manufacturing of items reserved for small scale sectors, and situations in which the proposed location is restricted.[171] These proposals are first considered at the national level by the SEZ Board of Approval, and then by the Secretariat for Industrial Assistance at the Department of Industrial Policy and Promotion, who grants the actual license. If the SEZ approval and the industrial license are granted, then the application is forwarded to the local Development Commissioner, who can then issue a letter of permission. The SEZ Act also specifies that the units must be net foreign exchange earners, but that they will not be subject to any predetermined minimum export performance requirements.[172]

While the Indian government continues to restrict FDI in industries that are considered sensitive outside of SEZs, such as agriculture and retailing, 100 percent investment is allowed through the automatic route for all activities in Special Economic Zones (SEZs), except for the manufacturing of weapons and defense equipment, hazardous chemicals, narcotics, alcohol, and tobacco products.[173]

Other FDI Incentives

India provides investment incentives outside of SEZs as well. These are generally designed to channel FDI to specific industries, promote development of economically impoverished regions, and encourage exports. The lack of reliable infrastructure outside of the SEZs is a significant factor preventing India from reaching its full growth potential. With this in mind, the Indian government has begun to remove restrictions on foreign investors in infrastructure. Beginning in March 2005, the government has allowed 100 percent FDI in infrastructure and construction development projects, as well as townships and housing projects, subject to minimum capitalization requirements.[174]

In addition to liberalizing ownership equity caps, there are a number of tax incentives for foreign firms to invest in infrastructure, including 10-year tax holidays that can be used anytime during the first 20 years of operation for enterprises that build, maintain, or operate infrastructure facilities. Other incentives include exemptions from income tax on interest and from long-term capital gains tax on infrastructure investments, and the ability to deduct 50 percent of profits for five years for setting up and operating large, specific types of infrastructure.[175]

Additional FDI incentives in India include accelerated depreciation and permitting tax deductions for R&D expenses. The specifics vary slightly depending on the region and industry. The FDI approval process has also been shortened and simplified through the implementation of the automatic route for approval in more and more industries. These incentives, along with the continued liberalization of caps on foreign firms' ownership equity in most industries, have contributed to the recent steep increases of FDI in India.[176]

5. FDI Regulation and Dispute Settlement

FDI Procedures

Foreign investment policy in India has been significantly liberalized since comprehensive macroeconomic reforms began in July 1991.[177] As of April 2007, 100 percent foreign equity is permitted in most sectors via automatic approval, with a handful of sectors subject to industrial licensing restrictions,[178] and only a few industries are entirely closed to foreign participation due to political or national security sensitivities (appendix A).[179] This chapter will review India's regulatory environment for FDI, including the approval process for new investments; regulation related to labor and intellectual property concerns; and legal alternatives for dispute settlement.

Foreign investment in India is approved through two routes: automatic and case-by-case government approval. Under the automatic route, foreign investment in an Indian entity does not require prior government approval. To qualify for the automatic route, companies investing in approved industries must notify the Reserve Bank of India (RBI) within 30 days of receipt of funds and issuance of shares to the foreign investor. In other cases, government approval by the Foreign Investment Promotion Board (FIPB) is required.[180] These cases include sectors that require industrial licenses, foreign investments exceeding 24 percent of equity in small-scale industries,[181] foreign investments where the foreign interest has an existing venture in the same field in India, and all proposals falling outside the predetermined sectoral caps or in sectors where FDI is usually not permitted, but authorized in certain cases at the discretion of the Indian government.[182] Foreign investments in existing companies and foreign technology collaboration agreements are also subject to case-by-case approval requirements.[183] There appear to be few or no limitations on forms of establishment.[184]

In addition to approving particular investment proposals, the FIPB is also the primary contact for large multinational companies planning extensive investment projects.[185] The Department of Industrial Policy and Promotion (DIPP), under the Ministry of Industry and Commerce, is responsible for all other foreign investment activity in India.[186] Within DIPP, the Secretariat for Industrial Assistance (SIA) provides a one-stop shop (or "single window facility") for entrepreneurial assistance, investor facilitation, project setup and monitoring, and application processing.[187] Further, the Foreign Investment Implementation Authority (FIIA), which is chaired by the SIA, provides proactive investor services for projects that have already received central government approval.[188] The FIIA helps investors obtain state-level clearances, assists with any operational problems, and liaises between various government agencies on behalf of investors to speed approval of FDI inflows.[189] Chapter 3 discusses the approval process for FDI in India's special economic zones (SEZs).

FDI Regulation

Although Indian business regulation principally falls under the jurisdiction of federal law, state governments are empowered to design and regulate their own FDI policies.[190] Consequently, the regulatory burden on foreign investors tends to be higher at the state level where application and approval procedures can vary widely across states. Moreover, FDI projects already approved at the central government level tend to bottleneck as they proceed since nearly 70 percent of the approvals and applications needed for eventual FDI implementation are obtained from state governments.[191] State-level impediments to FDI can be severe, to the point that companies have been known to abandon FDI projects mid-way through implementation due to issues such as onerous zoning, land-use, and environmental regulations.[192] In addition to difficult compliance procedures, such as the example mentioned, regulatory burden can take other forms in India. These can include long delays in getting new connections from public sector utilities, frequent visits by government inspectors, and the payment of bribes to avoid bureaucratic red tape.[193] As a result, the federal government has made efforts to establish independent regulators in sectors such as telecommunications, securities, and insurance in order to streamline supervision below the federal level.[194] Since it is impossible to comprehensively address all of the state FDI regulations here, appendix B provides website links to the investment promotion agencies for each of India's states and territories.

Labor Regulation

As described in chapter 4, the state of the labor market and related regulations are also an important factors for foreign investors to evaluate when making an FDI commitment. Similar to FDI policy, labor regulations are enacted at both the central and state government levels.[195] As of 2006, India maintains 47 national laws and 157 state regulations that directly or indirectly address labor markets (table 5-1).[196] India has a number of labor laws addressing issues such as the resolution of industrial disputes, the regulation of working conditions, labor compensation, insurance, child labor, and equal pay. Generally viewed as more protective of workers' rights, Indian laws such as the Minimum Wages Act, the Payment of Wages Act, and the Employees Provident Fund and Miscellaneous Provisions Act guarantee employee salaries regardless of whether companies are profitable, allow central or state governments to set worker wages in any type of business establishment, prohibit any unauthorized wage deductions or reductions, and ensure retirement savings and benefits for all permanent company employees.[197]

Table 5-1. Selected Indian Labor Laws

Law	Description
Employees Provident Fund and Miscellaneous Provisions Act of 1952	This Act ensures the financial security of employees by providing a compulsory savings system. It establishes a contributory Provident Fund where employees' contributions shall be at least equal to that made by the employer. The savings is payable to the employee after retirement or can be withdrawn partly for specified purposes.
Industrial Employment (Standing orders) Act of 1946	This Act requires employers in industrial establishments to clearly define the conditions of employment by issuing duly certified standing orders. Standing orders issued under this Act deal with the classification of workers, holidays, shifts, payment of wages, leave, termination, etc.
Industrial Disputes Act of 1947	Provides for the investigation and settlement of industrial disputes such as lockouts, layoffs, retrenchment, etc. The Act specifies the conditions that must be met before an employee is terminated. Terminations falling outside of these guidelines must receive government approval.
Minimum Wages Act of 1948	Prescribes minimum wages for all employees in any type of establishment. Central and state governments can revise specified wage levels.
Payment of Bonus Act of 1965	The Act provides for the payment of bonuses to persons employed in certain establishments on the basis of profit or productivity. This Act is applicable to establishments employing 20 or more people. A minimum bonus is required, even if the employer suffers a loss during the fiscal year.
Payment of Gratuity Act of 1972	Provides for the payment of gratuity to all employees in all establishments employing 10 or more people (regardless of the type of work). Gratuity is payable to an employee on his retirement or resignation at a rate of 15 days salary for each completed year of service, subject to a maximum of about $7,800.
Payment of Wages Act of 1936	Regulates the time limits within which wages shall be distributed to employees and that no unauthorized deductions are made by employers.
Workmen's Compensation Act of 1923	Provides that compensation will be given to any worker suffering an injury during the course of employment, or to his dependents in the case of death. The Act specifies the rate at which compensation shall be paid to the employee.

Source: Government of India, Ministry of Labor Web site.

Many of these labor laws are viewed as overlapping, potentially inconsistent, and cumbersome.[198] In particular, the Industrial Disputes Act (IDA) requires companies with more than 100 employees to secure state government permission to dismiss workers. Such permission can be difficult to obtain, but application of the IDA tends to vary across states.[199] According to recent research, Indian states with more restrictive labor laws tended to have fewer factories, with estimates suggesting that almost 3 million formal manufacturing jobs were lost due to the general application of IDA provisions.[200] Furthermore, businesses that hire contract workers to fill production gaps are subject to the Contract Labor Act, which gives state governments the right to abolish contract labor at any time, in any industry, in favor of permanent workers.[201] In states where contract labor is more restricted, keeping employment below the 100 employee threshold is the only way companies can maintain flexibility in the allocation of manpower. Consequently, Indian labor laws tend to reinforce exit barriers for investors and dampen overall FDI in labor-intensive industries.[202]

Intellectual Property Rights Regulation

Important improvements have been made in India's intellectual property rights (IPR) regime in recent years. India has substantially revised its laws to bring them into compliance with the requirements of the WTO's Agreement on Trade-Related Aspects of Intellectual Property Rights (TRIPS), which requires protections for various forms of intellectual property. However, according to the United States Trade Representative (USTR) and U.S. Department of Commerce (DOC), substantial concerns remain because of inadequate IPR protection and enforcement.[203] India's legal framework, and particular enforcement issues, in the predominant intellectual property areas of trademarks, copyrights, and patents are described below. The laws governing the protection of pharmaceutical products are explored in greater detail in the case study in chapter 8.

Trademark protection

The legal framework of India's trademark laws is generally considered consistent with international standards.[204] India revised its law with passage of the Trademarks Act of 1999, which came into effect in 2003, to comply with the requirements of TRIPS. The Act broadens the definition of a trademark and simplifies the procedural requirements for registration. It also provides civil and criminal remedies for trademark infringement.[205]

The actual level of protection afforded trademarks under the law is more problematic. According to a survey of business executives conducted by the International Chamber of Commerce, India is ranked as having the third worst IPR protection environment, following China and Russia, because of its disproportionate share of counterfeiting and piracy.[206] In the area of pharmaceuticals, the Pharmaceutical Research and Manufacturers of America (PhRMA) reports that while civil remedies for counterfeiting are generally available, the volume of litigation is substantial and judicial delays hinder the process of obtaining relief.[207] Although criminal remedies for counterfeiting hold the promise of a speedier resolution and a greater deterrent power, inadequate resources and low rates of conviction hamper their availability. Better results may be available in cases involving pharmaceutical counterfeiters whom criminal courts are more likely to convict because of health and safety risks.[208]

India exports a large amount of counterfeit products, although the situation may be improving.[209] In 2005, U.S. Customs and Border Protection reported that it seized counterfeit goods valued at about $2 billion from India. India was the fourth largest source of all counterfeits in the United States (behind China, Hong Kong, and the United Arab Emirates). Despite being fourth overall, India was the number one source of counterfeit pharmaceuticals in 2005, accounting for 61 percent of pharmaceutical seizures from all sources.[210] More positively, seizures of counterfeits from India were down in 2006; India fell to the eighth largest source of counterfeit products and pharmaceutical seizures in particular were substantially lower.[211]

Copyright protection

At the time India's amended Copyright Act went into effect in 1995, it was considered "one of the most modern copyright laws in any country," particularly because of its rigorous criminal enforcement provisions.[212] Today, the challenges of copyright protection in the digital environment reportedly require India to update its laws, for example, by joining and implementing the two World Intellectual Property Organization (WIPO) Internet Treaties.[213] Both treaties seek to ensure that traditional means for copyright protection apply to digital works and those transmitted on the Internet. The government of India recently released draft amendments to implement the provisions of the internet treaties; however, USTR has opined that the draft amendments are deficient.[214]

Problems with enforcement of the copyright laws are significant. According to the International Intellectual Property Alliance (IIPA), a coalition representing the U.S. copyright based industries, the principal challenge in India is "to make the criminal system work despite corruption, inefficient court procedures, lack of training, massively long delays, and few convictions." Piracy—the unauthorized distribution and use of copyrighted materials—remains a substantial problem for both U.S. and Indian producers. Piracy of software, film, popular fiction works, and television cable signals has been labeled "rampant."[215] Pirated movies and other content are available in the informal markets of major cities long before their domestic release in theaters. According to the IIPA, music file sharing and the online infringement of business and entertainment software, as well as deficiencies in the enforcement environment, substantially burden both foreign and local investors in copyright-based industries.[216]

Patent protection

India inherited its patent laws from the British and, until 1970, provided product and process protection for all inventions.[217] In 1970, India introduced the Patents Act which prohibited patents on products useful as medicines or foods, shortened the term of chemical process patents, and expanded the availability of compulsory licensing of patented inventions.[218] Effective January 1, 2005, India was required, pursuant to its WTO TRIPS commitments, to provide product protection for pharmaceuticals and agricultural chemicals. It did so through an interim measure adopted in December 2004 and a new patent law enacted in April 2005. This new law, including its impact on pharmaceutical FDI, is discussed in detail in the case study in chapter 8.

India and the United States entered into a Memorandum of Understanding (MOU) in December 2006. The purpose of the MOU is to further cooperation in the IPR field and to better promote innovation. The MOU provides for the training of patent personnel and the sharing of procedures and best practices.[219] It responds to the concern of U.S. industry, and particularly pharmaceutical firms, that Indian patent examiners are not trained or experienced in the review of pharmaceutical products and other complex technologies, and that there is a substantial backlog of patent applications awaiting review.[220] Moreover, the government of India reports that 25,000 new patent applications were filed in 2006; the amount of work and resources that will be required to handle these applications is substantial.[221] Patent infringement cases, like those involving trademarks and copyrights, are subject to lengthy judicial proceedings and delays. Industries that rely on IPR protections are severely hampered by the practical difficulties of enforcing these rights.

Other Regulatory Issues

Closing down a business in India involves a cumbersome regulatory process that poses expensive exit costs. Depending on the state, it takes an average of 10 years to complete bankruptcy procedures in India, with variations between 8 and 20 years. This compares to an average of about 4 years in South Asia, 2 years in East Asia, and 1 year in OECD countries.[222] Liquidations in India are governed by the Companies Act, which assigns official liquidators (OLs) to carry out the bankruptcy proceedings. Industry surveys report that OLs tend to follow cumbersome procedures and cause undue delays. Moreover, when a case is finally ready to be heard, courts and tribunals are often already overburdened with large caseloads, creating even longer delays[223]

Some regulatory impediments have been eliminated. Performance requirements, such as local sourcing, no longer exist in most sectors and requirements to hire Indian nationals have largely been eliminated.[224] FDI in the retail housing sector is restricted in most cases, but non-residents of Indian origin and foreign companies are permitted to acquire or hold real estate in India, except for farmland, farmhouses, and plantations.[225]

Implications of Recent FDI Policy Changes

Semiconductors

In February 2007, the government of India announced the establishment of the Special Incentive Package Scheme, which focuses on attracting greater investment in semiconductor manufacturing and other high technology industries in India. Broadly, the package provides subsidies in the form of tax breaks and interest-free loans to foreign companies interested in investing in Indian semiconductor plants with a minimum investment of $550 million. Loans are available for up to 20 percent of capital expenditures for projects in SEZs and up to 25 percent elsewhere.[226] This policy, which will extend through 2010, is expected to generate between $6 billion and $9 billion in new investments over the next three years.[227] The Special Incentive Package Scheme also covers LCD and plasma screens, storage devices, solar cells, photovoltaics, and nanotechnology products.[228] Following the announcement, Indian government officials were planning to reopen negotiations with Intel, which established a chip plant in Vietnam while waiting for India to formulate its long-delayed national semiconductor policy.[229] As noted in chapter 2, SemIndia, an Indian company setting up a $3-billion chip fabrication plant in Hyderabad, has received informal commitments from global semiconductor producers such as AMD, SanDisk, Flextronics, and Broadcom since the announcement.[230] However, as of April 2007, further details on these proposed ventures have not been disclosed.

Telecommunications

In late 2006, the Indian government announced plans to lower the price of bandwidth by up to 25 percent and allow for its resale to new operators, giving foreign firms greater access to the largely private-sector telecommunications infrastructure.[231] As a result, international firms such as BT and Cable & Wireless, which are both based in the United Kingdom, are reportedly interested in entering the Indian telecom market to provide broader advanced networking services, such as network integration and security. Additionally, current operators in India, such as AT&T,[232] which competes with Indian telecom companies in both domestic and international long distance services, believe that these changes will also improve overall service quality and reliability since end-to-end control of transmission systems are now possible. Moreover, broadband internet service, which has grown over 600 percent since 2005 to 1.5 million Indian subscribers, is seen as the primary driver of the bandwidth market in India.[233] Expansion in services such as Internet telephony (VoIP), which reached 1 billion minutes in India during the first quarter of 2006, reflecting six-fold growth from 160 million minutes in 2005,[234] will also likely provide greater investment opportunities in the Indian telecom sector as bandwidth prices continue to fall.

Retailing

Due to lingering political and social sensitivities within the retail sector, foreign investors in India's retailing industry remain limited to single-brand retail outlets. With a total of 12 million retailers in India (97 percent of which are small mom-and-pop style businesses), there is strong opposition to foreign involvement.[235] However, the Indian government is actively considering whether to allow greater foreign investments in specific products, namely, sporting goods, stationery, construction materials, and electronics.[236] As of March 2007, foreign investors were allowed to control a maximum of 51 percent equity in Indian retail ventures that sell products under a single international brand. In 2004, Arvind Brands, the second largest domestic apparel company in India, created a joint venture with Tommy Hilfiger licensor, Ganesh,[237] to establish Hilfiger-branded clothing and apparel stores throughout India.[238] In November 2006, Bharti Enterprises and Wal-Mart announced a joint-venture agreement where Wal-Mart would provide its goods wholesale to the Indian retailer and provide logistics and distribution services to the joint venture.[239] Specifically, Bharti, a major Indian telecom operator, is planning to invest $2.5 billion to create a national supermarket chain creating 10 million square feet of retail space and employ 60,000 people by 2015.[240] Industry sources estimate that retail sales in India will grow from $300 billion in 2006 to an estimated $427 billion by 2010 and $637 billion by 2015.[241] Overall, industry reports suggest that the biggest challenge for international retailers entering India will not be overcoming FDI restrictions, but rather, how quickly they will be able to adapt to local consumer buying habits and to the logistics infrastructure.[242]

Litigation and Alternative Dispute Resolution

Litigation in India

The Indian court system is severely backlogged and suffering from infrastructural difficulties. The Law Commission of India, a branch of India's Ministry of Law & Justice, reported that over 2 million cases in 13,000 district courts were pending in 2004. The Indian court system as a whole has an estimated backlog of 25 million cases which would take approximately 324 years to clear if the court system proceeds at its present rate.[243] Civil and criminal cases are reported to take between 10 and 20 years to be determined by a court.[244] Such long delays lead to further problems once the case finally reaches the court. Witnesses frequently lose recollection when they are called to give testimony so long after witnessing an event.[245] Similarly, evidence often becomes tainted or disappears over the many years prior to trial.[246] Such problems often lead to the adjournment of cases and further delays once the case finally reaches the court.

In an effort to address the longstanding problems with India's court system, the Indian national government issued a series of amendments to its Code of Civil Procedure. The two most pertinent amendments are the Code of Civil Procedure Amendment Act of 1999 (1999 Amendment) and the Code of Civil Procedure Amendment Act of 2002 (2002 Amendment). Both the 1999 Amendment and the 2002 Amendment came into force on July 1, 2002.[247]

The 1999 Amendment was designed to lessen the number of cases reaching the Indian courts by making Alternative Dispute Resolution (ADR) compulsory for certain civil disputes in India, and to lessen the time a judicial proceeding takes by limiting the allowable number of adjournments in a each litigation.[248] Moreover, the 1999 Amendment prevents further appeal for certain cases to lessen the burden on the court system.[249] The 1999 Amendment requires certain civil cases to attempt a resolution through ADR, and only if a case is not resolvable through ADR will it be allowed to proceed to the Indian courts for litigation.[250]

Similarly, the 2002 Amendment's objective is to shorten the length of judicial proceedings by placing limitations on a number of procedures, changing other procedures, and limiting certain appeals. The 2002 Amendment allows the service of summons by means of e-mail, fax, or private courier.[251] It also specifies that there shall be no second appeal from any decree "when the subject-matter of the original suit is for the recovery of an amount not exceeding Rs. 25,000."[252] Additionally, the 2002 Amendment specifies a series of strict time limitations for the submission of the commission report to the Court, the pronouncement of the judgment, and provides that the judge has the discretion to put time limitations on oral arguments.[253] Despite these efforts to expedite judicial proceedings, many foreign investors choose to resolve disputes arising in India through ADR mechanisms.

Alternative Dispute Resolution (ADR) in India

Foreign investors frequently choose to enter arbitration agreements when engaging in business in India, to avoid the problems of the judicial system. The terms of a potential arbitration are generally stipulated in a contract[254] by investors before any legal problems arise, although parties may also agree to arbitrate after a legal dispute occurs. Investors often contractually stipulate that arbitration will take place outside of India, opting instead for the more established arbitration venues of the United States or United Kingdom. In one recent example, a dispute between two private airline companies was brought to arbitration in London, rather than in New Delhi or Mumbai.[255]

The Indian government actively promotes alternative dispute resolution (ADR) mechanisms as an alternative to litigation. The Indian Arbitration and Conciliation Act of 1996 (IACA) creates a coherent system of arbitration of both domestic and international disputes. The IACA applies to both domestic arbitration between Indian parties and international arbitration, defined as arbitration occurring when one party is a non-resident of India, incorporated outside India, a foreign government, or a company whose central management is controlled outside of India.[256] The Act governs all major aspects of international commercial arbitration taking place in India.[257] The IACA also statutorily incorporated the New York Convention, the Geneva Convention, and the Geneva Protocol into the domestic laws of India, which gives investors recourse under both domestic and international law for violations of these conventions.[258]

Furthermore, in 2003, the Indian government set forth proposals to incorporate mediation and conciliation, two additional forms of ADR, more integrally into its legal regime (box 5-1).[259]

Additionally, India is a party to three international, multilateral treaties pertaining to arbitration. All three purport to recognize and/or enforce the arbitral awards of other countries signatory to each Convention. The conventions make it easier to enforce, and illegal not to enforce, arbitral awards issued in India within other nations that are parties to the conventions, as long as the requirements of the conventions are met.

The New York Convention, the largest multilateral convention governing the recognition and enforcement of foreign arbitral awards, presently has 142 parties, including the United States and India, and is the applicable law between the United States and India.[260] The New York Convention obliges its parties to recognize and enforce arbitral awards made in the territory of another party, subject to certain provisos.[261] The Geneva Protocol and the Geneva Convention were both ratified by India on October 23, 1937. The United States has not ratified either convention, but the two treaties are in force between India and other countries that have ratified the Convention or Protocol, but are not parties to the New York Convention.[262]

Box 5-1. Forms of ADR: Mediation, Arbitration, and Conciliation

Mediation is distinguished from arbitration in many ways, including:

- Under arbitration, an arbitrator or arbitration panel makes a binding decision, whereas decisions in mediation are made by the parties and the mediator acts as a catalyst;
- Under arbitration, the only settlement option is an arbitral award, whereas mediation has numerous settlement options;
- An arbitral award is generally rendered in favor of one party or the other whereas mediation generally reflects a compromise between the parties;
- The parties have less control over the arbitral process than the mediation process.

The conciliation process is closer to mediation than to arbitration, although the differences between conciliation and mediation vary among jurisdictions and venues.

In an effort to promote ADR in India, the Indian national and state governments founded the International Center for Alternative Dispute Resolution (ICADR) in 1995. The ICADR is an autonomous agency that works under the aegis of the Indian Ministry of Law & Justice, to encourage the use of ADR mechanisms for both international and domestic disputes, and to provide support services and a venue for these disputes.[263] The ICADR provides an optional forum for parties desiring to settle disputes via ADR mechanisms in India, rather than New York or London. The center is headquartered in New Delhi and has regional branches in Hyderabad and Bangalore.[264] Parties to a contract may contractually stipulate in their arbitration agreements that the ICADR will be the forum for dispute settlement. Additionally, parties may subsequently agree to settle an existing dispute in the ICADR. It was reported in November 2002 that the center has been receiving an average of only two to three cases per month.[265] According to the Indian government, the infrequent use of the ICADR can be attributed to "limited knowledge and awareness about this mechanism."[266] The report further suggests that all national and state governments should promote the use of the ICADR to investors, and tell investors to contractually stipulate its use as a forum in their arbitration agreements.[267] The ICADR, the Indian government suggests, offers a forum within which investors can settle their disputes in an expeditious manner.

ADR in Action: The Enron Dispute and the Dabhol Power Plant

The Dabhol dispute is the largest, most complicated investment dispute in recent Indian history, and has affected subsequent FDI dispute settlement procedures. The Dabhol project began as a joint venture to build a 2,200 megawatt power plant in the western Indian state of Maharashtra.[268] Enron was the majority investor with a 65 percent equity share in the Dabhol power project; General Electric (GE) and Bechtel Enterprise Holdings, Inc. (Bechtel) each maintained 10 percent equity; and the Maharashtra State Electricity Board (MESB) held the remaining equity share of 15 percent.[269] The $3 billion Dabhol power plant had nearly completed construction when the government of Maharashtra stopped paying its agreed amount under the power purchase agreement with U.S. investors, allegedly because the cost of power produced by the plant was too high.[270] Following these events, numerous lawsuits were initiated between the investors and the Indian government, and at least six international arbitral proceedings were initiated relating to the Dabhol breakdown.[271]

The Indian government placed anti-arbitration injunctions on Dabhol-related arbitration proceedings which were subject to jurisdiction in India, thus delaying arbitration indefinitely.[272] Nonetheless, GE and Bechtel were awarded $57.1 million from the U.S. Overseas Private Investment Corporation (OPIC) via arbitration, that side-stepped the Indian injunctions because none of the parties to this arbitral proceeding were subject to Indian jurisdiction.[273] Bechtel and GE brought the proceedings against OPIC in order to recover claims under a political risk insurance policy that was taken out to cover the Dabhol project. The OPIC-GE/Bechtel proceeding illustrates how arbitration can aid in the expedient resolution of disputes arising in India.

India and the United States entered into an Investment Incentive Agreement in 1997 in order to encourage OPIC to support U. S. investment in India, and to encourage investors to use OPIC when investing in India.[274] Under this agreement, if the national government of India is found in breach of its obligations under the agreement, it will be obliged to pay the insurer (OPIC) the amount OPIC has to pay the insured (in this case, GE and Bechtel). The $57.1 million award to GE and Bechtel in the present case, creates an obligation for the Indian government to pay OPIC that sum, free from the interference caused by the injunction on arbitrations issued by the Indian courts.[275]

The MESB was found in violation of a multitude of its obligations under the power purchase agreement in the OPIC arbitration. These obligations were counter-guaranteed by the Indian government, making the Indian national government responsible for reimbursement to GE and Bechtel.[276] The MESB was found responsible, in this arbitral proceeding, for over ten breaches of its obligations, including its failure to pay under the power purchase agreements and the rescission (denunciation) of the power purchase agreement.[277] The arbitral tribunal, chaired by a former U.S. federal judge, determined that because of the breaches by the MESB, OPIC must pay GE and Bechtel the $57.1 million under the political risk insurance policies that were issued by OPIC to the two companies in

1995.[278] Thus, GE and Bechtel recovered their costs from OPIC under their political risk insurance policy because MESB had breached its obligations under the power purchase agreement. The government of India is obliged under the Investment Incentive Agreement to reimburse OPIC for the money awarded to GE and Bechtel.

The OPIC-GE/Bechtel proceeding is one example of how arbitration agreements with a non- Indian venue can allow damaged parties to recover their losses from disputes arising in India in an expeditious manner. Recovery was granted to GE and Bechtel, even in face of a proceeding that would have been delayed indefinitely if it were brought in the Indian court system.

6. India's Investment-Related International Agreements

India is a founding member of both the General Agreement on Tariffs and Trade (GATT) and the World Trade Organization (WTO). India also is a signatory to the South Asia Free Trade Agreement (SAFTA), which promotes mutual trade, economic cooperation, and greater investment-related activities among its members.[279] India has entered into 57 bilateral investment treaties[280] (BITs) but does not have a BIT with the United states. India also maintains Double Tax Avoidance Agreements[281] (tax treaties) with 70 countries, including major trading and FDI partners China, Germany, Japan, Mauritius, the United Kingdom, and the United States (appendix C).

World Trade Organization

India's membership in the WTO benefits foreign investors primarily through two agreements: the Agreement on Trade Related Investment Measures (TRIMs), and the General Agreement on Trade in Services (GATS). In addition, WTO membership imposes the general obligations of most favored nation (MFN) treatment, market access (MA), and national treatment (NT) with regard to trade policy.[282] These also affect foreign investment, as India's obligations under these principles may affect investors' evaluation of India's investment environment. WTO rules allow certain exemptions from these principles for the benefit of developing country members, which make up approximately 75 percent of all WTO members, including India.[283] India's status as a developing country provides it with flexibility as to its obligations under both the TRIMs and the GATS.

Agreement on trade related investment measures

The TRIMs Agreement is the WTO agreement that most directly addresses investment, although only certain trade-related investment measures are covered by the agreement. It prohibits quantitative restrictions (quotas) and violations of the NT principle for investment measures related to trade in goods.[284] Moreover, the TRIMs includes an illustrative list of TRIMs that violate the NT principle and the prohibition on quantitative restrictions, including local content requirements[285] and trade balancing requirements.[286] In one significant WTO case, *Indonesia-Autos*, a dispute settlement panel defined such prohibited "trade- related investment measures" to include all measures posited on the TRIMs illustrative list, and thus these measures are open to action in the WTO.[287] If a measure is found to be in violation of the NT principle or the prohibition on quantitative restrictions, then the measure will have to be withdrawn by the nonconforming state.

The TRIMs agreement requires members to eliminate all non-conforming TRIMs, and contingent on the member's status within the WTO, the members were given variable amounts of time to eliminate all TRIMs. Developed country members were given two years, developing country members were given five years, and least developed countries were given seven years. Soon after the entry into force of the TRIMs Agreement, India notified the Committee of its three inconsistent TRIMs.[288] India, as a developing country member, was given the five year transition period for these TRIMs,which ended on December 31, 1999. None of these non-conforming TRIMs are presently in force in India.[289] The TRIMs Agreement allows developing countries to temporarily deviate from their national treatment obligations and the prohibition on quantitative restrictions in accord with certain exceptions, but to date, India has not pursued that option.[290]

General agreement on trade in services

The GATS is the second area of the WTO agreements to directly address investment. The GATS, which applies to all WTO members, outlines four modes through which member countries can trade services.[291] The third mode of trade in services applies to investment, and is defined as "the supply of a service. . . by a service supplier of one Member through commercial presence in the territory of any other Member."[292] This "commercial presence" mode brings foreign investment into the scope of the GATS.

The GATS is a "positive list" agreement. WTO members are only bound to MA and NT provisions for the service sectors that they choose to include in each country's Schedule of Commitments. Each WTO member develops a list of service sectors to be included in its commitments. For each sector, the schedule lists the sectors for which it has agreed to accept WTO obligations, and the limits to its MA and NT commitments for each sector. Table 6-1 outlines India's commercial presence (Mode 3) commitments included in its GATS Schedule.[293]

As a positive list system, the GATS is quite transparent regarding each member's commitments. For each sector that is included in India's Schedule of Commitments, the MA and NT limits are the maximum restrictions. So, for example, in business services, the only restriction listed on India's Schedule is that foreign firms can supply such services only through incorporation in India, with a maximum foreign equity limit of 51 percent. The Indian government is not then permitted to impose additional regulations limiting foreign investors in business services. By contrast, actual practice in India, as defined by local laws and regulations, may be less restrictive than those outlined in India's GATS Schedule. In the business services example above, the Indian government is free to remove the 51 percent equity cap on foreign investment. For industries identified as "unbound" in its Schedule, and for sectors not mentioned at all, India has not agreed to any limits to its potential restrictions on foreign investors, so India can and likely does restrict trade and investment of these services through its domestic laws and regulations.

Table 6-1. India, GATS Schedule of Commitments, Mode 3: Covered Service Sectors

Service Sector	Type of Restriction	Description
All industries on schedule	National Treatment	In case of collaboration with public sector enterprises or government undertakings as joint venture partners, preference in access will be given to foreign service suppliers/entities which offer the best terms for transfer of technology.
Business services	Market Access	Commitments apply to engineering, computer and related, R&D, and technical testing and analysis services. Foreign firms may establish only through incorporation, with a foreign equity limit of 51 per cent.[1]
	National Treatment	No restrictions.
Telecommunication services	Market Access	Commitments apply to local/long distance services, wire-based, circuit switched data transmission, facsimile, private leased circuit, and cellular mobile telephone services. GATS schedules lists licensing requirements, restrictions on new licenses, and subsector specific variant requirements. Foreign equity is limited to 25 percent for most subsectors.[1]
	National Treatment	Unbound for all subsectors.
Audiovisual services	Market Access	Commitments apply to motion picture or video tape distribution services. Commercial establishment permitted only through representative offices, which may function as branches of foreign companies, but may import no more than 100 titles per year.
	National Treatment	NT commitments subject to certification that the motion picture in question has won an award or otherwise been recognized by good reviews in prestigious journals or at an international film festival.
Construction services	Market Access	Commitments apply to construction of roads and bridges only. Foreign firms may establish only through incorporation, with a foreign equity limit of 51 per cent.[1]
	National Treatment	No restrictions.
Financial services: Insurance	Market Access	Unbound except for commitments on overseas brokers, which may establish representative offices in India to procure reinsurance business from Indian insurance companies, and place reinsurance business abroad.
	National Treatment	Unbound
Financial services: Banking & securities	Market Access	Commitments apply to 7 specified banking and securities subsectors, including deposit taking, lending, and securities underwriting and placement. The commitments specify limits on new banking licenses, limits on foreign equity of 51 percent for certain subsectors, and other restrictions.[1]
	National Treatment	Unbound except for entities established in accordance with the limits specified in India's market access commitments.
Tourism & travel related services	Market Access	Commitments apply to hotels and lodging; and travel agency and tour operator services. Foreign firms may establish only through incorporation, with a foreign equity limit of 51 per cent.[a]
	National Treatment	No restrictions.

Source: WTO, *India, Schedule of Specific Commitments*, GATS/SC/42, as revised by Supplements 1-4 (Suppl.1-Suppl.4).

[a] The actual permitted foreign equity cap under current Indian law may be higher. For instance, India has raised the permitted foreign equity to 74 percent in telecommunications companies.

India has scheduled the greatest number of commitments in the areas of communication services and financial services, so investors in these industries are provided the most open investment environment. India has also scheduled commitments in business services, construction and related engineering services, and tourism and travel related services.[294]

South Asia Free Trade Agreement

SAFTA, which entered into effect in January 2006, is South Asia's most prominent trade agreement. SAFTA requires the developing countries in South Asia (India, Pakistan, and Sri Lanka) to reduce their duties to 20 percent in the first phase of a two year period ending in 2007. In the final five year phase ending in 2012, the 20 percent duty will be reduced to zero in a series of annual cuts.[295] The least developed nations in South Asia (Nepal, Bhutan, Bangladesh and Maldives) have an additional three years to reduce tariffs to zero.[296] A complete elimination of tariffs is estimated to boost intra-regional trade by about 10 percent over its 2006 level. Although SAFTA does not have specific investment-related provisions, India has supported the agreement's general cooperative measures for "expanding investment and production opportunities. . ." among the contracting states and views it as an effective mechanism for future regional investment cooperation.[297] However, since FDI restrictions from Bangladesh and Pakistan into India remain in effect, much of the residual investment benefits gained from greater regional trade liberalization will likely go to SAFTA's least developed members.[298]

Bilateral Investment Treaties

In recent years, India has concluded BITs with both developed and developing nations.[299] The majority of India's BITs (30 of 57) involve developing countries from Asia (16), the Middle East (9), Africa (4), and Latin America (1). Generally, India's BITs focus on the protections of investments relating to expropriation (nationalization of investments), transfers of income or capital, and international arbitration and dispute settlement for both state-to-state and investor-to-state cases.[300] India's BITs also cover areas such as non-discrimination in treatment, the entry of personnel and foreign-controlled enterprises, and exceptions dealing with issues of national security or disease and pest prevention. The agreements have a standard duration of 10 years with their investment guarantees valid 15 years after termination.[301]

There is considerable uniformity in the broad principles underlying India's BIT. However, some specific differences arise when comparing agreements between developed and developing nations, differences which likely reflect India's relative negotiating position. For example, India's BITs with Ghana, Indonesia, Oman, and Thailand only apply to investors which are "nationals or a company of a contracting party."[302] However, India's agreements with Australia and other developed countries additionally include indirect or portfolio investments by third-party institutional investors. Further, under the India-Ghana BIT, claims or disputes taken or completed before the entry into force of the agreement will not be covered by the BIT's obligations. This clause contradicts the general rule that investment claims are protected equally, regardless of when the BIT takes effect.[303] With regard to the entry and temporary residence of personnel, India's BITs with Australia and France are particularly notable for two reasons. First, they permit investors to employ key technical and managerial personnel regardless of citizenship, and second, they promote "sympathetic" consideration to the requests for temporary entry and work in connection with the other party's investments.[304]

Double Tax Avoidance Agreements and CECA

Another policy tool India employs to promote FDI is the use of double tax avoidance agreements. Typically, these tax treaties provide relief from double taxation of income by providing exemptions and sometimes credits for taxes paid in one of the partner countries.[305] The laws of the two contracting states govern the taxation of income in their respective states. When an entity has income arising from both India and the partner country, the entity will be taxed under the tax laws of the country of residence.[306]

Mauritius, India's largest source of FDI in recent years, is the most prominent beneficiary of India's bilateral tax treaties. Due to the local tax benefits it provides and its close historic and cultural ties—68 percent of Mauritius' population is of Indian descent—Mauritius has been a primary destination for entities interested in entering the Indian market.[307] Specifically, companies planning to invest in India often first establish a holding company in Mauritius, which offers zero-tax status to overseas corporate bodies (OCBs).[308] An OCB in Mauritius then must obtain a tax residency certificate[309] to qualify for the tax treaty between Mauritius and India.

To avoid misuse of the treaty by Indian-based companies seeking to avoid paying taxes at home, the management of the Mauritian holding company must not be from India, and the company must not have a "permanent establishment" in India. In most cases, companies avoid "permanent establishment" status by establishing a subsidiary in India with limited corporate powers.[310] However, controversy over the India-Mauritius tax treaty has grown in India, as there are no strict legal definitions for the terms "management from Mauritius" or "permanent establishment."[311] Despite these legal uncertainties, FDI from Mauritius reached $2.6 billion during 2005–06.[312] In 2006, FDI approvals from Mauritius into India included Essar Communications (telecom) for $56 million in equity, ILM Trichy Ltd. (infrastructure) for $23 million, and Pacifica Infrastructure (construction) for $15 million.[313]

Notably, in June 2005, India and Singapore signed a Comprehensive Economic Cooperation Agreement (CECA), which integrated investment provisions, a broad package of trade liberalization, and a tax treaty similar to the one between India and Mauritius.[314] For India, this agreement was seen as the most ambitious and comprehensive economic agreement ever concluded with a foreign country.[315] CECA is India's first attempt to integrate "BIT-like" investment disciplines in a preferential trade agreement, focusing on new investment facilitation provisions for the movement of natural persons, e-commerce, education, and media.[316] Further, although the CECA with Singapore adopts tax concessions similar to those of the India-Mauritius tax treaty, the requirements for Singapore tax residency are much more rigorous compared to those for Mauritius. Specifically, Singapore companies must satisfy predetermined expenditure requirements and show that they have sustainable and continuous business operations within Singapore.[317] Nonetheless, Singapore is eager to overtake Mauritius as the primary investment route into India.[318] According to industry lobbying groups in India, Singapore's cumulative investment in India, which was about $3 billion in 2005, is expected to increase to $5 billion by 2010 and to $10 billion by 2015.[319] In addition, since it already acts as a major hub for investment in the region, Singapore is seen to be able to provide investors with a larger basket of financial services compared to Mauritius.[320] However, it is not yet known whether increased FDI from Singapore will correspond with decreased FDI from Mauritius.

Other Agreements

Similar to SAFTA, the majority of India's bilateral and multilateral trade agreements do not contain detailed clauses regarding investment. However, it is likely that investment opportunities between parties will grow as trade becomes more liberalized. Appendix B provides a comprehensive list of India's partners in trade and investment agreements.

7. Case Study 1: Automotive Investment in India

Introduction

Since the industry opened up to foreign direct investment (FDI) in 1996 and the government lifted all equity caps for foreign automotive investors in 2002, India has attracted a significant amount of FDI in the auto sector. Out of 42 separate industry sectors in India, the "transportation industry," which includes but is not limited to passenger vehicles and components, was the fourth largest recipient of FDI from August 1991 through December 2006. With a few exceptions, most FDI has been focused on sales to the local market, but recently, many automotive firms are investing in establishing production bases for export. FDI inflows in the sector totaled $3.5 billion, accounting for 7 percent of total FDI inflows from August 1991 through December 2006.[321] This case study will describe the factors contributing to the influx of FDI to the Indian automotive sector, including domestic market conditions and Indian government policies specific to the sector; and examine FDI by passenger vehicle manufacturers in the most recent 5 year period—2002 through 2006.

Background on the Domestic Indian Automotive Industry

While rapid growth and extensive FDI in the Indian automotive industry are fairly recent phenomena, the industry itself has a long history. Indigenous automakers Hindustan Motors Ltd., Mahindra & Mahindra Ltd., and Tata Motors Ltd. were all founded in the 1940s, with relative newcomer Maruti Udyog Ltd. founded in 1981. Overall economic liberalization, which began in 1991, led to the delicensing[322] of the passenger car sector in 1993; however, quantitative restrictions on vehicle imports remained. Many foreign-owned firms established Indian joint-venture subsidiaries in the 1990s. In 2001, quantitative import restrictions were removed and in 2002, 100 percent foreign ownership was permitted.

In the last 5 years, production of passenger cars more than doubled to over 1 million cars in FY 2005–06 (table 7-1).[323] Production of utility vehicles also nearly doubled, while multi-purpose vehicle (MPV) production increased only slightly. The compound annual growth rate (CAGR) over the 5 year period for total passenger vehicles is 18.2 percent, and PriceWaterhouseCoopers predicts that, in 2006–07, India's growth will only be surpassed by China and Slovakia.[324]

Maruti Udyog, majority owned by Suzuki (Japan) accounts for the largest percentage of local production, followed by Tata (India) and Hyundai (Korea) (figure 7-1). Maruti was founded by an Indian Act of Parliament in 1981; Suzuki's initial stake was 26 percent. Maruti was privatized in 2002 when Suzuki's stake rose to its current level of 54 percent.

Table 7-1. Indian passenger vehicle production, in units, FY 2001–02 through FY 2005–06

Type of vehicle	2001–02	2002–03	2003–04	2004–05	2005–06
Passenger cars	500,301	557,410	782,562	960,487	1,045,881
Utility vehicles	105,667	114,479	146,325	182,018	196,371
Multipurpose vehicles	63,751	51,441	60,673	67,371	66,661
Total passenger vehicles	669,719	723,330	989,560	1,209,876	1,308,913

Source: Society of Indian Automobile Manufacturers Web site.

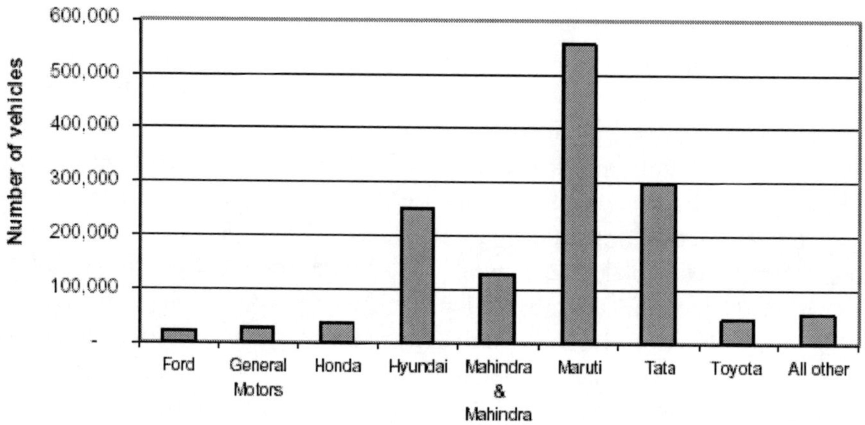

Source: Ward's Automotive Group, *World Motor Vehicle Data 2006.*

Figure 7-1. Indian car and light truck production, 2005

Table 7-2. Indian automotive parts production: FY2001–02 through FY2005–06, (million U.S. dollars)

Year	Production
2001–02	4,470
2002–03	5,430
2003–04	6,730
2004–05	8,700
2005–06	10,000

Source: Automotive Component Manufacturers Association of India, "Industry Statistics."

Table 7-3. Indian passenger vehicle exports, in units, FY 2001–02 through FY 2005–06

Type of vehicle	2001–02	2002–03	2003–04	2004–05	2005–06
Passenger cars and multipurpose vehicles	50,088	70,828	126,249	160,677	170,193
Utility vehicles	3,077	1,177	3,067	5,736	5,579
Total passenger vehicles	53,165	72,005	129,316	166,413	175,772

Source: Society of Indian Automobile Manufacturers Web site.

The Indian automotive parts industry exhibited growth similar to that of the auto industry during the 2001–06 period, more than doubling output to an estimated $10 billion, a response in large part to the strong local automotive market and greater outsourcing by automakers to their suppliers (table 7-2). According to Indian sources, Indian industry output is likely to total $18.7 billion by 2009 and then reach an estimated $40 billion by 2014.[325]

Indian exports of passenger vehicles grew consistently at a CAGR of 34.8 percent from FY 2001–02 to FY 2005–06 (table 7-3). Maruti Udyog, Tata Motors, and Hyundai are the key exporters; leading markets include Sri Lanka, Algeria, South Africa, United Kingdom, and Italy. By 2010, industry observers predict that capacity will surpass domestic sales by 1 million, leaving a significant quantity of vehicles available for export.[326] Stringent government automotive emission regulations have ensured that vehicles assembled in India meet developed market standards, making them exportable. FDI in the automotive sector is clearly contributing to India's export growth, with many foreign automakers announcing that new FDI is aimed, at least partially, at production for export.[327]

Indian exports of automotive components more than tripled during the period, with a CAGR of 20 percent, and reached an estimated $1.8 billion in FY 2005–06 (table 7-4). A growing share of Indian production is destined for export markets, which accounted for an estimated 18 percent of Indian production in 2006. Approximately 75 percent of these exports were shipped to OEMs, with the remaining 25 percent heading to the aftermarket,[328] compared with a 35 percent share to OEMs in the 1990s.[329] Because original equipment manufacturers (OEMs) maintain relatively stringent product and quality specifications, the market shift likely represents, in part, the effect of quality improvements in association with the influx of FDI. Indian auto parts exports are likely to continue to see significant growth, according to at least one industry analyst, who has offered an "industry vision" of such exports reaching $20–25 billion by 2015.[330]

Table 7-4. Indian exports of automotive parts: FY 2001–02 through FY 2005–06, (million U.S. dollars)

Year	Exports
2001–02	578
2002–03	760
2003–04	1,000
2004–05	1,400
2005–06	1,800

Source: Automotive Component Manufacturers Association of India at http://www.acmainfo.com.

India as an Automotive FDI Destination

The Indian domestic market

India is one of the fastest growing auto markets in the world, with sales registering a CAGR of 14.1 percent in the last 5 years (table 7-5), and projected sales of 3 million by 2015.[331] Catalysts for increased sales of passenger cars currently include new model offerings, expanding purchase finance options and low interest rates,[332] and reductions in motor vehicle- related taxes.[333] Maruti is the market leader in passenger car sales by a wide margin (figure 7-2). Other important brands in terms of sales are Hyundai, Tata, and Mahindra & Mahindra.

Table 7-5. Indian passenger vehicle sales, in units, FY 2001–02 through FY 2005–06

Type of vehicle	2001–02	2002–03	2003–04	2004–05	2005–06
Passenger cars	509088	541491	696153	820179	882094
Utility vehicles	104253	113620	146388	176360	194577
Multipurpose vehicles	61775	52087	59555	65033	66366
Total passenger vehicles	675116	707198	902096	1061572	1143037

Source: Society of Indian Automobile Manufacturers Web site.

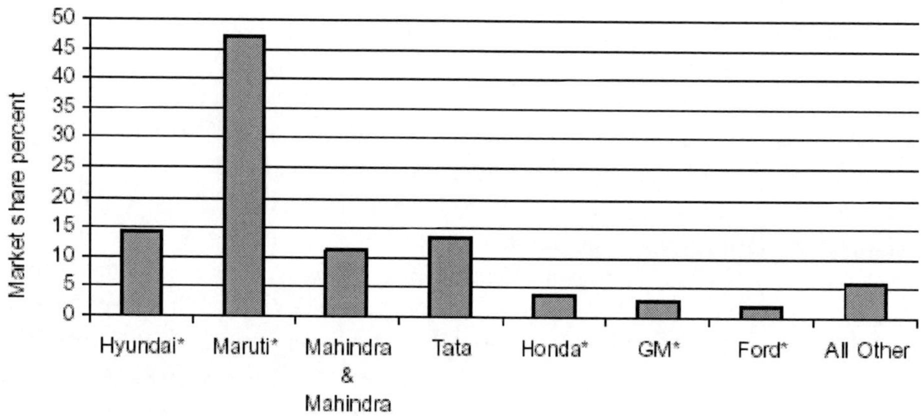

Source: Ward's Automotive Group, *World Motor Vehicle Data 2006*.

Figure 7-2. Indian car and light truck market share, by company, 2005

The composition of the domestic market makes India an attractive FDI destination for automobile components manufacturers. The middle class is expanding, and is estimated to reach 450 million in 2007, or about 45 percent of the total population,[334] and the potential pool of drivers—the segment of the population aged 20–60 years—is growing.[335] Disposable incomes in India are reportedly rising quickly, and Indian consumers tend to be more likely to channel their increased income toward a vehicle purchase than other Asian consumers.[336] The market has much room to expand, as the vehicle penetration rate is just 7 cars per 1,000 people[337]—one of the lowest rates in the world.

India is also attractive to the world's automakers because it has a large pool of high technology engineering talent, and its location in the populous Asia-Pacific region allows it to serve as a regional export base. According to the Indian government, the increasing competition in the Indian automotive industry has spurred significant improvements in productivity, making it one of the most productive manufacturing sectors in India.[338]

In addition to the favorable market and manufacturing environment in India, the presence of a large number of leading motor vehicle manufacturers has attracted a substantial base of non-Indian automotive parts producers.[339] Because of automakers' specific product, material, and quality requirements, they generally purchase components from established producers with the necessary certifications, reputation, and experience. Moreover, automakers prefer to source components locally to benefit from just-in-time delivery and supplier support. To meet these objectives, automakers often encourage their suppliers to invest in greenfield operations or form joint ventures with local manufacturers, particularly when entering new markets with limited or developing component industries. The size of the local vehicle assembly industry also offers sufficient production volumes to warrant the level of investment necessary to support component manufacturing operations in India.

Indian Government Policies Affecting Auto FBI

As noted above, since the 1990s, Indian government policies have been aimed at promoting a globally competitive auto sector, and FDI is a critical component of this plan. In the past 5 years, the government of India has taken a number of steps toward expanding the domestic automotive industry and promoting it as a globally competitive player. These policies are summarized below.

Automotive policy of 2002

The primary goal of this policy was "to establish a globally competitive automotive industry in India and to double its contribution to the economy by 2010."[340] Key objectives outlined in the 2002 policy included modernizing the domestic industry; fostering domestic design, research, and development; developing alternate propulsion technologies; and establishing domestic environmental and safety standards on par with international standards.[341] In an important change, the 2002 policy permitted 100 percent foreign ownership of automotive and automotive parts manufacturing firms without minimum investment criteria. The policy also addressed import tariffs, with a stated objective of "facilitat(ing) development of manufacturing capabilities as opposed to mere assembly without giving undue protection; ensur(ing) balanced transition to open trade, promot(ing) increased competition in the market and enlarg(ing) purchase options to the Indian customer."[342] Import duties on components and completely knocked down (CKD) kits[343] were reduced to 30 percent in 2003 and to 15 percent in 2005.[344] Coupled with a reduction in local content requirements, these changes encouraged FDI by making it more economical to assemble vehicles in India. The 2002 automotive policy also provided for incentives for R&D and tax concessions.

Automotive mission plan 2006–2016

Recognizing that "the concept of attaining competitiveness on the basis of cheap and abundant labour, favourable exchange rates, low interest rates and concessional duty structure is becoming inadequate and therefore, not sustainable,"[345] the Indian government introduced the Automotive Mission Plan (AMP) in September 2006, and finalized in March 2007. The policy states that industry investment in R&D is needed to "increase innovative breakthroughs for vehicle design as well as in manufacturing technology" and that the Indian government has a role to play in attracting this investment.[346] The vision statement of the AMP is:

> To emerge as the destination of choice in the world for design and manufacture of automobiles and auto components with output reaching a level of $145 billion accounting for more than 10% of the GDP and providing additional employment to 25 million people by 2016.[347]

These goals are expected to be addressed via large investments from both industry and the government; according to the AMP, output targets "would require incremental investment of $35–40 billion. . . by 2016."[348] If successful, India would emerge, in 2016, as the world's seventh largest passenger car producer, compared to its current rank of eleventh.[349]

The AMP envisions that the role of the Indian government would entail facilitating infrastructure creation, promoting the country's capabilities, creating a favorable and predictable business environment, attracting investment, and promoting R&D. Under this scenario, the role of industry would include designing and manufacturing world-class vehicles, improving cost competitiveness and labor and capital productivity, achieving economies of scale and R&D capabilities, and showcasing India's products in potential markets.[350] Specific portions of the AMP are summarized in box 7-1 below.

Box 7-1. Key Recommended Interventions in the AMP

Investment Incentives

- A tax holiday for auto industry investment exceeding $133 million.
- One-stop clearance of FDI proposals.
- Tax deductions of 100 percent of export profits.
- 30 percent deduction of net (total) income for 10 years for new industrial undertakings.
- Duty suspension for machinery for a greenfield plant or for expansion of an existing operation.
- 50 percent deduction on foreign exchange earnings.
- Actions on the part of state governments to ensure power supply and/or promote captive generation and provide preferential land allotment.

Export Measures

- Reforming the tariff and tax structure.
- Creating a Special Auto-Component Parks system to promote components exports.
- Creating 'virtual SEZs'.
- Adjusting existing export promotion schemes to ensure that they are WTO compatible.
- Extending product and market focus schemes to the auto sector.

Research and Development

- Implement the National Automotive Testing and R&D Infrastructure Project[a].
- Encourage collaboration between industry and research and academic institutions.
- Further develop the facilities and programs of the technical institutes.
- Emphasize fuel economy and alternate propulsion technologies.

- Consideration by the Ministry of Finance of R&D tax concessions, grants of 100 percent for fundamental research, 75 percent for precompetitive technology/application, and 50 percent for product development; zero taxes on technology transfers (products, features, alternate fuel, etc.); increased weighted deduction for expenditures incurred on R&D from 150 percent to 200 percent; and excise duty concession for 'Made-In-India' products.

Education, Training, and Labor Law Reform

- Creation in the Eleventh Five-Year Plan period a National Level Specialized Education and Training Institute for Automotive Sector.
- Providing for multi-year sabbaticals for national laboratory and university R&D personnel to work in industry.
- Expansion of working hours from 48 to 60 per week with a concomitant expansion of allowable hours per day.
- Allowing contract labor in core areas for temporary periods.
- Allowing fixed term contacts in certain core activities.
- Increasing flexibility in recruitment and lay-off of workers in response to changes in market demand.
- Creation by companies of a supplementary unemployment benefits fund.

Infrastructure Development

- Continued government investment in road, rail, port, and power infrastructure.
- Creation of three auto export hubs near Mumbai, Chennai, and Kolkatta, able to each handle 500,000 vehicle exports annually by 2015.
- Allowances for automobile retail trade and service infrastructure.

Sources: Government of India, Ministry of Heavy Industries and Public Enterprises, *Automotive Mission Plan 2006–2016*; *Autocar Professional*, "Mega Auto Project Well On Course"; and Wells and Sadana, "Hub or Hubris? India and the Automotive Mission Plan 2006–2016," 29.

[a] The Indian government established the $400 million National Automotive Testing and R&D Infrastructure Project (NATRIP), jointly funded by industry and government. NATRIP's detailed project implementation report was approved on July 25, 2006, by the governing council, which comprises representatives both from the Indian automotive industry and the Government of India. NATRIP will set up world-class R&D, testing, and proving grounds facilities in the automotive clusters that will be available to all automakers. The first center is scheduled to open in 2008, with the remaining facilities opening by 2011.

Foreign Investment in the Indian Auto Industry

Automaker FDI decisions are primarily driven by market factors, including proximity to markets, market size, cost of production, and favorable infrastructure. For example, automakers tend to assemble vehicles in or near their major markets, or may choose to invest in a foreign market because of that country's tariff structure or to improve access to local markets. Foreign automakers direct their investment toward manufacturing plants, and also seek to expand their dealer networks and their network certified repair shops. Investments can also go into R&D facilities, training centers, and purchase financing operations. Because of India's improving technical capabilities and low costs, global automakers are increasingly outsourcing R&D, design, and engineering to their Indian partners or subsidiaries.[351] For example, Suzuki has been increasingly outsourcing more R&D and design work for its global operations to its Indian subsidiary, Maruti, and scaling back on such operations in Japan. Since its inception in 2000, Maruti's R&D staff grew to 250 employees in 2006.[352]

Several special economic zones (SEZs) are targeted specifically at the automotive industry, such as the Mahindra World City Auto Ancillary SEZ, which advertises its proximity to Ford and Visteon as one of the many reasons that automotive suppliers would choose to set up operations there,[353] and Adityapur Industrial Area Development Authority, which boasts competencies in sheet metal pressed fabricated components and subassemblies; light and heavy fabrication; castings, forgings and machining; and polymer components.[354] Despite the financial incentives offered by Indian SEZs, these zones have been less successful in attracting foreign and domestic investment than other economic zones, such as those operating in China. The Indian zones reportedly lack sufficient size to achieve economies of scale, have been subject to restrictive labor laws, and lack efficient infrastructure to facilitate communication and shipment of goods.[355]

As discussed in chapter 3, foreign investors in India face issues related to infrastructure and corruption in India, but these are not enough to dissuade investors. Power, road, rail, and port infrastructure all pose challenges for the automotive industry, raising the cost of production and lowering efficiencies. Some automotive industry observers consider the unreliable power supply to be the most significant infrastructure constraint. One source reports that, "on average, a company can expect nearly 17 significant power outages per month, against one per month in Malaysia and fewer than 5 in China. At the same time, costs are higher."[356] Many companies reportedly maintain their own private power supplies to compensate for the national shortcomings;[357] one study on the Indian manufacturing sector asserts that over 60 percent of companies rely on private power generation.[358] The transportation infrastructure is also inadequate. An industry official states that India's weak infrastructure is "the biggest challenge for industry," noting that political disagreements between India's state and federal governments exacerbate the problems.[359]

Corruption also adds to automotive companies' cost of doing business. An official of DaimlerChrysler acknowledged that corruption exists and that the company's policy is not to tolerate it. According to the official, "Now you can't say, I won't invest in India because there is corruption. You just have to accept the fact that you will have to find your own way."[360]

U.S.-based passenger vehicle investment

Both GM and Ford have invested in India through their wholly owned subsidiaries, General Motors India and Ford India Pvt Ltd., respectively. General Motors India was incorporated in 1994 as a 50–50 joint venture company with the C.K. Birla Group of Companies (Hindustan Motors), and became a wholly owned subsidiary of General Motors Co. in 1999 (table 7-6). GM's technical center in Bangalore employs 800 and conducts engineering and R&D for local as well as global applications. Company officials recently announced that they plan to add 200 engineering jobs at the center per year.[361] This clearly indicates that GM is ramping up its presence in the Indian market; the company is introducing the Chevrolet Spark small car, and hopes to achieve a 10 percent share of the Indian market by 2010.[362] GM's total investment of $750 million[363] is geared toward reaching an installed annual capacity of 225,000 automobiles by 2010.[364] According to GM's chairman and CEO, "India is 'the' candidate for GM's future investments."[365] While current assembly and domestic sales plans do not leave room for exports, company officials have said that India could become an export hub for mini cars in the future.[366]

Ford commenced operations in India in 1996 through a joint venture with Mahindra & Mahindra; Ford India became a wholly owned subsidiary of Ford Motor Co. in March 2005. Two of the three reported M&A deals from the United States name Ford as the acquirer—the acquisition of Mahindra' s 15.88 percent share of Ford India Pvt. Ltd. to make it wholly owned by Ford Motor Co. in 2005, and, later in 2005, a $75 million equity infusion by Ford Motor Co. into Ford India Pvt Ltd.[367] Ford is striving for installed annual capacity of 150,000 vehicles by 2010.[368]

Table 7-6. U.S. Automakers with Assembly Operations in India

Automaker	Year operations commenced	JV partner "ownership share/JV partner"	Number of plants/ location	Total installed capacity[a]	Examples of recently announced investments
General Motors	1994	NA	1/Gujarat	85000	• Expanded Gujarat from 60,000 to 85,000 in 2007 • Greenfield plant in Talegaon to begin production in late 2008—capacity of 140,000
Ford	1996	NA	1/Maraimalai, near Chennai	100000	• Planning diesel engine plant to produce 100,000 engines/year

Source: Various industry reports, company Web sites, press releases, LocoMonitor, *FDI database*, and SIAM Web site.

Note: NA—not available.

[a] Total installed capacity refers to the total number of vehicles that could be assembled per year if plants were running at full capacity.

European-based passenger vehicle investment

A total of 12 European-based automakers (counting subsidiary investments as distinct from parent company investments) are invested in India; they include Audi, Bentley, BMW, DaimlerChrysler, Fiat, Mercedes-Benz, Porsche, Renault, Rolls Royce, Skoda, Volkswagen, and Volvo. Of these 12, the investments of Bentley, Mercedes-Benz, Porsche, and Rolls Royce are in retail outlets only; they are not assembling cars in India. Similarly, in 2006, Volvo announced an investment in a new subsidiary, Volvo Cars India, that will be selling the XC90 and S80 models imported from Sweden; Volvo has no immediate plans for production in India.[369]

Among the 7 EU- 15 automakers assembling or planning to assemble cars in India, the individual level of investment and commitment to the market varies considerably (table 7-7). BMW and Audi, for example, are just beginning assembly operations, and DaimlerChrysler produces less than 3,000 vehicles per year. Conversely, Fiat, Renault, Volkswagen, and Skoda are more heavily invested. Fiat has had the longest presence in India, dating to the

1950s, and is currently aligned with indigenous automaker Tata Motors; Renault, by far the largest European player in India, is also allied with an indigenous automaker—Mahindra & Mahindra.[370] Volkswagen, although a newcomer, is building a greenfield plant with an installed annual capacity of 110,000 vehicles, and its subsidiary, Skoda, has an annual capacity of 30,000 vehicles with a goal of increasing to 50,000 vehicles by 2010.

The M&As reported for European acquirers include a deal in which Fiat SpA of Italy increased its minority share in Fiat India Ltd. from 19.44 percent to 44.61 percent in 2005; and a deal in which a 10 percent stake in International Cars and Motors Ltd. was acquired by 3i Group plc, a private equity/venture capital firm in the United Kingdom in 2006.[371]

Table 7-7. EU automakers with assembly operations in India

Automaker	Year operations commenced	JV partner "ownership share/JV partner"	Number of plants/ location	Total installed capacity	Examples of recently announced investments
Audi	2006 (announced investment)	NA	NA	NA	• Plans to start producing cars in autumn 2007 at a Skoda facility in Aurangabad
BMW	2005 (announced investment)	NA	1/Pune	1700	• Greenfield plant for CKD assembly in Pune came online in March 2007
DaimlerChrysler	1994	NA	1/Pune	2,000 (at a rented Tata facility)	• Constructing a greenfield plant in Chakan for assembly of Mercedes-Benz models—5,000 per year expected to begin rolling off assembly line in early 2009
Fiat	1951 (Fiat licensed Premier Automobiles to produce a Fiat model)	Tata	NA	NA	• Announced JV plant with Tata in Ranjangaon—to be operational in 2008 with 100,000 annual capacity, shared with Tata, as well as 200,000 engines
Renault	N/A	Mahindra	1/Nashik	NA	• JV greenfield plant in Chennai—Mahindra (50%), Renault (25%), and Nissan (25%)—annual capacity of 400,000—to be fully integrated and operational in 2009—capacity rumored to be increased to 700,000 by 2012
Skoda	1999	NA	1/Aurang abad	30000	NA
Volkswagen	2006 (announced investment)	NA	NA	NA	• Greenfield construction to begin in Pune—full-scale manufacturing plant—annual capacity to be 110,000 by 2009

Source: Various industry reports, company Web sites, press releases, *LocoMonitor FDI database,* and SIAM Web site.
Note: NA—not available.

Asia-Pacific-based passenger vehicle investment

According to LocoMonitor, a total of 9 Asian-Pacific automakers invested in India from 2002 through 2006: Honda, Mazda, Nissan, Suzuki, Toyota, and Daihatsu of Japan; Hyundai of Korea; Naza of Malaysia; and MG Rover a subsidiary of Nanjing Auto of China.[372] Details of the investment made by MG Rover, (in 2002) are not available and may not have come to fruition.

Suzuki and Hyundai are the leading Asian-Pacific automakers in India (table 7-8). Suzuki owns 54 percent of India's Maruti Udyog Ltd., the leading passenger car maker in India, and has been a player in the Indian automotive industry since 1982. Hyundai Motor India Limited (HMIL), a wholly owned subsidiary of Hyundai Motor Company, is the second largest carmaker in India and accounts for 60 percent of all cars exported from India.[373] Honda, Toyota, and Hyundai entered the industry in the mid to late 1990s, and Nissan and Naza are the most recent Asian-Pacific automakers to begin Indian operations.

Table 7-8. Asia-Pacific automakers with assembly operations in India

Automaker	Year operations commenced	JV partner ownership share	Number of plants/ location	Total installed capacity	Examples of recently announced investments
Honda	1995	Siel/99%	1/Noida	50000	• Greenfield plant in Rajasthan announced in 2006—50,000 initial capacity online by 2010, eventually reaching 200,000 • Expanding Noida to 100,000 by 2007 and to 150,000 by 2010 • Expanding dealership network from 53 to 100 by 2010
Nissan	2004	Ownership/ 100%	NA	NA	• JV greenfield plant in Chennai—Mahindra (50%), Renault (25%), and Nissan (25%)—eventual annual capacity of 400,000—to be operational in 2009, reaching full capacity by 2016
Suzuki	1982	Maruti/ 54%	4/Gurgaon & Manesar	600000	• Upgrading Gurgaon • Expanding the new Manesar plant opening in 2007 to 300,000 by 2009—large supplier park included at new facility • Plan to build R&D center, test track, and collision evaluation facility • Expanding dealership network from 405 to 600 by 2010
Toyota	1997	Toyota/ 89% Kirloskar/ 11%	1/Bangalore	60000	• Considering a greenfield plant as an expan-sion of its current facility—annual capacity would be 100,000—decision awaiting government approval of site selection • Expanding dealership network from 63 to 200 by 2010
Hyundai	1998	NA	1/Chennai	300000	• Greenfield plant in Chennai being completed in 2007 to expand total capacity to 600,000 • Adding a $40 million R&D center, to employ 800 • Expanding dealership network from 183 to 250 • Expanding service network to 1,000 in 2007
Naza	2006 (announced)	NA	NA	NA	• Greenfield plant in Tamil Nadu announced in 2006; output expected in late 2008

Source: Various industry reports, company Web sites, press releases, *LocoMonitor FDI database,* and SIAM Web site.

Note: NA—not available.

Component industry

From FY 2001–02 through FY 2005–06, total investment in the Indian automotive components industry nearly doubled to an estimated $4.4 billion.[374] Of known foreign direct investment, roughly one-half of such projects were in higher technology items such as engine components, drive trains, and electronic systems. Most of the FDI represented new projects rather than expansions of existing operations, and focused on manufacturing rather than R&D and other automotive-related activities. As would be expected because of their leading positions in the global automotive industry, U.S., German, and Japanese firms were the principal sources of foreign investment in the Indian components industry.[375]

Additionally, foreign firms increased their total investment in Indian automotive parts producers by a minimum of $600 million from 2002 through YTD 2007[376] with 44 announced or completed acquisitions.[377] U.S. firms led in total number of deals for single countries, with 10 reported acquisitions, and Japanese firms were involved in 8 deals. Europe as a whole took part in 17 acquisitions, with the United Kingdom and Germany accounting for 5 and 4 acquisitions, respectively. The largest deal for which value was reported was the $128 million acquisition of the majority stake of Ashok Leyland by the Hinduja Group, a London- based multinational with interests in manufacturing, banking, and trade, completed in August 2006.

Table 7-9. Examples of global automotive parts suppliers manufacturing in India

Company	Country	Product examples
Aisin Seiki	Japan	Door latches, window regulators, door hinges
Bosch	Germany	Development center for electronic diesel injection systems
Dana	United States	Clutches, piston rings, axle housings
Delphi	United States	Steering systems, wiring harnesses, driveshafts, catalytic converters, technology center
Denso	Japan	Auto electrical components, fuel pumps, radiators, HVAC units, and heaters
Faurecia	France	Automotive seating and interior components
Siemens VDO	Germany	Dashboard instruments and accessories
Visteon	United States	AC systems, engine cooling systems, instrument panels
Yazaki	Japan	Wiring harnesses

Source: Automotive Component Manufacturers Association of India, http://www.acmainfo.com.

Many multinational automotive parts producers from these and other major producing countries have been manufacturing in India for years, producing a wide range of products from basic commodities such as castings and forgings to highly sophisticated electronic systems (table 7-9). Some of these firms have also located technology or development centers in India. Of the 400 substantive Indian component producers, roughly 40 percent are joint ventures with foreign manufacturers.[378] The Indian government has encouraged local industry to partner with foreign firms to enhance its potential as an outsourcing location and global R&D resource center.[379]

Conclusion

The key to continued FDI in India's auto sector rests with continued expansion of the domestic market, which seems ensured, and the further development of India as an automotive export hub. "Much will depend upon individual corporate strategies, particularly in terms of manufacturing locations in relation to market served."[380] Moreover, because of extensive forward and backward linkages, the viability of the AMP and the accomplishment of its goals are reliant on related industries and domestic developments.[381] The slow progress on improvements to the transportation infrastructure and the uncertain availability of inputs such as steel may make it difficult for India to meet its AMP targets. Like the auto industry, the steel industry also has a national plan specifying production and other targets.[382] However, meeting these targets depends on expansion of the railway network in order to move iron ore, coking coal, and finished steel around the country. The supply of fuel for individual motorists is also problematic in India.[383] Some automakers also note that frequently changing government policies have a negative impact on their investment decisions.[384]

8. Case Study 2: Pharmaceutical FDI in India

This case study traces the impact of India's changing patent laws on FDI in the pharmaceutical sector. India's patent laws have evolved from a model protective of pharmaceutical patents during the colonial period (1856–1947), to a legal regime intended to foster the establishment and growth of a domestic industry by excluding pharmaceuticals from patent protection (1972–2005), and finally to the present law (2005), which reestablishes patent protection for pharmaceutical products to comply with the requirements of the international intellectual property system.

The evolution of the patent law appears to have had a substantial impact on domestic and foreign pharmaceutical investment. Foreign firms dominated the market during the colonial period. When there was no pharmaceutical product patent protection in India, domestic firms flourished by reverse engineering patented products to make generic pharmaceuticals, and the market share of multinational pharmaceutical firms declined. While it is still too early to definitively identify the impact of the 2005 change to the patent law, it appears to be motivating increased foreign investment in India's pharmaceutical sector. In anticipation of the new law, pharmaceutical FDI increased sharply in 2004, declined in 2005 and then rebounded in 2006. The decline in 2005 may be attributable to substantial uncertainty as to how India will implement and interpret its new patent law.

Over the last five years (2002-06), FDI and strategic alliances between foreign and domestic firms in the areas of clinical trials, data management services, new drug discovery, and the manufacturing of pharmaceuticals and ingredients all have been on the increase. The valuable intellectual property connected to these activities is protected through operational security procedures, contractual protections and due diligence to ensure trustworthy partners. Multinational firms conduct R&D and manufacturing in India because of cost savings, the skilled labor force and the country's disease profile, among other reasons. These firms have, however, waited to see how the patent law will be interpreted and enforced before expanding their product patenting and commercialization activities in India.

India is charting a new intellectual property path, attempting to foster access to medicine and the growth of the domestic pharmaceutical industry while also phasing in compliance with the requirements of the international intellectual property system. The ultimate impact of India's calibrated approach on the quantity and quality of FDI in the pharmaceutical sector remains to be seen.

The Evolution of India's Patent Laws

The patent laws under british rule (1856-1947)

India enacted its first patent law in 1856 while the country was under British rule, a period that lasted until India's independence in 1947. While the patent laws were amended throughout the colonial period, they consistently provided for the patenting of pharmaceutical products. Most patents granted during this period went to foreigners. At the time of independence, India's pharmaceutical sector was dominated by multinational companies with only limited participation by domestic firms.[385]

The post-independence patent laws (1947-1995)

With independence in 1947, the Indian Government began preparing a new patent law, with a goal of fostering the development of an indigenous pharmaceutical industry. In 1972, after repeated expert reports and deliberations in Parliament, the India Patents Act of 1970 came into force.[386]

The 1970 Act imposed substantial limits on patent rights; these limits were intended to encourage indigenous inventions and secure their production in India on a commercial scale.[387] First, and most importantly, pharmaceutical products could not be patented. Second, firms were permitted to patent only a single process for making a pharmaceutical; a firm could not block competitors by patenting all possible processes for making a particular drug. Third, the term for pharmaceutical process patents shortened to 5 years from the grant of the patent or 7 years from application filing, whichever was less, compared to 14 years from application filing for all other inventions. And fourth, the Act imposed very broad "compulsory licensing" provisions for pharmaceutical manufacturing process patents. Within 3 years of the grant, the patents were deemed "licenses of right," meaning that anyone could use the process if they paid a royalty.[388] In sum, pharmaceutical products had no protection, and pharmaceutical processes were protected only for 3 years if a royalty was paid and for 5 years if no royalty was paid.

The post-trips patent laws (1995-present)

In January of 1995, India became a founding member of the World Trade Organization (WTO) and agreed to the requirements of TRIPS, the WTO intellectual property agreement Because India was a developing country that did not provide for pharmaceutical product patenting when TRIPS came into force, it obtained a 10 year transition period, until January 2005, to put in place pharmaceutical patent protections.[389] During this transition period, India was required to provide a means for applications to be filed and assigned a filing date, a "mailbox" facility. TRIPS also required that "exclusive marketing rights"—the sole right to sell the invention for a specified time—be provided for certain mailbox applications filed during the transition period.[390] India complied with these requirements through the Patents Act of 1999, after a WTO complaint was filed and resolved against India.[391]

In 2002, India amended its patent law to provide the TRIPS-mandated 20 year patent term for all inventions, to be applied to pharmaceutical patents at the conclusion of the transition period. The amendments also include new compulsory license provisions. These provisions permit a compulsory license application 3 years after a patent is granted if the "reasonable requirements of the public" regarding the invention have not been satisfied, the invention is not available at a reasonably affordable price, or the invention is not being "worked" or produced in India.[392] The law also provides for immediate compulsory licensing in cases of a governmental notification of a public health crisis or public non-commercial use, or where the product will be exported to countries with insufficient manufacturing capacity to address public health problems.[393] The compulsory license provisions of India's law are, by far, the broadest of all the world's patent systems.[394] As such, they raise substantial concerns among multinational pharmaceutical companies; to date, however, no compulsory licenses have been sought or issued under the new law.

The critical step in India's implementation of its TRIPS commitments came in January 2005 with the end of the transition period and the required amendment of its law to provide patent protection for pharmaceutical products. According to Indian industry representatives, India now is taking a "calibrated approach" to intellectual property protection that seeks to take into account concerns for public health and access to medicine as well as the interests of the domestic industry.[395] Notwithstanding this focus on domestic issues, India now has in place an IP regime that addresses the requirements of the international IP system.

Ongoing patent law controversies

Despite the substantial patent law changes since India's entry into the WTO, there are still gaps and provisions that raise objections from multinational pharmaceutical companies. First and foremost, multinationals seek a law to protect the clinical trial and other data used to obtain marketing approval of pharmaceuticals that utilize new chemical entities. Clinical trial data is extremely expensive to amass. The fully capitalized cost to develop a new drug has been estimated at an average of $847 million, with a substantial portion of these costs attributable to the conduct of clinical trials.[396] Conducting clinical trials in India can significantly reduce these costs.

TRIPS requires the protection of such data against "unfair commercial use." However, because TRIPS does not define the critical terms included in this requirement, the obligation's precise nature arguably is unclear. The United States, the European Union, and many multinational pharmaceutical firms interpret TRIPS Article 39.3 to require "data exclusivity," meaning that data submitted to a marketing authority cannot be used by another company or person for a particular period (ranging from 5 years in the United States to up to 10 years in European Union countries). Others assert that developing countries can flexibly interpret TRIPS to protect test data only against misappropriation or other circumstances in which it is unfairly obtained.[397] Data protection measures have been under consideration in India for years, with no resolution to date.

Moreover, a substantial backlog of unexamined patents, a lack of patent examiner experience, lengthy pre-grant opposition proceedings, and limited resources raise the concern that the patent law changes have not yet yielded meaningful patent protection.[398] Under these circumstances, the need for data protection—to provide certainty that there will be some return on the investment necessary to support new drug discoveries—may be considered particularly acute. According to Pfizer India, the lack of data protection is part of the reason that "people are talking about India but investing in China."[399]

Box 8-1. The Novartis Challenge to India's Patent Law

Novartis is challenging in the Indian courts the refusal of the patent office to grant a patent for its cancer drug, Glivec. The patent office found that Glivec was not patentable under Section 3(d) of the Patents Act, which requires that a new form of a known compound demonstrate improved efficacy, and also found that the drug did not satisfy the requirements for novelty and an inventive step. The Novartis case challenges the constitutional validity of the patent law and its TRIPS compatability. The dispute is pending in the Madras High Court which, in April of 2007, referred part of the case to a newly constituted Intellectual Property Appellate Board.

Novartis asserts that this is not a case of "evergreening." Although Glivec is patented around the world, the pre-2005 bar on product patents precluded Novartis from obtaining a patent in India. Novartis further alleges that it has demonstrated that the new version of the drug is more effective than a previous version, contrary to the findings of the patent office. NGOs and health advocates object to the Novartis challenge on the grounds that it undermines access to medicines and India's ability to place limits on the patenting of essential drugs.

Ironically, although Section 3(d) was intended to limit "evergreening" by multinational companies, it also limits the ability of domestic firms to obtain patents for incremental innovations. Domestic firms are in the early stages of investing the large amounts of money and scientific expertise necessary to discover new drugs. For example, the Indian firm Ranbaxy has reported that its patent applications in 2004 focused primarily on process discoveries for generics. In 2007, its patent filings focused on new drug delivery systems and other incremental innovations. Ranbaxy anticipates it will not be in a position to seek patents for new drug discoveries until 2012.

By limiting the availability of patents in cases of incremental innovation, Section 3(d) may have the opposite effect of that India intended. It may concentrate valuable pharmaceutical product patents in the hands of multinational companies because they have access to the resources and expertise needed for the most complex and costly inventions, at the expense of domestic firms undertaking incremental innovations.

Sources: Novartis, "Questions and Answers"; and Technical Expert Group on Patent Law Issues, "Report of the Technical Expert Group on Patent Law Issues."

Another controversial aspect of India's Patent Act is the exclusion from patentability for derivatives of known substances, unless it can be shown that they are significantly more efficacious than the original substance.[400] This exclusion was meant to preclude "evergreening"—the practice of extending the terms of patents through related patents on modified forms of the same drug, new drug delivery systems or new uses.[401] The types of efficacy data needed to show that a derivative is patentable, the ability of patent examiners to evaluate medical efficacy data, and the standards governing the patent examiner's data evaluation are all unclear.[402] The Government of India charged a Technical Expert Group with determining whether this exclusion from patentability was TRIPS compatible. The Expert Group issued its opinion in December 2006, concluding that it was not, but they later withdrew the report due to "technical inaccuracies."[403] The multinational pharmaceutical firm Novartis is in the midst of a high profile challenge to the provision's legality (box 8-1).

The perceived inadequacies in India's patent law described above, as well as the Novartis experience, appear to have impacted multinational pharmaceutical companies' evaluation of the investment environment in India. Novartis has stated in the press that it constructed its new research institute in Singapore rather than India because of its concerns about patent protection. Also, Novartis announced the creation of a Shanghai research institute because of its perception that, unlike India, China has a system in place to improve intellectual property protection. Moreover, Novartis has asserted that because of intellectual property insecurity, its R&D collaborations in India are limited to supportive work rather than the development of new medicines.[404] More generally, according to a survey conducted by Ernst & Young and the Economist, more than 62 percent of multinational pharmaceutical companies surveyed in India consider threats to intellectual property a business risk, and 63 percent believe that their companies risked losing intellectual property rights when trying to integrate with local suppliers and third party service providers.[405] The final chapter on the actual level of patent protection that India will accord pharmaceuticals has not yet been written.

The Evolution of the Pharmaceutical Industry in India

The domestic pharmaceutical industry

The composition of India's pharmaceutical industry has changed with the patent laws. Multinational firms dominated the Indian market during the colonial period. The removal of patent protection fostered the growth of the domestic industry and a corresponding decline in the market share of the multinationals. During the years after enactment of the 1970 India Patents Act, Indian scientists became particularly adept in the reverse engineering and production of pharmaceutical products patented outside of India and in the development of non-infringing production processes. By contrast, the withdrawal of patent protection caused many multinational pharmaceutical companies to limit their product portfolio in India to patent-expired products, or to pull out of the market altogether.[406] In 1970, foreign firms accounted for two thirds of the market; by 2004, they held only a 23 percent market share.[407]

Pharmaceutical firms operating in India are a diverse group with varied interests in the new patent law. Although there are approximately 6,000 active firms, the top 300 make up most of the Indian market. In the top tier are approximately 100 domestic and foreign-owned companies, with annual sales greater than $650,000. The top tier firms, both foreign and domestic, with their own research agendas and discoveries generally support the amended patent law, believing that it provides a necessary incentive for innovation.[408]

The top three domestic firms, in terms of operating revenues, are Ranbaxy Laboratories, Cipla Ltd., and Dr. Reddy's Laboratories. The only Indian subsidiary of a multinational firm with operating revenues sufficient to place it within the top ten firms in India is ninth-ranked

GlaxoSmithKline Ltd. (GSK-India), a subsidiary of UK-based Glaxosmithkline (GSK) (figure 8-1).[409] The top domestic firms compete with multinational corporations in the global generics market, often have significant investments outside of India, and engage in R&D, including strategic alliances with foreign and domestic firms.[410] In general, the R&D budgets of domestic firms are substantially smaller than those of the multinationals. Ranbaxy, for example, had R&D expenditures of 7 percent of sales in 2005, and Dr. Reddy's Laboratories' expenditures were 10 percent, as compared to an average R&D expenditure of 15 percent for the top 15 global pharmaceutical companies in 2005.[411]

In the second tier are approximately 200 medium-sized companies including generic producers and firms that specialize in niche areas such as contract research, with annual sales ranging from $210,410 to $650,000.[412] Many of the mid-sized domestic generics firms have been exclusively focused on the reverse engineering and manufacturing of patented and unpatented drugs. These firms generally oppose the new patent law; they do not have inventions of their own to protect and the new law undercuts what has been a successful market niche.[413]

In the third tier are the remaining firms (approximately 5,700 small firms with annual sales less than $210,410), some of which perform contract manufacturing services for foreign and domestic pharmaceutical makers. More than the new patent law, contract manufacturing firms are impacted by the revisions to India's Drug and Cosmetics Act, which as of 2005, require the implementation of Good Manufacturing Practices and have necessitated the substantial upgrading of facilities.[414] Although many smaller firms have been forced to shut down because they could not meet these enhanced standards, upgrading has provided some remaining manufacturers with increased opportunities to provide contract services to foreign firms.

Foreign direct investment in the drug and pharmaceutical sector

Annual FDI inflows into India's drug and pharmaceutical sector have grown steadily from $12 million in 1994 to $342 million in 2004, declining to $116 million in 2005, and rebounding to $216 million in 2006 (figure 8-2). In 2004, FDI inflows increased 463 percent over 2003 levels, in large part in anticipation of the "advent of the product patent era."[415] Ongoing uncertainty, perhaps attributable to perceived inadequacies in India's law in the areas of data protection, the standards for patentability, and compulsory licensing appears to have tamped down FDI in 2005 and 2006.

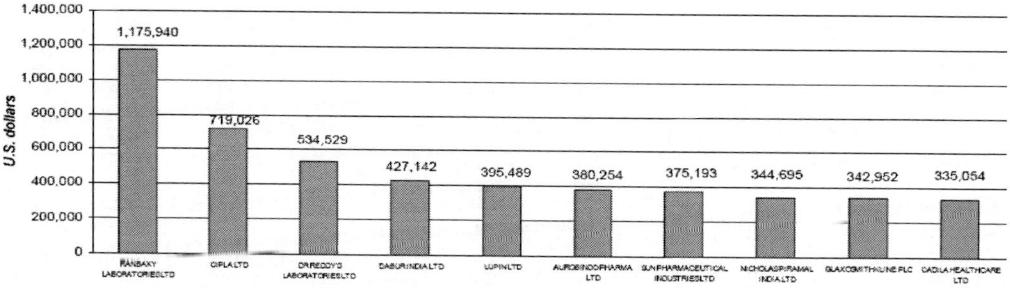

Source: Bureau van Dijk, *Orbis Companies database* .

Figure 8-1. India's top ten pharmaceutical firms by operating revenue, 2005

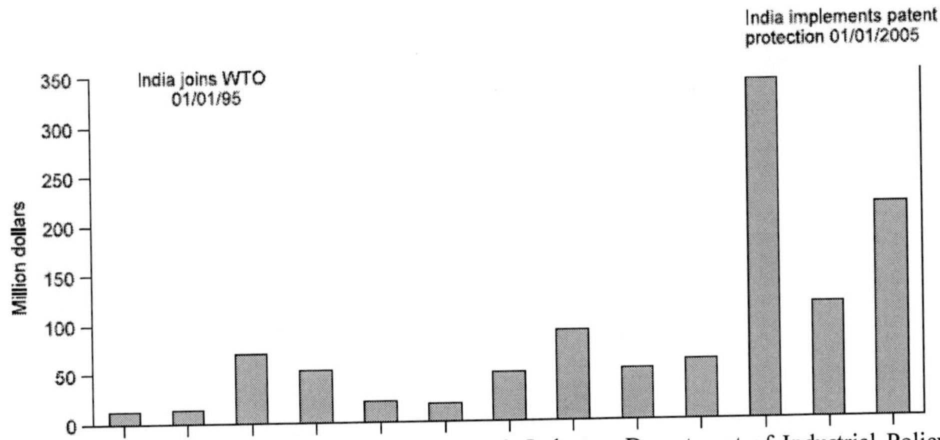

Source:Government of India, Ministry of commerce & Industry, Department of Industrial Policy & promotion.

Figure 8-2. India's FDI inflows, Drugs & Pharmaceuticals, 1994-2006

The largest souce of FDI in India's pharmaceutical industry is Mauritius.[416] The United States is the second largest source, followed by the United Kingdom and Singapore (figure 8-3). FDI in India takes various forms including greenfield projects (both the establishment of new facilities and the expansion of existing ones), strategic alliances between foreign and domestic firms, and mergers and acquisitions (M&A).[417]

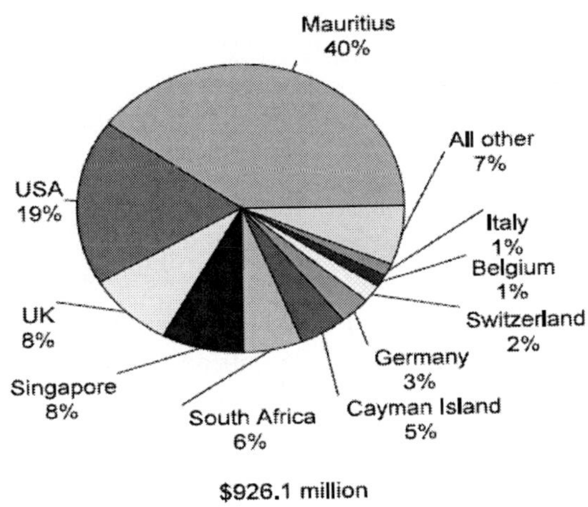

Source: Government of India, Ministry of Commerce & Industry, Department of Industrial Policy & promotion.

Figure 8-3. Drugs and Pharmaceutical FDI bycountry , 2002-06

Greenfield projects

During the period from 2002–06, foreign firms undertook about 80 greenfield investment projects in the pharmaceutical and health biotechnology sectors. The annual number of projects more than doubled between 2003 and 2004, and remained at high levels in 2005 and

2006 (figure 8-4). Most of the projects were for new facilities (83 percent) rather than expansions of existing facilities (17 percent). R&D was reported as the focus of most of the projects (59 percent), followed by manufacturing (26 percent) and sales and service (9 percent).[418]

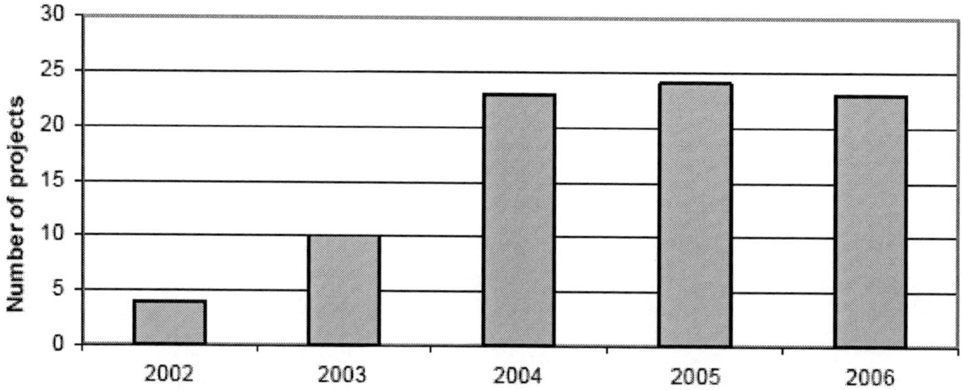

Source: OCO Cons ulting Ltd., *LocoMonitor FDI database.*

Figure 8-4. Greenfield FDI in India's pharmaceutical industry, by year, 2002–06

Table 8-1. Greenfield FDI in the pharmaceutical and health biotechnology sectors by source region and activity, 2002-06

	North America		Europe		Asia Pacific		Middle East	
	No. of projects	% of projects	No. of projects	% of projects	No. of projects	% of projects	No. of projects	% of projects
R&D	27	66	18	62	0	0	2	67
Manufacturing	6	15	10	34	4	57	1	33
Sales and Service	8	20	1	3	3	43	0	0
Total projects	41		29		7		3	

Source: OCO Consulting Ltd., *LocoMonitor FDI database.*

Note: Because of rounding figures may not total 100 percent.

The majority of projects were undertaken by North American firms (51 percent), followed by European firms, including those outside of the European Union (36 percent). North American and European firms concentrated their investment activities in R&D, with 66 percent of all North American projects in this sector and 62 percent of all European projects. For North American firms, the next most frequent investment activity was in sales and service (20 percent) followed by manufacturing (15 percent). By contrast, for European firms, most of the remaining investment activity was focused on manufacturing (34 percent) while only 3 percent was focused on sales and service activities (table 8-1).[419]

Strategic alliances in R&D

Strategic alliances between multinational and domestic firms are an important part of FDI in the R&D and manufacturing sectors. In the R&D area, contract research organizations (CROs) offer pharmaceutical firms a range of services including product development, clinical trial management, laboratory services, and data management.[420] The top three reasons multinational companies cite for performing clinical trials in India are the number of potential clinical trial subjects, cost savings, and the country's disease profile.[421] These reasons must be compelling; despite China's much larger market size, there are presently 251 clinical trials ongoing in India compared to 227 in China. Companies with a substantial number of clinical trials ongoing in India include GSK with 25, Bristol-Myers Squibb (BMS) with 21, Johnson & Johnson with 16, and Pfizer with 14.[422]

Prominent examples of contract research services being performed in India include the recent contract between India-based Tata Consultancy Services (TCS) and U.S.-based Eli Lilly (Lilly), in which TCS's services will include "clinical trial data management, statistical analysis and medical writing."[423] In 2007, Lilly also announced a new agreement with the Indian firm Nicholas Piramal (NPIL), in which NPIL will design and execute Lilly's global clinical development program, including investigational drug applications and human clinical trials.[424] The U.S.-based biotechnology firm Amgen recently announced its entry into the Indian market with the opening of a wholly owned subsidiary in Mumbai. The new investment will initially focus on strategic alliances with CROs, particularly in the area of clinical development.[425]

Already among India's top ten pharmaceutical firms, GSK-India recently increased its presence in Bangalore by expanding its clinical trial data management, analyses and reporting activities to account for more of the data services required for GSK's global clinical trials.[426] In addition, GSK-India has signed a new R&D agreement with India-based Ranbaxy to expand their 2003 agreement to increase Ranbaxy's drug-development responsibilities. Under the 2003 agreement, Ranbaxy developed drug leads only to the stage of candidate selection. Under the expanded agreement, Ranbaxy will "advance the leads beyond candidate selection to completion of clinical proof of concept."[427]

Similarly, Wyeth USA and India-based GVK Biosciences entered into a five year agreement under which GVK will set up an R&D center in Hyderabad and hire 150 scientists in 2007 to work on Wyeth's drug discovery projects. According to Wyeth, the driving factors behind its decision to partner for contract research services were the growing skill base in Asia, India's 2005 revision of its patent laws, and the high quality of science at GVK.[428] Most recently, in March 2007, U.S.-based BMS and Indian biotechnology firm Biocon broke ground on a new research facility planned to house 400 scientists working on early drug development for BMS in India.[429]

These new and increasingly sophisticated R&D projects may be surprising given the reported inadequacies in India's patent law described above, and the fact that India does not have a data protection law. However, different IP protection mechanisms are relevant to the R&D projects described here than to projects which involve product patenting and commercialization. R&D projects depend on the relationship between the parties, pre-contract due diligence, strong contractual protections, operational security practices, and documented compliance with international standards such as ISO 27001, which addresses information security management systems, to ensure the confidentiality of proprietary data. India's Contract Act and Information Technology Act may also provide statutory bases for the protection of sensitive R&D data and proprietary information; to date, these statutes have been used to protect sensitive information shared in the course of BPO projects.[430]

By contrast, the data protection law sought by multinational firms would govern the commercialization of a product and the submission of clinical trial data to drug regulatory authorities in India. Clinical trial data developed in R&D projects may or may not be submitted to Indian regulatory authorities. If the data supports global trials, it likely will be submitted in regulated markets, such as those of the United States and the European Union, where there are data protection laws. Thus, the lack of a data protection law in India may not be of critical importance to a company's decision to conduct preliminary R&D there.

Table 8-2. Selected contract manufacturing deals in pharmaceuticals in India

Indian contract manufacturer	Multinational company	Product
Lupin Laboratories	Fujisawa (Japan)	Cefixime
	Apotex (Canada)	Cefuroxime Axetil, Lisinopril
	DMS (USA)	API for cephalosporings
Nicholas Piramal	Allergran (USA	Bulk and formulations
	Advanced Medical Optics (USA)	Eye products
	AstraZeneca (Sweden)	APIs
	Pfizer (USA)	APIs
Wockhardt	Ivax (USA	Nizatidine (anti- ulcerant)
Dishman Pharmaceuticals	Solvay Pharmaceuticals (Belgium)	APIs and formulations
	GSK (UK)	Intermediates and APIs
	AstraZeneca (Sweden)	Nexium
	Merck (USA	Losartan
IPCA Labs	Merck (USA)	Bulk Drugs
	Tillomed (UK)	Atenelol
Orchid Chemicals and Pharmaceuticals	Apotex (Canada)	Cephalosporin and other injectables
Sun Pharma	Eli Lilly (USA)	Cardiovascular products, anti-infective drugs and insulin
Kopran	Synpac Pharmaceuticals (USA)	Penicillin
Cadila Healthcare	Altana Pharma (Germany)	APIs and intermediates
	Boehringer Ingelheim (Germany)	Gastrointestinal and cardiovascular products
	Mayne (Australia)	Intermediates for oncology products
Blocon	Bristol Myers Squibb (USA)	Bulk Drugs
Shasun Chemicals	Eli Lilly (USA)	APIs
	GSK (UK)	APIs
	Reliant Pharma (USA)	APIs
	Alpharma (USA)	Generics & APIS
	Boots (S Africa)	APIs
Jubilant Organosys	Novartis	Intermediates and APIs

Sources: Government of India, Ministry of External Affairs, ITP Division, and Greene, William.

This said, this case study reports numerous instances in which multinational pharmaceutical firms have stressed the importance of a strong IP protection environment to their investment decisions. Multinational firms remain wary of investing in countries where the fruits of their investment will be used to foster low cost competitors.[431] The IP landscape in India prior to 2005 gave rise to substantial uncertainty about whether Indian courts would protect sensitive information developed in pharmaceutical R&D projects. Under the 1970 Patents Act pharmaceutical products were not entitled to patent protection, thus there would be little motivation for a court to protect the R& D used to develop these products under existing contract laws—one could even envision a public policy-based challenge to a contract that attempted to do so. Now that the law does provide patent protection for pharmaceutical products, contract law protections for pharmaceutical R&D also may be more available.

Strategic alliances in manufacturing

A second major focus of FDI by multinational companies in India is outsourced contract manufacturing. This contract manufacturing includes the production of intermediates, active pharmaceutical ingredients (APIs), bulk drugs, formulations, and generic drugs. U.S.-based Pfizer, for example, maintains a single drug manufacturing facility in India, but also outsources manufacturing to about 20 Indian companies.[432] U.S.-based Merck has recently decided to outsource 35 percent of its manufacturing processes to developing countries, and particularly India, in order to substantially reduce costs. According to Merck, "the critical factor" driving the decision to increase Indian investment was the patent law change.[433] The Indian government has noted that "top MNCs like Pfizer, Merck, GSK, Sanofi Aventis, Novartis, Teva, etc. are largely depending on Indian companies for many of their APIs and intermediates" (table 8-2).[434]

One reason for India's strength in the area of contract manufacturing compared to other emerging markets is the large number of manufacturing facilities that the U.S. Food and Drug Administration (FDA) has certified.[435] FDA certification allows pharmaceutical products to be imported into the United States. Outside of the United States, India has the largest number of FDA- approved manufacturing facilities, numbering 75 in 2006.[436] Another reason for the strength of contract manufacturing is the large number of scientists and engineers with unique skills in the areas of process chemistry and biochemistry.

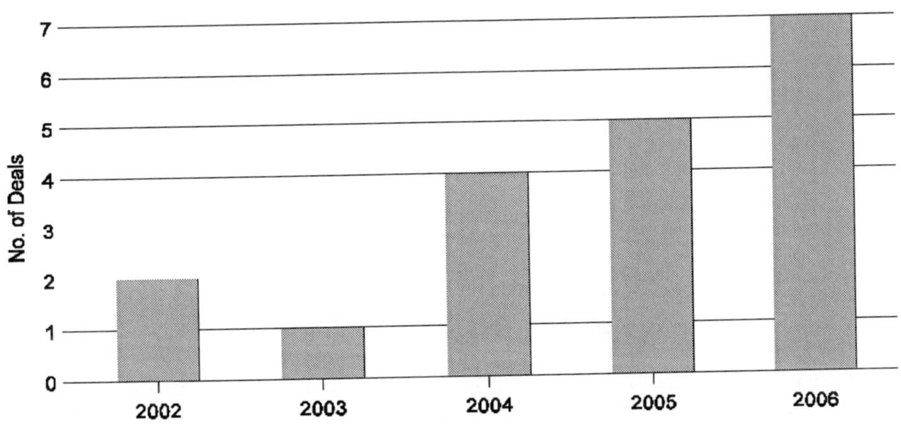

Source: Bureau van Dijk, Zephyr Mergers andAcquisitions database.

Figure 8-5. Pharmaceutical M&A Activity, 2002-06

As with contract R&D, contract manufacturing permits the segmentation and protection of production processes so that valuable intellectual property is not lost. For example, different variants of a molecule may be tested in different locations, fire walls may be set up between production functions, and the contract relationship may begin with commodity style production services and evolve only upon the establishment of trust. Indian expertise in BPO also has resulted in a demonstrated competence in security practices and contractual provisions such as non-disclosure agreements, as well as comfort with global standards that cover security domains.[437] The gaps identified by multinationals in India's IP regime do not appear to substantially affect collaborations in the manufacturing of pharmaceuticals. In fact, the success of manufacturing relationships for the production of pharmaceuticals has been the precursor to increasingly complex and sophisticated R&D and manufacturing collaborations.

Pharmaceutical M&A

Cross-border M&A deals in India's pharmaceutical sector have been on the upswing since 2003 (figure 8-5). European companies have been the most active acquirers with 61 percent of all deals, followed by North American firms with 26 percent.[438]

The most significant deal in terms of scale and value has been the January 2007 acquisition by Mylan, one of the largest generic drug providers in the United States, of a majority stake in Indian-based Matrix, the world's second largest API manufacturer, in a $548 million deal. According to Mylan, the merger was needed to expand its manufacturing platform, obtain a presence in key markets, and tap into local technical expertise in the production of generic biologics.[439] U.S.-based Watson Pharmaceuticals similarly expanded its operations in India by acquiring two Indian companies. In 2005, it acquired a finished dosages manufacturing plant from Dr. Reddy's. Then, in 2006, it acquired Sekhsaria Chemicals, a company focused on process R&D and contract manufacturing services. Watson Pharmaceuticals reported that the two acquisitions would improve efficiencies and cost management and enhance the company's competitive position.[440] In 2003, U.S.-based Healthscribe reported that it would buy out its Indian joint venture partner in a $10.3 million deal. The Indian affiliate would continue to provide BPO services to the healthcare sector.[441]

Acquisitions by European companies also focused on expanding Indian operations including three acquisitions by Iceland-based Actavis during the period from 2005–07. In 2005, it acquired Lotus Laboraties, a CRO, in a $27 million deal. In 2006, it acquired a manufacturing plant from Grandix Pharmaceuticals to obtain "backward integration" with an API and a finished dose development and manufacturing unit. Then, in 2007, it acquired Sanmar Specialty Chemicals, a developer and manufacturer of API, with the goal of continuing its backward integration and reducing costs. In 2006, the French company, Merieux Alliance, acquired a majority stake in Shantha Biotechnics, an Indian company focused on R&D for infectious disease vaccines, to get access to proprietary research and a branded product base. M&A activity during this period also enabled European firms—including AstraZeneca and Solvay—to increase their majority stakes in Indian affiliates.[442]

The globalization of clinical research and manufacturing operations—with the goal of reducing costs and accessing Indian expertise—has resulted in increased M&A activities in India over the last five years. As with other types of FDI, these M&A activities have increased in size and scope with the evolution of India's intellectual property laws towards compliance with international standards under TRIPS.

CONCLUSION

India has charted its own path over the last 35 years, attempting to foster the growth of a domestic pharmaceutical industry and access to medicine while, more recently, also addressing the requirements of the international intellectual property regime. Multinational pharmaceutical firms have responded to India's movement towards TRIPS compliance by increasing the quantity and quality of FDI in the areas of R&D and manufacturing. Multinational firms have adopted a more cautious attitude toward investment in the patenting and commercialization of pharmaceutical products in India, waiting to see how Indian courts and patent offices interpret the new laws, and until India enacts data exclusivity legislation. The ultimate success of India's "calibrated approach" to fostering the domestic industry and access to medicine while also addressing international intellectual property requirements remains to be seen.

BIBLIOGRAPHY

3i Web site. http://www.3i.com/portfolio (accessed March 30, 2007).

Abdullah, Omer. Inaugural address to the 35th Annual General Meeting of The Indian Council of Arbitration.

Adityapur Industrial Area Development Authority Web site, http://www.aiadaonline.com/facts.php (accessed June 8, 2007).

Altbach, Philip G. "Higher Education in India (2005)." *The Hindu*, April 12.

American Arbitration Association. International Centre for Dispute Resolution (2005). "Bechtel Enterprises International (Bermuda) Ltd.; Ben Dabhol Holdings, Ltd.; and Capital India Power Mauritius I, claimants against Overseas Private Investment Corp., Respondent. AAA Case No. 50, T195 0050902, September 3, http://www.opic.gov/insurance1.pdf (accessed June 8, 2007).

Anderson, W. Geoffrey ((2004). *"Legal and Practical Protection of U.S. Foreign Investment."* 18 Transnational Lawyer 133.

Asian Development Bank Web site. http://www.adb.org (accessed January 11, 2007).

_________. "Key Indicators 2005: Labor Markets in Asia: Promoting Full, Productive, and Decent Employment," 2005.

Asia Pacific Bulletin. "Can India Revitalize its Special Economic Zones to Rival those in China?" Asia Pacific Foundation of Canada, February 1, 2006. http://www.asiapacificbusiness.ca/apbn/pdfs/bulletin244.pdf (accessed June 8, 2007).

AstraZeneca. "AstraZeneca Inaugurates State-of-the-Art Global Process R&D lab in Bangalore (March 21)," 2007. http://www.astrazeneca.com/pressrelease/5315.aspx (accessed April 16, 2007).

Kearney, A. T. Inc. (2005). "FDI Confidence Index." *Global Business Policy Council. Volume 8*.

Autocar Professional. "Mega Auto Project Well On Course," August 15, 2006. http://www.natrip.in/newscontent.aspx?newsid=N:34 (accessed January 19, 2007).

Automotive Component Manufacturers Association of India. *"Industry Statistics."* http://www.acmainfo.com.

Barnes, David. Remarks at the 5th Summit of the U.S.-India High Technology Cooperation Group, Washington, DC, February 22, 2007.

Basu, Indrajit. "India, Singapore Ink Pact." *Asia Times Online,* July 2, 2005. http://www.atimes.com/ (accessed January 12, 2007).

Basu, Kaushik. "Why India's Labour Laws Are a Problem." *BBC News*, May 18, 2006. http://news.bbc.co.uk/2hi/south Asia/4984256.stm (accessed December 6, 2006).

Bellman, Eric. "As Economy Grows, India Goes for Designer Goods." *Wall Street Journal Online,* March 27, 2007. http://www.wsj.com/ (accessed April 2, 2007).

Bhalla, Nita & Jonathan Allen. "GM Says to Buy More Auto parts from India." *Reuters India*, April 17, 2007. http://in.today.reuters.com (accessed April 18, 2997).

Bhati, Usha. *Foreign Direct Investment: Contemporary Issues.* New Delhi, India: Deep & Deep Publications, 2006.

Bilaterals.org. "India and Mauritius Close to Economic Treaty," February 13, 2007. http://www.bilaterals.org (accessed March 16, 2007).

———. "*Saudi, Kuwait want India to give 'S'pore Treatment'*," August 16, 2005. http://www.bilaterals.org (accessed January 12, 2007).

Bindra, Satinder. "India Battles Infrastructure Woes." *CNN*, October 25, 2005. http://edition.cnn.com/2005/WORLD/asiapcf/09/21/india.eye.infrastructure (accessed January 16, 2007).

Biocon. *"Biocon Conducts Ground Breaking Ceremony of New Research Facility at Biocon Park* (March 21)." Bangalore, 2007. http://www.biocon.com/biocon press releases details.asp?Fileid=252 (accessed May 8, 2007).

Biotechmedia. "CRO, Contract Research Organization." http://www.biotechmedia.com/ definitions-c.html CR), (accessed April 13, 2007).

Bissinger, Maria. *Dream Machines: Emerging Markets Beckon the World's Carmakers.* Standard & Poor's, March 8, 2006.

Bombay Stock Exchange Web site. http://www.bseindia.com (accessed January 30, 2007).

Bonasia, J. "Indian Outsourcers Scramble to Meet Need for More Staff." *Investor's Business Daily,* March 2, 2007. http://www.investors.com/ (accessed March 6, 2007).

Boston Consulting Group. *Harnessing the Power of India,* May 2006. http://www.bcg.com/publications/files/Rising to the Productivity Challenge in Biopharma RD May06.pdf (accessed April 16, 2007).

Bureau van Dijk. *Orbis Companies database*. https://orbis.dvdep.com/ (accessed various dates).

———. *Zephyr Mergers and Acquisitions database*. https://zephyr.bvdep.com/ (accessed various dates).

Business India Intelligence. "India Automotive: Burning Rubber." The Economist Intelligence Unit, December 10, 2006.

———. "Hotels," April 17, 2007. http://dialog.newsedge.com (accessed April 23, 2007).

Business Monitor Food & Drink Insight. "Bharti Confirms Wal-Mart Plans," February 21, 2007. http://dialog.newsedge.com/ (accessed February 21, 2007).

Business World, The (India). "We Are Not Doing This Out of Spite," February 16, 2007. http://www.drugwonks.com/2007/02/ (accessed March 25, 2007).

BusinessStandard.com. "Industrial Corridor to Get $50 Billion Investment," April 15, 2007. http://dialog.newsedge.com (accessed April 19, 2007).

________. "Semiconductor Policy Notified," March 23, 2007. http://www.business-standard.com/ (accessed March 2, 2007).

Caterpillar Inc. "Caterpillar Completes Purchase of Former Joint Venture Engine Business in India (November 16, 2006)." Mathagondapalli, India, 2006. http://cat.com/cda/components (accessed June 4, 2007).

Central Intelligence Agency (CIA). "India." *The World Factbook,* 2006. http://www.cia.gov/cia/publications/factbook/geos/in.html (accessed November 22, 2006).

Chakrabarti, Rajesh. (2006). *The Financial Sector in India Emerging Issues.* New Delhi, India: Oxford University Press.

Chaudhuri, Sudip. (2005). *The WTO and India's Pharmaceuticals Industry: Patent Protection, TRIPS, and Developing Countries.* Oxford: Oxford University Press.

Chatterjee, Moumita. "TCS Wins $35 Mn Eli Lilly Contract." *The Economic Times,* November 13, 2006.

Confederation of Indian Industry. Northern Region. "Special Economic Zones—Engines for Growth," May 2006. http://www.ciionline.org/Northern/regionalfocus/836/images (accessed November 2, 2006).

David, Ruth. "India Sets Semi Subsidy Policy." *Forbes.com,* March 22, 2007. http://www.forbes.com/ (accessed March 2, 2007).

Data, P.T. Jyothi. "More Global Buys by Pharma Cos Likely." *Hindu Business Line (Internet Edition)*, July 22, 2005.

Deccan Gold Mines, Ltd. Company press releases http://www.deccangoldmines.com/media33.htm (accessed May 14, 2007).

Deloitte. *China and India: The Reality Beyond the Hype*. Deloitte, 2006. Deutsche Bank Web site. http://www.db.com (accessed March 5, 2007).

Dikshit, Sandeep. "Ban on FDI from Bangladesh May Go." *The Hindu Times,* April 4, 2007. http://www.thehindu.com/ (accessed April 12, 2007).

DiMasi, J. A., Hansen, R. W. & Grabowski, H. G. (2003). "The Price of Innovation: New Estimates of Drug Development Costs." *Journal of Health Economics*, *22(2)*, 151–85.

Doi, Ayako. "Suzuki Will Build Suppliers Industrial Park Next Door to its New Indian Swift Plant." *The Japan Automotive Digest*, June 12, 2006.

Economic Times, The. "Hindustan Semiconductor to Chip In $4 B for Indian Fabs," March 29, 2007. http://economictimes.indiatimes.com/articleshow/1825640.cms (accessed April 4, 2007).

________. "Pharma Tops the FDI Chart in '04 With $340 Mn Inflow," April 18, 2005. http://ibef.org (accessed March 5, 2007).

________. "Patent Pat: Pharma MNCs Prefer Tiger to Dragon," February 13, 2005. http://ibef.org (accessed March 5, 2007).

________. "India's on Merck's Outsourcing Radar," June 23, 2006. http://economictimes.indiatimes.com/News/CompaniesA-Z/M_Companies_/Merck_Pharma/Indias on Mercks outsourcing radar/articleshow/1 672701 .cms (accessed March 20, 2007).

Economist.com. "Indian Retailing: Getting Cheaper and Better," February 1, 2007. http://www.economist.com/ (accessed February 1, 2007).

Economist Intelligence Unit (EIU). *Business India Intelligence,* November 8, 2006.

———. "Country Report India—Main report: December 4, 2006." http://www.eiu.com/ (accessed various dates).

EIU, *India: Country Commerce 2006*, 22.

Embassy of India. "FDI Policy and Procedure." http://www.indianembassy.org/newsite//Doing business In India/FDI Policy Procedures.asp#6 (accessed February 13, 2007)

———. "U.S. Investments in India." http://www.indianembassy.org/newsite//Doing business In India/ (accessed various dates).

Ernst & Young. *Unveiling India's Pharmaceutical Future*, 2005. http://www.ey.com/global/download.nsf/International_/Industry_Pharmaceuticals_Unveiling_India_Pharma_Future/$file_/NM_Pharma_Report_Unveiling_India_Future.pdf (accessed February 1, 2007).

European Commission (EC). "Bilateral Trade Relations - India." http://ec.europa.eu/trade en.htm (accessed March 7, 2007).

———. *EU 2005 Breakdown of Number of Cases Registered*. Brussels: EC, 2006. http://ec.europa.eu/taxation_customs/resources/documents/customs/customs_controls/counterfeit_piracy/statistic s/counterf_comm 2005_en.pdf (accessed February 5, 2007).

Fenwick & West L. L. P. (2006). *Structuring Venture Capital and Other Investments in India.*

Fillmore, Ken. "Indian Capacity Will Rise to 3 Million a Year by 2010, Says Nikkei." *The Japan Automotive Digest*, December 11, 2006.

———. "Short of Engineers at Home, Suzuki Will Shift More Design Chores to Maruti." *The Japan Automotive Digest*, January 22, 2007.

Financial Express, The. "EADS to Open Technology Centre in Bangalore." April 4, 2007. http://www.financialexpress.com/fe full story.php?content id=160135 (accessed May 3, 2007).

Financial Times, The. "FDI in India Expected to Double," December 28, 2006. http://www.ft.com/ (accessed January 18, 2007).

Flextronics International Ltd. "SemIndia Announces Flextronics as a Strategic Partner (April 4)." New Delhi, 2006. http://www.flextronics.com/en/portals/0/press%20releases/20060404SJA.pdf (accessed April 2, 2007).

Ford Motor Co. "Volvo to Sell Cars in India (July 5)." *Dearborn,* 2006. http://media display.cfm?release=23361.

Fraser, Cameron, Axel Berkotsky, Maya Bhandari, Diane Halley. European Policy Centre "EU-India Relations (including EU-India Journalists' Conference report, 30–31 May") EPC issue paper no. 35, June 2005.

Frontline. Volume 19 - Issue 14, July 6–19, 2002. http://www.hinduonnet.com/fline/fl1914/19141020.htm (accessed April 9, 2007).

General Electric Web site. http://www.ge.com/in (accessed December 6, 2006). Geneva Convention on the Execution of Foreign Arbitral Awards of 1927. Geneva Protocol on Arbitration Clauses of 1923.

Global Trade Information Service, Inc. (GTIS). *World Trade Atlas database*. Government of Goa Web site. http://www.edc-goa.com (accessed January 12, 2007).

Government of India. "Committee Report on Reforming Investment Approval & Implementation Procedures." http://dipp.nic.in/implrepo/implrepo2.pdf (accessed March 30, 2007).

———. Indian Arbitration and Conciliation Act of 1996 (IACA).

________. "SEZ Rules 2006, Chapter 2, Procedure for Establishment of Special Economic Zone." www.seznews.com/acts-and-rules/sez-rules-2006/procedure-for-establishment-of-sez.htm.

________. Labour Bureau. *Annual Survey of Industries Scheme.* http://labourbureau.nic.in/asitab%20new%20sep06.htm (accessed October 27, 2006).

________. Ministry of Civil Aviation. "Policy on Airport Infrastructure." http://civilaviation.nic.in/moca/airppol.htm (accessed March 21, 2007).

________. Ministry of Commerce & Industry. "2006 Year of Record FDI Inflows." http://pib.nic.in/release/release.asp?relid=23630 (accessed April 17, 2007).

________. Ministry of Commerce & Industry. *Economic Survey 2006–2007.* http://indiabudget.nic.in/es2006-07/esmain.htm (accessed April 17, 2007).

________. Ministry of Commerce & Industry. "Fact Sheet on Foreign Direct Investment from August 1991 to December 2006." http://dipp.gov.in/fdi statistics/india fdi dec 2006.pdf (accessed April 7, 2007).

________. Ministry of Commerce & Industry. "SEZs Future Vehicle of Economic Activity, Says Kamal Nath (November 16)." New Delhi, 2006. http://commerce release.htm#h1 3, (accessed December 5, 2006)

________. Ministry of Commerce & Industry. "Special Economic Zones in India—About." http://www.sezindia.nic.in/HTMLS/about.htm (accessed April 2, 2007).

________. Ministry of Commerce & Industry. "Special Economic Zones in India—Facilities and Incentives." http://www.sezindia.nic.in/HTMLS/set-sez.htm (accessed November 16, 2006).

________. Ministry of Commerce & Industry. "Special Economic Zones in India—Home Page." http://sezindia.nic.in/ (accessed November 14, 2006).

________. Ministry of Commerce & Industry. "Special Economic Zones in India—How to Apply." http://www.sezindia.nic.in/howapply_enterprise.asp. (accessed November 28, 2006).

________. Ministry of Commerce & Industry. Department of Commerce. *Annual Report 2005–2006.* http://commerce (accessed April 17, 2007).

________. Ministry of Commerce & Industry. Department of Commerce. *CECA Between India and Singapore*. http://commerce.nic.in/ (accessed various dates).

________. Ministry of Commerce & Industry. Department of Industrial Policy and Promotion. *Investing in India: Foreign Direct Investment Policy & Procedures*, 2006.

________. Ministry of Commerce & Industry. Department of Industrial Policy and Promotion. http://dipp.nic.in/fdistatistics/indiafdiindex.htm)

________. Ministry of Commerce & Industry. Department of Industrial Policy and Promotion. Secretariat for Industrial Assistance. "*Destination India.*" Issue No. 2, 2004.

________. Ministry of External Affairs. ITP Division. "Drugs & Pharmaceuticals." http://www.indiainbusiness.nic.in/industry (accessed April 16, 2007).

________. Ministry of Finance. Income Tax Department Web site. http://incometaxindia.gov.in/ (accessed various dates).

________. Ministry of Heavy Industries and Public Enterprises. *Automotive Mission Plan 2006–2016: A Mission for Development of Indian Automotive Industry.* http://www.siam.in/Upload/AMP.pdf.

________. Ministry of Heavy Industries and Public Enterprises. Department of Heavy Industry. *Auto Policy*, March 2002. http://www.dhi.nic.in/autopolicy.htm.

———. Ministry of Human Resource Development. Sourced from Reserve Bank of India. Handbook of Statistics on Indian Economy, September 18, 2006. http://www.rbi.org.in (accessed January 18, 2007).

———. Ministry of Labor Web site. http://labour (accessed various dates).

———. Ministry of Law and Justice. "Civil Procedure Code As Amended Enforced as of Today (July 1)." New Delhi, 2002. http://pib.nic.in/archieve/lreleng/lyr2002/rjul2002/01072002/r010720022.html (accessed April 9, 2007).

———. Ministry of Law and Justice. "Landmark Legal Reforms in the Social Sector, (October 7)." New Delhi, 2002. http://pic.nic.in/arcieve/lreleng/1yr2002/roct2002/07102002/r071020021.html (accessed April 9, 2007).

———. Ministry of Shipping, Road Transport and Highways. Department of Road and Transport and Highways. *"Externally Aided Projects."* http://north.nic.in/externalproj.htm (accessed January 12, 2007).

———. Ministry of Shipping, Road Transport and Highways. Department of Road and Transport and Highways. *"Opportunities for Private Sector Participation."* http://morth.nic.in/pub pvt participation.htm (accessed January 12, 2007).

———. Ministry of Shipping, Road Transport and Highways. Department of Road and Transport and Highways. "Status of BOT Projects Awarded." http://morth.nic.in/BOT Proj NHAI.htm (accessed January 12, 2007).

———. Ministry of Steel, National Steel Policy 2005. http://www.steel (accessed June 29, 2007).

———. Planning Commission. *Foreign Investment, India*, August 2002.

Grace, Cheri. "The Effect of Changing Intellectual Property on Pharmaceutical Industry Prospects in India and China," June 2004. http://www.dfid.gov.uk/pubs/files/ndiachinadomproduce.pdf (accessed March 19, 2007).

Greene, William. *The Emergence of India's Pharmaceutical Industry and Implications for the U.S. Generic Drug Market*, USITC Publication 2007-05-A. Washington, DC: USITC, 2007. http://www.usitc.gov/ind_econ_ana/research_work_papers/documents/EC200705A.pdf (accessed May 7, 2007).

Grocer. "Bharti to Invest $2.5 Billion in Chain," February 24, 2007. http://dialog.newsedge.com/ (accessed April 12, 2007).

GulfNews.com. "Japan to Help India Build $50 Billion Industry Corridor," April 15, 2007. http://archive.gulfnews.com/articles (accessed April 17, 2007).

Gupta, Ritesh. "India Gears Up For Retail." *Chain Store Age,* February 2007.

Gutierrez, Carlos, Secretary of the U.S. Department of Commerce, and David Sampson, Deputy Secretary of the U.S. Commerce Department, Remarks at the 5th Summit of the U.S.-India High Technology Cooperation Group, Washington, DC, February 22, 2007.

HSBC Web site. http://www.hsbc.com (accessed March 5, 2007).

The Hindu. "New Hunt for the Yellow Metal." December 15, 2003. http://www.hindu.com/biz/2003/12/15/stories/2003121500241600.htm (accessed May 14, 2007).

Hindu Business Line. "GVK Biosciences to Provide Research Services for Wyeth Pharma," January 14, 2006. http://www.thehindubusinessline.com/2006/01/14/stories/2006011403320200.htm.

Hindustan Lever Limited Web site. http://www.hll.com (accessed October 5, 2006).

Huber, Hans-Michael. "The Indian Automotive Scenario: Past – Stable, Present – Bright, Future – Promising!" http://www.fadaweb.com/indian_auto_scenario.htm

Human Rights Features, *Legal Reform and Investment Prospects in India*, HRF/1 54/06, November 30, 2006.

Iloveindia Web site. http://www.iloveindia.com/finance (accessed March 5, 2007).

India Brand Equity Foundation. *Auto Components*. http://www.ibef.org/industry

________. *Pharmaceuticals*, July 2006. http://www.ibef.org/download/Pharma sectoral.pdf (accessed March 19, 2007).

India Mart. *Taxation - Tax Treaties*. 2007. http://www.finance (accessed January 12, 2007).

Indian Express. *"Work on Delhi-Mumbai Corridor from January,"* April 14, 2007. http://dialog.newsedge.com (accessed April 19, 2007).

Indian Insurance Regulatory and Development Authority Web site, http://www.irdaindia.org/hist.htm (accessed April 5, 2007).

Indo-Asian News Service. *"India Woos Foreign Equity in Infrastructure,"* February 23, 2007. http://www.hindustantimes.com/news (accessed May 31, 2007).

Industries Commission rate, Government of Gujarst, *New Initiatives* Special Economic Zones, http//www.icgujarst.gov.in/new-initiatives/SEZ-intro.htm.

Intel. "Intel Outlines $1 Billion Multi-year Investment Plans, Highlights India's Importance (December 5)." City of release, 2005. http://www.intel.com/pressroom/archive/releases/20051205corp b.htm (accessed May 8, 2007).

International Bank for Reconstruction and Development (IBRD)/World Bank. *Doing Business in South Asia 2007*. Washington, DC: The World Bank, 2007.

International Center for Alternative Dispute Resolution (ICADR) Web site. http://www.icadr.org/aboutus/about.html (accessed March 23, 2007).

International Chamber of Commerce (ICC). *Global Survey on Counterfeiting and Piracy*. London: ICC, 2007. http://www.iccwbo.org/bascap (accessed February 27, 2007).

International Finance Corporation Web site. http://www.ifc.org (accessed January 11, 2007).

International Intellectual Property Alliance (IIPA). *2003 Special 301 Report: India*. Washington, DC: IIPA, 2003. http://www.iipa.com/rbc/2003/2003SPEC301INDIA.pdf (accessed February 5, 2007).

________. *2007 Special 301 Report: India*. Washington, DC: IIPA, 2007. http://www.iipa.com/rbc/2007/2007SPEC301INDIA.pdf (accessed February 14, 2007).

International Monetary Fund (IMF). *India: Selected Issues*, March 2005.

Islamic Republic News Agency. "India Attractive Destination for PGCC Investments," February 12, 2007. http://www2.irna.ir/en/ (accessed February 14, 2007).

iTWire. "Google Likely to Set Up $1 Billion Datacenter in India," August 11, 2006.

Jacob, Jayanth. "India to Advance Zero-Tariff SAFTA Date." *The Indian Express*, April 1, 2007. http://www.indianexpress.com/ (accessed April 12, 2007).

Jayakumar, P.B. "Amgen Opens Subsidiary in India," March 30, 2007. http://www.business-standard.com/general/pintpage.php?autono=279348 (accessed April 10, 2007).

Jha, "UAE, India to Expand Ties."

Johnson, Jo. "India Lifts Freeze on Enterprise Zones." *Financial Times*, April 6, 2007. http://www.ft.com/cms/s/c45ad352-e408-11db-bf06-000b5df10621,-i-rssPage=ff3cbaf6-3024-11da-ba9f00000e2511c8.html (accessed June 8, 2007).

Just-auto.com editorial team. "Hyundai Has Ambitious Plans," August 25, 2006. http://www.just-auto.com/article.aspx?id=88826&lk=s.

Just-auto.com editorial team. "ACMA-McKinsey's Vision 2015 for the Indian Supplier Industry: How Achievable Is It?" http://www.just-auto.com/article.aspx?id=86273&lk=s (accessed March 14, 2007).

Kanellos, Michael. "India's Tech Renaissance—U.S.-Style Labor Pains from Mumbai to Bangalore." *CNET News. com*, June 28, 2005. http://news.com.com/Indias+renaissance+ U.S.-style+labor (accessed December 6, 2006).

Kantor, Mark. *"Arbitration Award May Alter Dabhol Debate." 1* Transnational Dispute Management 2 (May 2004).

Kapur, Devesh. Center for Advanced Study of India. University of Pennsylvania. Remarks at a conference at the Woodrow Wilson International Center for Scholars, Washington, DC, April 13, 2007.

Kaushik, Neha & Sasi, Anil "Indian Wages Cheaper Than Chinese." *Hindu Business Line*, November 15, 2005. http://www.thehindubusinessline.com (accessed November 7, 2006).

Khaleej Times. "DP World's India Foray Runs Into Murkier Waters," March 30, 2006. http://www.khaleejtimes.com (accessed May 17, 2007.

———. "Gulf Arab Investors Target Asia as US Ties Wane," March 28, 2007. http://www.khaleeitimes.com (accessed May 17, 2007.

———. "Upbeat India Scales Up FDI Projections by 25 Percent," March 28, 2007. http://www.MENAFN.com (accessed April 2, 2007).

KPMG. *Automotive and Components Market in Asia*. KPMG International, 2005.

———. *Manufacturing in India: Opportunities, Challenges, and Myths*. KPMG International, 2005. http://www.kpmg.ca/en/industries/cib/industrial/documents/ ManufacturingInIndia.pdf.

———. *The Indian Pharmaceutical Industry: Collaboration for Growth*. KPMG International, 2006. http://www.kpmg.de/library/pdf/060618 KPMG IndiaPharma en.pdf (accessed April 16, 2007).

Kumar, Sushil. "How to Protect Data in Outsourcing Deals." *Supplement - India IP Focus 2007 4th edition*, March 2007. http://www.managingip.com/?Page=16&ISS=23507 (accessed April 16, 2007).

LaReau, Jamie. "GM Want More Engineers in India." *Automotive News*, April 30, 2007.

Law Commission of India, *On Revision of Court Fees Structure* (189th Report), February 2004.

Law Commission of India Web site. http://lawcommissionofindia.nic.in/adr conf/adr index.htm (assessed March 23, 2007).

Lopez-Claros, Augosto, Michael E. Porter, Xavier Sala-i-Martin & Klaus Schwab. *The Global Competitiveness Report 2006–2007*. New York, NY: Palgrave Macmillan, 2006.

Mahindra World City Web site. http://www.mahindraworldcity.com/chennai/ (accessed June 8, 2007).

Maddox, Jeff. "From Single Brand to Open Season." *FinancialTimes.com*, February 20, 2007. http://www.ft.com/ (accessed February 27, 2007).

Matthew, Joe. "GSK Identifies Asia, Eastern Europe as Major Centres for Clinical Research," September 25, 2006. http:www.gsk-india.com/News/GSK news.asp (accessed April 7, 2007).

McKenzie, Michael. "2007 Global Outlook." *PwC Automotive Institute Analyst Note*, January 18, 2007.

McKinsey & Co., McKinsey Global Institute. *New Horizons: Multinational Company Investment in Developing Economies*. San Francisco: McKinsey & Co., 2003.

Microsoft Web site. http://www.microsoft.com/India (accessed September 26, 2006). Motorola Web site. http://www.motorola.com (accessed September 21, 2006).

Mueller, Janice M. "The Tiger Awakens: The Tumultuous Transformation of India's Patent System and the Rise of Indian Pharmaceutical Innovation." *68 U. Pitt. L. Rev.* (forthcoming 2007), http://ssrn.com/abstract=923538 (accessed March 15, 2007).

Nair, M.S. "India: Mashelkar Committee Withdraws Its Report." *Lex Orbis Intellectual Property Practice*, March 1, 2007. http://www.mondaq.com/article.asp?articleid=46480& lastestnews=1 (accessed March 7, 2007).

National Stock Exchange Web site. http://www.nseindia.com (accessed March 5, 2007).

newKerala. com. "India—The New Hub of the Automotive Industry," October 6, 2006. http://www.newkerala.com/news4.php?action=fullnews&id=32376.

New York Convention of 1958 on the Recognition and Enforcement of Foreign Arbitral Awards.

Novartis. "Questions and Answers." http://www.novartis.com/downloads/about-novartis/india-glivec-patent-case-faq.pdf (accessed May 2, 2007).

Nokia. "Nokia Taps Chennai as New Nokia Global Networks Solutions Center Site, (December 16)." Chennai, 2005. http://www.nokia.com/link?cid=Editorial 4326 (accessed September 20, 2006).

OCO Consulting Ltd. *LocoMonitor FDI database*. http://www.locomonitor.com/ (accessed various dates).

OECD. *Counterfeiting and Piracy: Measurement Issues*. Geneva: OECD, 2005. http://www.oecd.org/dataoecd/42/44/35651123.pdf (accessed April 17, 2007).

OECD. Directorate for Financial and Enterprise Affairs, Investment Committee. "Salient Features of India's Investment Agreements." DAF/INV/WD(2006)3, March 23, 2006.

Overseas Private Investment Corporation (OPIC). *Annual Reports for 2004, 2005,* and *2006*. Washington, DC: OPIC, 2004, 2005, and 2006.

Patent Office, India. *Manual of Patent Practice and Procedure*. Mumbai: India Patent Office, 2005. http://www.patentoffice.nic.in/ipr/patent/manual-2052005.pdf (accessed March 3, 2007).

Pharmabiz.com. "Pharmabiz Studies of Top Cos." April 17, 2006. http://www.pharmabiz.com (accessed March 7, 2007).

Pharmaceutical Research and Manufacturers of America (PhRMA). *PhRMA Special 301 Submission: India*. Washington, DC: PhRMA, 2007.

PhRMA. *PhRMA Survey of Pharmaceutical Counterfeiting Laws and Remedies: China, India, Russia, Brazil and Mexico*. Washington, DC: PhRMA, 2006.

Prasad, Ashish S. & Balan, Violeta I. (2007). "Strategies for U.S. Companies to Mitigate Legal Risks from Doing Business in India." 1587 PLI/Corp 9.

Press Trust of India. "Delphi to Invest $10 Mn in India, Double Halfshaft Production," April 12, 2006. http://www.newsedge.com.

_________. "Morgan Stanley, Citigroup, Actis Pick Up 6 pc Stake in NSE," March 9, 2007. http://dialognewsedge.com (accessed March 12, 2007).

———. "Orissa to Pursue POSCO Project with 'Humane' Face: Naveen," April 18, 2007. http://dialognewsedge.com (April 19, 2007).

———. "VP Writes to PM on POS CO Issue: Demands Intervention," April 18, 2007. http://dialognewsedge.com (April 19, 2007).

PriceWaterhouseCoopers. *"Offshoring in the Financial Services Industry: Risks & Rewards."* PriceWaterhouseCoopers Global Financial Services Briefing Programme, September 2005.

Ramachandran, Sudha. "A Grand Plan for Indian Automobiles." *Asia Times Online*, February 1, 2007. http://www.atimes.com/atimes/South Asia/IB0_1Df0 1_.html.

Ranbaxy Laboratories Ltd. "Ranbaxy Signs New R&D Agreement with GSK," February, 2007. http://www.ranbaxy.com/newsroom/pressrelease_det.asp?sno=322 (accessed March 19, 2007).

Rathore, Deepesh & Swarup, Tilak *A Review of India's Automotive Industry*. Bromsgrove, UK: Aroq Limited, June 2006.

Reuters. "World bank Halts India Health Funds on Fraud Claim." April 4, 2006.

Roumeliotis, Gregory. "Mylan in India's Biggest Pharmaceutical Takeover as it Enters the Matrix." *In-Pharma Technologist.com*, August 30, 2006. http://www.in-pharmatechnologist.com/news/ng.asp?id=70188-mylan-matrix (accessed April 7, 2007).

"Royal Indian Raj International Corporation Pens Estimated $4 Billion Deal with Choice Hotels for at Least 12,000 Budget Hotel Rooms Throughout India, Vancouver, Bristish Columbia and New Delhi, India (April 12).", 2007. http://dialog.newsedge.com (accessed _____, 2007).

Sahoo, Pravakar. "Foreign Direct Investment in South Asia: Policy Trends, Impact and Determinants." *ADB Institute Discussion Paper No. 58,* November 2006.

Sampath, P. "Indian Pharma within Global Reach." In J. Chataway, D. Kale and D. Ried, *The Indian Pharmaceutical Industry Before and After Trips*, Special Issue of the Journal of Technology Analysis and Strategic Management. September 2007. http://www.merit.unu.edu/publications/wppdf/2006/wp2006-031.pdf (accessed February 14, 2007).

Samsung Electronics Co., Ltd. "Samsung Dedicates a Mobile Phone Plant in India (April 3)." Seoul, 2006. http://www.samsung.com/in/products/gsm/news (accessed September 28, 2006).

SemIndia. *"Empowering India: The Semiconductor Way,"* http://www.semindia.in/ (accessed April 2, 2007).

Shared Expertise Forums. "Survey: Pharmaceutical Companies Cautious of Investments in Emerging China and India Markets," December 2, 2005. http://www.sharedservicesbpo.com/file/2998/survey-pharmaceutical-companies-cautious-of-investments-in-eme rging-china-and-india-markets.html (accessed April 12, 2007).

Sikarwar, Deepshikhas. "Mauritius Overhauls DTAA Agreement." *Economic Times*, February 27, 2007. http://dialog.newsedge.com (May 2, 2007).

Singh, Harsimran. "Analysts Skeptical of Chip Fab in India." *IndiaTimes.com*, February 6, 2007. http://infotech.indiatimes.com/ (accessed March 12, 2007).

Singh, Seema. "It's Pharmaceutical Giant's Third Drug Development Alliance in India in Six Months." *Red Herring*, January 12, 2007.

http://www.redherring.com/Article.aspx?a=20712&hed=Lilly+Signs+India (accessed April 7, 2007).

Society of Indian Automobile Manufacturers (SIAM). "Auto Policy of Government of India." http://www.siamindia.com/scripts/PrintView.aspx (accessed January 17, 2007).

Society of Indian Automobile Manufacturers Web site. http://www.siamindia.com (accessed various dates).

South Asian Association for Regional Cooperation. *Agreement on South Asian Free Trade Area.* http://www.saarc-sec.org/ (accessed April 2, 2007).

Srinivasan, T.N. "China, India and the World Economy." Working Paper No. 28. Stanford Center for International Development, July 2006. http://scid.stanford.edu/pdf/SCID286.pdf (accessed June 8, 2007).

Statesman, The (India). "India Attracts $1 5b FDI During 2006–07," April 14, 2007. http://dialog.newsedge.com (accessed April 17, 2007).

Swire, Mary. *"Singapore and Mauritius Vie To Supply India's FDI."* LawAndTax-News.com, October 25, 2005. http://www.tax-news.com/ (accessed various dates).

Technical Expert Group on Patent Law Issues. "Report of the Technical Expert Group on Patent Law Issues." December 2006. http://www.patentmatics.org/pub2007/pub2c.pdf (accessed May 2, 2007).

Thomas, Dorothy. "Singapore, New Tax Haven for Offshore Investors." *The Hindu Times,* January 8, 2005. http://www.thehindu.com/ (accessed January 12, 2007).

Thomas, John. *Proprietary Rights in Pharmaceutical Innovation: Issues at the Intersection of Patents and Marketing Exclusivities.* CRS Report for Congress RL33288. Washington, DC: Congressional Research Service, 2006.

Thomson Scientific, "I.P. Overload?—Thomson Scientific 2007 Patent Focus Report." *Knowledge Link*, January 2007. http://scentific.thomson.com/newsletter (accessed March 5, 2007).

Tippu, Sufia. "India's Coming Bandwidth Boom." *Business Week.com,* February 7, 2007. http://www.businessweek.com/ (accessed March 9, 2007).

UNCTAD. "Foreign Direct Investment Rose by 34% in 2006 (January 9)." Geneva, 2007. http://www.unctad.org/templates/webflyer.asp?docid=7993&intItemID=1634&lang=1, (accessed June 11, 2007).

UNCTAD. "UNCTAD Proposes Ways to Limit Excessive Incentives Competition to Attract Foreign Direct Investment, (March 28)." Geneva, 1996. http://www.unctad.org/Templates/webflyer.asp?docid=3391&intItemID=2298&lang=1, (accessed February 15, 2007).

UNCTAD, *World Investment Report 2006.* (United Nations, Geneva and New York, 2006).

United Nations Web site. http://untreaty.un.org/ENGLISH/bible/englishinternetbible/partI/chapterXXII/treaty1.asp (accessed March 23, 2007).

United Nations. Economic and Social Council. Commission on Human Rights. Civil and Political Rights. Including the Questions of the Judiciary, Administration of Justice, Impunity. Written Statement Submitted by the Asian Legal Resource Centre (ALRC), E/CN.4/2005/NGO/107, February 15, 2007.

U.S. Customs and Border Protection (USCBP). *FY 2005 Top IPR Commodities Seized.* Los Angeles: USCBP, 2005. http://www.cbp.gov/linkhandler/cgov/import/commercial enforcement/ipr/seizure/trading/fy05 midyear stats.c tt/fy05 ipr midyear.pdf (accessed February 5, 2007).

———. *FY 2006 Top IPR Commodities Seized*. Los Angeles: USCBP, 2006. http://www.cbp.gov/linkhandler/cgov/import/commercial_enforcement/ipr/seizure_trading/fy06 midyear stats.c tt/fy06 ipr midyear.pdf (accessed February 5, 2007).

U.S. Department of Commerce (USDOC). *The Agreement on Trade Related Investment Measures*. http://commerce (accessed March 23, 2007).

. Bureau of Economic Analysis (BEA). International Economic Accounts. "Operations of Multinational Companies." http://www.bea.gov/international/index.htm#omc (accessed varous dates).

———. U.S. Commercial Service. *India: Architecture/Construction/Engineering Services,* June 2006.

———. U.S. Commercial Service. *India Country Commercial Guide.* Washington, DC: U.S. Department of Commerce, 2006. http://www.buyusa.gov/india/en/88.html (accessed March 15, 2007).

———. U.S. Commercial Service. *Doing Business in India: A Country Commercial Guide for U.S. Companies 2006.*

———. U.S. Commercial Service. *India: Electric Power Equipment,* August 2006.

U.S. Department of Labor. *A Chartbook of International Labor Comparisons*: *The Americas, Asia- Pacific, Europe*, January 2007.

U.S. Department of State. "Congress Passes U.S.-India Civilian Nuclear Cooperation Bill (December 9)." Washington, DC, 2006. http://usinfo.state.gov/ (accessed April 5, 2007).

. "President Bush Signs U.S.-India Civil Nuclear Agreement (December 18)." Washington, DC, 2006. http://usinto.state.gov/ (accessed April 5, 2007).

U.S. India 2006 CEO Forum. "U.S. India Strategic Economic Partnership," March 2006. http://planningcommission.nic.in/reports/genrep/USIndia.pdf (accessed on January 18, 2007)

U.S. India Business Council. *Recommendations of the Breakout Session on Biotechnology/Life Sciences/Medical Devices Breakout Session*, February 2007. http://www.usibc.com/documents/Feb%20Life%20Sciences.pdf (accessed March 25, 2007).

U.S. National Institutes of Health. "ClinicalTrials.gov." http://www.clinicaltrials.gov (accessed May 1, 2007).

U.S. Patent and Trademark Office (USTPO). "U.S. and India Sign Historic Memorandum of Understanding on Bilateral Cooperation on Intellectual Property (December 20)." Washington, DC, 2006. http://www.uspto.gov/web (accessed February 14, 2007).

United States Trade Representative (USTR). *2006 Special 301 Report*. Washington, DC: USTR, 2006. http://www.ustr.gov (accessed February 2, 2007).

———. "Brazil." *2006 National Trade Estimate Report on Foreign Trade Barriers*. Washington, DC: USTR, 2006. http://www.ustr.gov/Document Library/Reports Publications/2006/2006 NTE Report/Section Index.html?ht= (accessed March 7, 2007).

———. "India." *2007 National Trade Estimate Report*. Washington, DC: USTR, 2007. http://www.ustr.gov/assets Library/Reports Publications/2007/2007 NTE Report/asset upload file 452 1095 1.pdf (accessed April 17, 2007).

———. *2007 Special 301 Report,* 26.

Van den Bossche, Peter. *The Law and Policy of the World Trade Organization: Text, Cases and Materials*. United Kingdom: Cambridge University Press, 2006.

Venkatesan, V. "Trial and Execution." *Frontline. Volume 19*-Issue 14, July 6–19, 2002. http://www.hinduonnet.com/fline/fl1914/19141020.htm (accessed April 9, 2007).

VoIP Now. *"VoIP in India,"* October 12, 2005. http://www.voipnow.org/ (accessed April 9, 2007).

Wakhlu, Bharat. Tata, Inc. Remarks at a conference at the Woodrow Wilson International Center for Scholars, Washington, DC, April 13, 2007.

Ward's Automotive Group. *World Motor Vehicle Data 2006*. Southfield, MI: Ward's Automotive Group, 2006.

Ward's Automotive Reports. "Chevy's Spark Key to GM's Growth in India," April 30, 2007.

Wells, Dr. Peter and Shanivi Sadana. "Hub or Hubris? India and the Automotive Mission Plan 2006–20 16." *World Commercial Vehicles*, November 2006.

Wells, Dr. Peter. "Hub or Hubris? Prospects for the AMP to 2016." *Automotive World* December 21, 2006. http://www.automotiveworld.com/wcv/print.asp?contentid=57070 (accessed January 17, 2007).

World Bank Web site. http://www.worldbank.org (accessed October 30, 2006 and January 18, 2007).

World Bank. "Doing Business Report 2007." http://www.worldbank.org (accessed October 30, 2006).

_________. "Do the Benefits of Special Economic Zones Outweigh Their Costs?" Archives discussion moderated by James Crittle and Gokhan Akinci, July 2004. http://rru.worldbank.org/Discussions/Topics/Topic40.aspx (accessed November 14, 2006).

_________. "Enterprise Surveys, India 2006." http://www.enterprisesurveys.org/Explore Economies/Default.aspx?economyid=89&year=2006, (accessed February 20,2007).

_________. "Enterprise Surveys, What Businesses Say." http://www.enterprisesurveys.org/exploreeconomies (accessed January 4, 2007).

_________. "India, Inclusive Growth and Service Delivery: Building on India's Success." Report No.34580-IN, May 29, 2006.

_________. "India Transport Sector." http://web PORT/0,,contentMDK:20703625~menuPK:868822~ pagePK:340041 73~piPK:34003707~theSitePK:579598,00. html (accessed various dates).

_________. *Sustaining India's Services Revolution,* 2004. http://web.worldbank.org/ (accessed March 9, 2007).

_________. *The Investment Climate in Brazil, India, and South Africa: A Contribution to the IBSA Debate,* September 2006.

_________. *World Development Indicators database.* http://ddp-ext.worldbank.org/ext/DDPQQ/report.do?method=showReport (accessed various dates).

World Bank/International Finance Corporation (IFC). *India: Investment Climate and Manufacturing Industry,* November 2004.

WTO. "India—Patent Protection for Pharmaceutical and Agricultural Chemical Products." WT/DSSO/AB/R, January 16, 1998.

_________. "Indonesia—Certain Measures Affecting the Automobile Industry." Report of the Panel, WT/DS54/R, WT/DS55/R; WT/DS59/R; WT/DS56/R, July 2, 1998 (98-2505)

_________. "Understanding the WTO, Services: Rules for Growth and Investment." http://www.wto.org/english/thewto e/whatis e/tif e/agrm6 e.htm (accessed various dates).

APPENDIX A. SECTOR-SPECIFIC GUIDELINES FOR FDI IN INDIA

Sector/Subsector	FDI Equity Cap	Entry Route	Notes
Air transport services	49% for FDI; 100% for non-resident Indian investment	Automatic	No direct or indirect equity participation by foreign airlines allowed.
Airports • Greenfield projects • Existing airports	 100% 100%	 Automatic FIPB beyond 74%	 Subject to Ministry of Civil Aviation regulations. Subject to Ministry of Civil Aviation regulations.
Alcohol distillation and brewing	100%	Automatic	Subject to licensing by appropriate authority.
Asset reconstruction companies	49% for FDI only	FIPB	Individual investments beyond 10% of equity subject to regulation.
Atomic minerals	74%	FIPB	Subject to Department of Atomic Energy guidelines.
Atomic energy	FDI Prohibited		
Banking (private sector)	74% for FDI + foreign institutional investors (FII)	Automatic	Branches and subsidiaries of foreign banks subject to RBI guidelines.
Broadcasting			
• FM radio	20% for FDI + FII	FIPB	Subject to Ministry of Information and Broadcasting guidelines.
• Cable network	49% for FDI + FII	FIPB	Subject to Cable Television Network Rules (1994) by the Ministry of Information and Broadcasting.
• Direct-to-home	49% for FDI + FII (FDI not to exceed 20%)	FIPB	Subject to Ministry of Information and Broadcasting guidelines.
• Hardware setup (Up-linking, HUB, etc.)	49% for FDI + FII	FIPB	Subject to Up-linking Policy by the Ministry of Information and Broadcasting.
• Up-linking news and current affairs channel	26% for FDI + FII	FIPB	Subject to Ministry of Information and Broadcasting guidelines.
• Up-linking of non-news and current affairs channel	100%	FIPB	Subject to Ministry of Information and Broadcasting guidelines.
Cigars and cigarettes manufacturing	100%	FIPB	Subject to industrial licensing.
Coal and lignite mining for captive consumption by power projects, iron, steel, and cement production, and other approved activities	100%	Automatic	Subject to the Coal Mines Act (1973).
Coffee and rubber processing and warehousing	100%	Automatic	

(Continued)

Sector/Subsector	FDI Equity Cap	Entry Route	Notes
Construction development projects.	100%	Automatic	Subject to minimum capitalization and land size requirements.
Courier services for carrying items not covered by the Indian Post Office Act (1898)	100%	FIPB	Subject to existing laws and any related activities exclusively reserved for the State.
Defense production	26%	FIPB	Subject to licensing under the Industries (Development and Regulation) Act (1951) and further guidelines on the production of arms and ammunition.
Floriculture, horticulture, development of seeds, animal husbandry, pisciculture, aquaculture, and the cultivation of vegetables and mushrooms under controlled conditions	100%	Automatic	
Gambling and betting sector	Prohibited		
Hazardous chemicals –	100%	Automatic	Subject to licensing under the Industries (Development and Regulation) Act (1951) and other sectoral regulations.
Industrial explosives – manufacture	100%	Automatic	Subject to licensing under the Industries (Development and Regulation) Act (1951) and regulations under the Explosives Act (1898).
Insurance	26%	Automatic	Subject to licensing by the Insurance Regulatory and Development Authority.
Investing companies in infrastructure/services sector (except telecom sector)	49%	FIPB	FDI in an investing company will not be counted toward sectoral caps in infrastructure/services sector provided that the investment is no larger than 49% and company management is Indian.
Lottery business Mining	Prohibited		
	100%	Automatic	Subject to Mines and Minerals Act (1957) and applicant must declare no existing joint venture for the same area/and or mineral.
Non-bank finance companies	100%	Automatic	Subject to minimum capitalization norms, subsidiary and joint venture regulations, and Reserve Bank of India guidelines.
Sector/Subsector	FDI Equity Cap	Entry Route	Notes

(Continued)

Sector/Subsector	FDI Equity Cap	Entry Route	Notes
Petroleum and natural gas sector			
• Other than refining – includes market study and formulation, investment/financing, setting up infrastructure for marketing	100%	Automatic	Subject to sectoral regulations by the Ministry of Petroleum and Natural Gas and future divestment requirements in petroleum product trading and marketing.
• Refining	26% for public sector enterprises (PSUs); 100% for private companies	FIPB for PSUs and Automatic for private companies	Subject to sectoral regulations.
Power, including generation (except atomic energy), transmission, distribution, and power trading	100%	Automatic	Subject to the Electricity Act (2003).
Print media			
• Publishing of newspapers and periodicals dealing with news and current affairs	26%	FIPB	Subject to Ministry of Information and Broadcasting guidelines.
• Publishing of scientific magazines, specialty journal/periodicals	100%	FIPB	Subject to Ministry of Information and Broadcasting guidelines.
Satellites – establishment and operation	74%	FIPB	Subject to sectoral regulations by the Department of Space.
Special economic zones and free trade warehousing zones, covering setting up of units	100%	Automatic	Subject to Special Economic Zones Act (2005) and foreign trade policy.
Tea sector, including tea plantations	100%	FIPB	Subject to state government approval and future divestment requirements.
Telecommunications services, except ISP without gateway	74%	Automatic up to 49%; FIPB beyond 49%	Subject to licensing and security requirements by the Department of Telecommunications
• ISP without gateway, infrastructure providing dark fiber, electronic mail, and voice mail	100%	Automatic up to 49%; FIPB beyond 49%	Subject to licensing, security, and future divestment requirements.
• Manufacture of telecom equipment	100%	Automatic	Subject to sectoral requirements.
Trading			
• Wholesale, cash and carry trading	100%	Automatic	Subject to investment guidelines.
• Trading for exports	100%	Automatic	Subject to investment guidelines.
• Trading of items sourced from the small scale sector	100%	FIPB	Subject to investment guidelines.

(Continued)

Sector/Subsector	FDI Equity Cap	Entry Route	Notes
• Test marketing of pre-approved manufactured items	100%	FIPB	Subject to investment guidelines.
• Single brand product retailing	51%	FIPB	Subject to investment guidelines.
• Multiple brand product retailing	Prohibited		

Source: Government of India, Ministry of Commerce & Industry, DIPP, *Investing in India: Foreign Direct Investment Policy and Procedures* .

Note: Those sectors not specifically covered here are allowed 100 percent equity, through the automatic route, without additional restrictions. FDI and FII represent the maximum combined equity limit for direct and foreign institutional investments.

Appendix B. Web site Addresses of State and Union Territory (UT) Governments and their Investment Promotion Agencies in India

Andaman & Nicobar (UT)
Government: http://www.and.nic.in
Investment Promotion Agency: http://www.aniidco.nic.in

Andhra Pradesh
Government: http://www.aponline.gov.in/apportal/index.asp
Investment Promotion Agency: http://www.apidc.org

Arunachal Pradesh
Government: http://arunachalpradesh.nic.in

Assam
Government: http://assamgovt.nic.in

Bihar
Government: http://gov.bih.nic.in
Investment Promotion Agency: http://www.bicico.com

Chandigarh (UT)
Government: http://chandigarh.nic.in
Investment Promotion Agency: http://www.citco.nic.in

Chhattisgarh
Government: http://chhattisgarh.nic.in
Investment Promotion Agency: http://www.csidcindia.com

Dadra and Nagar Haveli (UT)
Government: http://dnh.nic.in
Investment Promotion Agency: http://www.oidc.nic.in

Daman and Diu (UT)
Government: http://goidirectory.nic.in/daman.htm
Investment Promotion Agency: http://www.oidc.nic.in

Delhi (UT)
Government: http://delhigovt.nic.in/index.asp
Investment Promotion Agency: http://www.dsidc.org

Goa
Government: http://goagovt.nic.in
Investment Promotion Agency: http://www.goaidc.com

Gujarat
Government: http://www.gujaratindia.com
Investment Promotion Agency: http://www.gidc.gov.in

Haryana
Government: http://haryana.gov.in
Investment Promotion Agency: http://hsidc.nic.in/hfi.htm

Himachal Pradesh
Government: http://himachal.nic.in/welcome.asp
Investment Promotion Agency: http://hpsidc.nic.in

Jammu and Kashmir
Government: http://jammukashmir.nic.in

Jharkhand
Government: http://jharkhand.nic.in

Karnataka
Government: http://www.karnataka.gov.in
Investment Promotion Agency: http://www.ksiidc.com

Kerala
Government: http://www.kerala.gov.in
Investment Promotion Agency: http://www.kinfra.com

Lakshadweep (UT)
Government: http://lakshadweep.nic.in
Investment Promotion Agency:
http://www.lakshadweep.nic.in/depts/industries/home.htm

Madhya Pradesh
Government: http://mpgovt.nic.in
Investment Promotion Agency: http://www.mpsidc.org

Maharashtra
Government: http://www.maharashtra.gov.in
Investment Promotion Agency: http://www.midcindia.org

Manipur
Government: http://manipur.nic.in

Meghalaya
Government: http://meghalaya.nic.in
Investment Promotion Agency: http://www.meghalaya.nic.in/MIDC/midc.htm

Mizoram
Government: http://mizoram.nic.in

Nagaland
Government: http://nagaland.nic.in

Orissa
Government: http://orissagov.nic.in
Investment Promotion Agency: www.idcoindia.com/

Pondicherry (UT)
Government: http://pondicherry.nic.in
Investment Promotion Agency: http://www.pipdic.com

Punjab
Government: http://punjabgovt.nic.in
Investment Promotion Agency: http://www.punjabgovt.nic.in/Industry/ind552.htm

Rajasthan
Government: http://www.rajasthan.gov.in/Rajasthan1024.asp
Investment Promotion Agency: http://www.riico.co.in

Sikkim
Government: http://sikkim.gov.in
Investment Promotion Agency: http://www.sikkiminfo.net/sidico/

Tamil Nadu
Government: http://www.tn.gov.in
Investment Promotion Agency: http://www.tidco.com

Tripura

Government: http://tripura.nic.in
Investment Promotion Agency: http://www.tripura.nic.in/tidc/

Uttar Pradesh
Government: http://upgov.nic.in
Investment Promotion Agency: http://www.upsidc.com

Uttaranchal
Government: http://www.ua.nic.in
Investment Promotion Agency: http://www.sidcul.com

West Bengal
Government: http://www.wbgov.com/e-gov/English/EnglishHomePage.asp
Investment Promotion Agency: http://www.wbidc.com

Source: Embassy of India, Washington, DC.
Note: Not all states have investment promotion agency Web sites.

Appendix C. Bilateral International Agreements That Affect Investment in India

Country	Bilateral Investment Agreement	Double Tax Avoidance Agreement	Free Trade Agreement	Notes
Argentina	X			
Armenia	X*	X		
Australia	X	X		
Austria	X	X		
Bahrain	X*		X	Framework Agreement for establishing a free trade area completed. India-Gulf Cooperation Council (GCC) FTA under negotiation.
Bangladesh		X	X	Under the South Asia Free Trade Agreement (SAFTA) and Asia Pacific Trade Agreement (APTA).
Belarus	X	X		
Belgium	X	X		
Bhutan			X	Under SAFTA.
Brazil		X		
Bulgaria	X	X		
Canada		X		Bilateral investment agreement under negotiation.
Chile			X	Framework Agreement on Economic Cooperation.
China		X		
Croatia	X			
Cyprus	X	X		
Czech Republic	X	X		
Denmark	X	X		
Djibouti	X*			

(Continued)

Country	Bilateral Investment Agreement	Double Tax Avoidance Agreement	Free Trade Agreement	Notes
Egypt	X	X		
Finland	X	X		
France	X	X		
Germany	X	X		
Ghana	X*			
Greece		X		
Hungary	X*	X		
Indonesia	X	X		
Ireland		X		
Israel	X	X		
Italy	X	X		
Japan		X		
Jordan		X		
Kazakstan	X	X		
Kenya		X		
Korea	X	X	X	Under APTA.
Kuwait	X		X	Framework Agreement for establishing a free trade area completed. India-Gulf Cooperation Council (GCC) FTA under negotiation.
Kyrgyzstan	X	X		
Laos	X			
Libya		X		
Luxembourg	X			
Malaysia	X	X		
Maldives			X	Under SAFTA.
Malta		X		
Mauritius	X	X	X	Comprehensive Economic Cooperation and Partnership Agreement (CECPA) under negotiation.
Mongolia	X	X		
Morocco	X	X		
Namibia		X		
Nepal		X	X	Under SAFTA.
Netherlands	X	X		
New Zealand		X		
Norway		X		
Oman	X	X	X	Framework Agreement for establishing a free trade area completed. India-Gulf Cooperation Council (GCC) FTA under negotiation.
Pakistan			X	Under SAFTA.
Philippines	X	X		
Poland	X	X		
Portugal	X*	X		
Qatar	X	X	X	Framework Agreement for establishing a free trade area completed. India-Gulf Cooperation Council (GCC) FTA under negotiation.
Romania	X	X		
Russia	X	X		

(Continued)

Country	Bilateral Investment Agreement	Double Tax Avoidance Agreement	Free Trade Agreement	Notes
Saudi Arabia		X	X	Framework Agreement for establishing a free trade area completed. India-Gulf Cooperation Council (GCC) FTA under negotiation.
Serbia and Montenegro X Singapore		X	X	India-Singapore Comprehensive Economic Cooperation Agreement
Slovenia		X		
South Africa		X		
Spain	X	X		
Sri Lanka	`	X	X	Under SAFTA and APTA.
Sudan	X*	X		
Sweden	X	X		
Switzerland	X	X		
Syria		X		
Taiwan (China)	X			
Tajikistan	X			
Tanzania		X		
Thailand	X	X	X	Framework Agreement for establishing a free trade area completed.
Trinidad and Tobago		X		
Turkey	X*	X		
Turkmenistan	X*	X		
Uganda		X		
Ukraine	X	X		
United States		X		
United Arab Emirates		X	X	Framework Agreement for establishing a free trade area completed. India-Gulf Cooperation Council (GCC) FTA under negotiation.
United Kingdom	X	X		
Uzbekistan	X	X		
Vietnam	X	X		
Yemen	X*			
Zambia		X		
Zimbabwe	X*			

Sources: Government of India, Ministry of Finance, *Economic Survey 2006–2007*; Government of India, Income Tax Department; and OECD, Directorate fore Financial and Enterprise Affairs, Investment Committee, "Salient Features of India's Investment Agreements."

Notes: (*) As of June 2006, agreement has not entered into force.

India is also in framework/free trade agreement negotiations with ASEAN (Association of South East Asian Nations), BIMSTEC (Bangladesh, Bhutan, Myanmar, Nepal, Sri Lanka, and Thailand), MERCOSUR (Argentina, Brazil, Paraguay, and Uruguay), and SAARC/SAPTA (Bangladesh, Bhutan, Maldives, Nepal, Pakistan, and Sri Lanka).

End Notes

[1] Most official Indian statistics are presented on a fiscal year basis. India's fiscal year runs from April 1st through March 31st. According to the standard IMF definitions, FDI is defined as investment equal to or greater than a

10 percent equity share in a single firm. By contrast, portfolio investment (the remaining $12.5 billion) is defined as acquisition of an equity stake of less than 10 percent. FDI data represent inflows net of outflows.

[2] Government of India, Ministry of Commerce & Industry, *Economic Survey 2006–2007,* 127–28; and *Financial Times,* "FDI in India Expected to Double."

[3] Government of India, Ministry of Commerce & Industry, "Fact Sheet on Foreign Direct Investment."

[4] Under the treaty, foreign investors are able to invest in holding companies in Mauritius which then sell shares in India, but pay taxes in Mauritius. Since Mauritius has no capital gains tax, the companies have no capital gains tax obligations. EIU, "Country Report India." (See chapter 6).

[5] Government of India, Ministry of Commerce & Industry, "Fact Sheet on Foreign Direct Investment from August 1991 to December 2006."

[6] FDI approvals data measure the intentions of foreign firms to invest in India. However, many firms never actually proceed with investment projects that have received approval, so approvals data do not indicate actual FDI trends.

[7] The sectors are defined by India's Ministry of Commerce & Industry, and do not match U.S. Government statistical classifications. Government of India, Ministry of Commerce & Industry, Department of Commerce, *Annual Report 2005–2006,* 88.

[8] U.S. Department of State, "Congress Passes U.S.-India Civilian Nuclear Cooperation Bill"; and U.S. Department of State, "President Bush Signs U.S.-India Civil Nuclear Agreement."

[9] Gutierrez and Sampson, Remarks at the 5th Summit.

[10] An additional 17 percent of FDI is invested in electrical equipment, including computer software and electronics. It is not clear whether some offshore services FDI is included in the electrical equipment sector. Government of India, Ministry of Commerce & Industry, "Fact Sheet on Foreign Direct Investment."

[11] Offshoring refers to the process whereby a company based in one country outsources certain functions to an affiliate or domestic company in another country. BPO includes information technology-enabled services such as insurance claims processing, and other types of back office processing.

[12] McKinsey & Co., McKinsey Global Institute, *New Horizons,* 499.

[13] See, e.g., PriceWaterhouseCoopers, "Offshoring in the Financial Services Industry."

[14] McKinsey & Co., McKinsey Global Institute, *New Horizons,* 501.

[15] Barnes, Remarks at the 5th Summit; and Bonasia,"Indian Outsourcers Scramble to Meet Need."

[16] Bonasia,"Indian Outsourcers Scramble to Meet Need."

[17] Government of India, Ministry of Commerce & Industry, "Fact Sheet on Foreign Direct Investment."

[18] Bureau van Dijk, *Zephyr Mergers and Acquisitions database*.

[19] *Press Trust of India,* "Morgan Stanley, Citigroup, Actis Pick Up 6 pc Stake in NSE."

[20] Government of India, Ministry of Commerce & Industry, *Economic Survey 2006–2007,* 154; and EIU, "Country Commerce India - Main report: November 20, 2006."

[21] *Business Monitor Food & Drink Insight,* "Bharti Confirms Wal-Mart Plans."

[22] Major international insurance firms investing in the Indian market include Chubb, New York Life, AIG, Metlife (all based in the United States); Old Mutual, Standard Life, and Royal & Sun Alliance (United Kingdom); ING (Netherlands); Allianz (Germany); Tokio General and Mitsui Sumitomo (Japan); and AMP (Australia). Indian Insurance Regulatory and Development Authority Web site.

[23] The list includes ICICI Prudential Life, AMP Sanmar Life, Metlife India, IFFCO-Tokio General, Cholmandalam General, and Tata AIG Life. Bureau van Dijk, *Zephyr Mergers and Acquisitions database*.

[24] Most countries, including the United States, report FDI data on a calendar year basis. India reports FDI data on a fiscal year basis, with the fiscal year beginning April 1st.

[25] The databases are Zephyr, a mergers and acquisitions (M&A) database published by Bureau van Dijk, and LocoMonitor, a greenfield FDI database published by OCO Consulting Ltd.

[26] *The Statesman (India),* "India attracts $15b FDI During 2006–07.

[27] UNCTAD, *World Investment Report 2006*. UNCTAD data are based on official Indian government statistics, but are adjusted to provide calendar year totals and prepared according to international practices, which makes the data comparable to international FDI statistics. The majority of data in this chapter is taken from Government of India statistical publications, which report on a fiscal year basis, and are not prepared according to international practices (see fn. 4). India's fiscal year runs from April 1 to March 31.

[28] Government of India, Ministry of Commerce & Industry, Department of Industrial Policy and Promotion. Fact sheet on Foreign Direct Investment.

[29] Includes new equity capital flows only. According to international standards, FDI flows include new equity capital flows, reinvested earnings, and intra-company loans. Most Indian FDI statistics reflect equity capital flows only. According to Kamal Nath, India's Minister of Commerce and Industry, FDI inflows including reinvested earnings totaled $18 billion during the 2006–07 fiscal year. *The Statesman (India),* "India attracts $15b FDI During 2006–07."

[30] Government of India, Fact Sheet on Foreign Direct Investment (FDI) from August 1991 to March 2007.

[31] UNCTAD, "Foreign Direct Investment Rose by 34% in 2006."

[32] OCO Consulting Ltd., *LocoMonitor FDI database*; and Bureau van Dijk, *Zephyr Mergers and Aquisitions database*.

[33] Excludes deals that have been announced but not completed, or deals that are awaiting regulatory approval as of March 2007.

[34] Approximately one-half of transactions do not have reported values.

[35] OCO Consulting Ltd., *LocoMonitor FDI database*.

[36] Industry designations for greenfield FDI data are determined by OCO Consulting, and do not necessarily reflect the industry classifications used either by the U.S. or the Indian governments. Heavy industry includes energy, manufacturing of machinery and industrial goods, metals, and mining.

[37] Includes hotels, restaurants, and real estate.

[38] Includes business machines and equipment, consumer electronics, electronic components, and semiconductors.

[39] LocoMonitor data by country do not match official Indian government statistics, which show almost 40 percent of incoming FDI originating in Mauritius. Government of India, Ministry of Commerce & Industry, Department of Industrial Policy & Promotion, Foreign Direct Investment Statistics. Although the funding for many FDI projects may come through offshore holding companies in Mauritius in order to maximize tax benefits, an analysis based on the investing company's home office is likely more revealing.

[40] OCO Consulting Ltd., *LocoMonitor FDI database*.

[41] India is divided into 28 states, six union territories (UTs) and 1 national capital territory. States have their own government, whereas UTs are administered by the central government. However, Puducherry, a UT, has its own elected government. The National Capital Territory of Delhi is a special region that has its own elected government and retains a status that is a hybrid between a state and a union territory.

[42] Indian brand Equity Foundation (IBEF). Indian States, Business and Economy. *Maharashtra.*

[43] Bureau van Dijk, *Orbis Companies database*.

[44] Ibid.

[45] IBEF. Indian States, Business and Economy. *Delhi.*

[46] Kripalani, "IBM's India Pep Rally."

[47] Goodyear India, "History by Year."

[48] *The Hindu Business Line*. "Goodyear India Changes Retailing Strategy."

[49] IBEF. Indian States, Business and Economy. *Uttar Pradesh.*

[50] Ibid., *Haryana.*

[51] See chapter 7 for a discussion of FDI in the passenger cars and automotive components industry.

[52] IBEF. Indian States, Economy and Business. *Tamil Nadu.*

[53] OCO Consulting Ltd., *LocoMonitor FDI database*; and *Agence France-Presse English Wire,* "India's Steel Production Set to Triple by 2015 As Demand Booms."

[54] *Press Trust of India,* "Orissa to Pursue POSCO Project with 'Humane' Face"; and *Press Trust of India*, "VP Writes to PM on POSCO Issue.

[55] OCO Consulting Ltd., *LocoMonitor FDI database*.

[56] Representative of Arcelor-Mittal, telephone interview by Commission staff, April 20, 2007.

[57] Department of Industrial Policy and Promotion. Fact Sheet on Foreign Direct Investment.

[58] The projects were small, with a combined value of $31 million. Two of the projects were in software development, one was in financial services, and the last was in gold mining.

[59] Round-tripping is a process whereby a company operating in India registers a subsidiary in Mauritius, and then routes profits through the subsidiary in order to avoid paying capital gains taxes on its profits in India.

[60] Sikarwar, "Mauritius Overhauls DTAA Agreement."

[61] FDI inflows are allocated to the countries which have direct transactions with India, not to the ultimate source of the capital. For a corporation based in the Netherlands with a holding company in Mauritius, for example, the direct transaction takes place between Mauritius and India, even though the capital may ultimately have originated in the Netherlands.

[62] Fuel includes power and oil refineries; telecommunications includes radio paging, cellular mobile and basic telephone services; electrical equipment includes computer software and electronics; services includes financial and non-financial services. Embassy of India. "U.S. Investments in India."

[63] Bureau van Dijk, *Zephyr Mergers &Acquisitions database*.

[64] iTWire, "Google Likely to Set Up $1 Billion Datacenter in India."

[65] OCO Consulting Ltd., *LocoMonitor FDI database*.

[66] Intel, "Intel Outlines $1 Billion Multi-Year Investment Plans."

[67] According to U.S. government statistical standards, consistent with IMF standards, an affiliate is any firm with an equity share of 10-percent or more. The U.S. Department of Commerce compiles statistics on both U.S.-owned affiliates and majority-owned affiliates (MOFAs), with greater detail available for MOFAs. USDOC, BEA. International Economic Accounts, "Operation of Multinational Companies."

[68] The U.S. Department of Commerce does not provide a breakdown of the information category, but there is a significant amount of U.S. FDI in India's telecommunications industry. The information category also includes publishing, motion picture and sound recording, broadcasting, and data processing services.

[69] The R&D figure for professional, scientific, and technical services was suppressed to avoid disclosing individual company information.
[70] EC. "Bilateral Trade Relations - India."
[71] OCO Consulting Ltd., LocoMonitor FDI database.
[72] Government of India, Ministry of Commerce & Industry, Department of Industrial Policy and Promotion. Fact Sheet on Foreign Direct Investment.
[73] Department of Industrial Policy and Promotion. "FDI Synopsis on Japan."
[74] "Upbeat India Scales Up FDI Projections by 25 Percent," *Khaleej Times*.
[75] OCO Consulting Ltd., *LocoMonitor FDI database*.
[76] Ibid.
[77] *BusinessStandard.com*, "Industrial Corridor to Get $50 Billion Investment"; *Indian Express*, "Work on Delhi-Mumbai Corridor from January"; and *Gulf News.com*, "Japan to Help India Build $50 Billion Industry Corridor."
[78] Jha, "UAE, India to Expand Ties."
[79] *Khaleej Times*, "Upbeat India Scales Up FDI Projections by 25 Percent."
[80] OCO Consulting Ltd., *LocoMonitor FDI database*.
[81] *Khaleej Times*, "DP World's India Foray Runs into Murkier Waters."
[82] Ibid., "Gulf Arab Investors Target Asia as US Ties Wane."
[83] Government of India, Ministry of Commerce & Industry, Department of Industrial Policy and Promotion, *FDI Statistics 2006*
[84] The definition of industry sectors in the Zephyr database follows the North American Industry Classification System (NAICS) followed by U.S. government statistical agencies.
[85] Flextronics International Ltd., "SemIndia Announces Flextronics as a Strategic Partner."
[86] *The Economic Times*, "Hindustan Semiconductor to Chip In $4 B for Indian Fabs."
[87] OCO Consulting Ltd., *LocoMonitor FDI database*.
[88] Ibid.
[89] Business India Intelligence, "Hotels."
[90] Royal Indian Raj International Corp., "Royal Indian Raj International Corporation."
[91] The Global Competitiveness Index, developed by the World Economic Forum from responses to an executive opinion survey, ranks a country's competitiveness based upon nine factors: institutions, infrastructure, macroeconomy, health and primary education, higher education and training, market efficiency, technological readiness, business sophistication, and innovation. These nine factors each consist of a number of items relevant to that particular factor. For example, institutions include such things as property rights, judicial independence, and the strength of auditing and accounting standards. Innovation includes such things as the availability of scientists and engineers and the quality of scientific research institutions, and macroeconomy includes government surplus/deficit, national savings rate, and inflation. Lopez-Claros, et al., *The Global Competitiveness Report*, xiv, xvi, xvii, 242–43.
[92] A.T. Kearney's annual Foreign Direct Investment Confidence Index is based upon survey responses received from top executives of the world's largest 1,000 firms concerning their FDI plans and their opinions of the economic and business environment in 68 countries which account for virtually all worldwide FDI. In the 2004 survey, India ranked third, behind China and the United States. A.T. Kearney, Inc., "FDI Confidence Index," 1–2.
[93] The Doing Business Report 2007, an annual report developed by the World Bank and the IFC, ranks 175 countries on the ease of doing business and the pace of reforms. Ten factors are considered in the rankings, including starting a business, employing workers, registering property, getting credit, protecting investors, enforcing contracts, and closing a business. World Bank, "Doing Business Report 2007."
[94] FDI regulations in India, another significant factor in determining a country's overall FDI attractiveness, are addressed in chap. 5 of this study.
[95] CIA, "India."
[96] Purchasing power parity is the number of foreign currency units required to buy goods and services in a foreign country equivalent to what can be bought with one dollar in the United States. U.S. Department of Labor, *A Chartbook of International Labor Comparisons*.
[97] U. S. Department of Commerce, U.S. Commercial Service, *Doing Business in India*.
[98] Inflation as measured by the Indian GDP deflator. World Bank, *World Development Indicators database*.
[99] GTIS, *World Trade Atlas database*.
[100] CIA, "India."
[101] World Bank, *World Development Indicators database*.
[102] U.S. Department of Commerce, U.S. Commercial Service, *Doing Business in India*.
[103] Government of India, Labour Bureau, *Annual Survey of Industries Scheme*. Average wages per day, reported by the Labour Bureau, converted to annual salaries by multiplying daily wages by 250 (5 days per week, 50 weeks in a work year).
[104] Kanellos, "India's Tech Renaissance—U.S.-Style Labor Pains."

[105] Kaushik and Sasi, "Indian Wages Cheaper Than Chinese."
[106] World Bank, *World Development Indicators database*.
[107] The formal sector consists of establishments using electric power and employing 10 or more workers, and establishments not using electric power and employing 20 or more workers. This sector accounts for about 40 percent of Indian output. Two-thirds of the employees in the formal sector work in the public sector. Asian Development Bank, "Key Indicators 2005: Labor Markets in Asia," 46.
[108] In a recent survey, 17 percent of Indian managers stated that labor regulations were a major business constraint. World Bank, *World Development Indicators database*.
[109] Asian Development Bank, "Key Indicators 2005: Labor Markets in Asia," 46–51; and Basu, "Why India's Labour Laws Are a Problem."
[110] Wakhlu, Remarks.
[111] Kanellos, "India's Tech Renaissance—U.S.-Style Labor Pains."
[112] Kanellos, "India's Tech Renaissance—U.S.-Style Labor Pains."
[113] Kaushik and Sasi, "Indian Wages Cheaper Than Chinese."
[114] *Indo-Asian News Service*, "India Woos Foreign Equity in Infrastructure."
[115] Power generation in India is principally a central government and state government function, although private energy producers play an increasingly important role.
[116] U.S. Department of Commerce, U.S. Commercial Service, *Doing Business in India*.
[117] World Bank, "Enterprise Surveys, What Businesses Say."
[118] World Bank, *World Development Indicators database*.
[119] World Bank, "India, Inclusive Growth and Service Delivery."
[120] World Bank, "India Transport Sector."
[121] Ibid.
[122] World Bank, "India, Inclusive Growth and Service Delivery."
[123] World Bank, "India Transport Sector."
[124] Government of India, Ministry of Shippping, Road Transport and Highways, Department of Road Transport and Highways, "Opportunities for Private Sector Participation," and "Status of BOT Projects Awarded."
[125] Government of Goa Web site.
[126] U.S. Department of Commerce, U.S. Commercial Service, *India: Architecture/Construction/Engineering Services*.
[127] Government of India, Ministry of Civil Aviation, "Policy on Airport Infrastructure."
[128] U.S. Department of Commerce, U.S. Commercial Service, *India: Electric Power Equipment*.
[129] Colleges generally fall under the purview of state governments; universities/institutes generally fall under the purview of the central government.
[130] Government of India, Ministry of Human Resource Development.
[131] Altbach, "Higher Education in India."
[132] Government of India, Ministry of Commerce & Industry, Department of Industrial Policy and Promotion, Secretariat for Industrial Assistance, "Destination India."
[133] Altbach, "Higher Education in India"; and Kapur, Remarks.
[134] World Bank, "India, Inclusive Growth and Service Delivery."
[135] U.S. Department of Commerce, U.S. Commercial Service, *Doing Business in India*.
[136] Ibid.
[137] Chakrabarti, *The Financial Sector in India Emerging Issues*, 176; Deutsche Bank Web site; HSBC Web site; and Iloveindia Web site.
[138] Government of India, Ministry of Commerce & Industry, Department of Industrial Policy and Promotion, Secretariat for Industrial Assistance, "Destination India"; U.S. Department of Commerce, U.S. Commercial Service, *Doing Business in India*; Bombay Stock Exchange Web site; and National Stock Exchange Web site.
[139] OPIC, *Annual Reports for 2004, 2005, and 2006*.
[140] Asian Development Bank Web site.
[141] As part of India's National Highway Development Program, 29 road projects are currently being funded by the ADB. Nineteen of these projects involve Indian and foreign firms, eight projects involve only foreign firms, and two projects involve only Indian firms. Foreign firms include firms from South Korea, China, Denmark, Switzerland, Malaysia, and the United States. Government of India, Ministry of Shipping, Road Transport and Highways, Department of Road Transport and Highways, "Externally Aided Projects."
[142] World Bank Web site.
[143] As part of India's National Highway Development Program, 27 road projects are currently being funded by the World Bank. Seventeen of these projects involve Indian and foreign firms, one project involves only foreign firms, and nine projects involve only Indian firms. Foreign firms from France, the United Kingdom, Malaysia, Russia, Singapore, Canada and Thailand are represented. Government of India, Department of Road Transport and Highways, "Externally Aided Projects."
[144] IFC financial support was provided to a United Kingdom oil and gas company to expand its production capacity in India, a U.S. engineering and environmental consulting firm to construct small hydroelectric generation

facilities in India, and a Chinese carbon black producer to upgrade and expand the capacity of its carbon black plant in India. International Finance Corporation Web site.

145 U.S. Department of Commerce, U.S. Commercial Service, *India: Architecture/Construction/Engineering Services.*

146 U.S. Department of Commerce, U.S. Commercial Service, *Doing Business in India.*

147 Reuters, "World Bank Halts India Health Funds on Fraud Claim."

148 Inadequate supply of infrastructure and restrictive labor regulations were the first and third most problematic factors, respectively, for doing business in India, as reported by the survey respondents. For purposes of the survey, respondents were asked to choose the five most problematic factors for doing business in India from a list of 14 factors. Some of the other factors included tax regulations, tax rates, crime and theft, government instability/coups, inadequately educated workforce, and policy instability. This survey of business executives, assessing the business climate in 125 countries, is conducted annually by the World Economic Forum. Lopez-Claros, et al., *The Global Competitiveness Report,* 140, 242.

149 Government of India, Ministry of Commerce & Industry, "SEZs Future Vehicle of Economic Activity."

150 Government of India, Ministry of Commerce & Industry, "Special Economic Zones in India—About."

151 Confederation of Indian Industry, Northern Region, "Special Economic Zones—Engines for Growth," 4.

152 Fraser, et al. European Policy Centre, "EU-India Relations ."

153 Government of India, Ministry of Commerce & Industry, "Special Economic Zones in India—Facilities and Incentives."

154 The Foreign Investment Promotion Board oversees cases which are approved outside this "automatic route," a process which takes approximately 6 weeks.

155 Government of India, Ministry of Commerce & Industry, "Special Economic Zones in India—Facilities and Incentives."

156 Confederation of Indian Industry, Northern Region, "Special Economic Zones—Engines for Growth," 1.

157 U.S. India 2006 CEO Forum, "U.S. India Strategic Economic Partnership."

158 By comparison, China reportedly spends $260 billion on infrastructure annually. Bindra, "India Battles Infrastructure Woes."

159 World Bank, "Enterprise Surveys, India 2006."

160 World Bank, "India Transport Sector."

161 This information was acquired from the various Web sites of operational SEZs. These sites include http://www.sez2.com, http://www.leandlasez.com, http://www.csez.com, http://www.surssez.com, and http://www.nap2.com.

162 Government of India, Ministry of Commerce & Industry, "Special Economic Zones in India—Home Page."

163 Government of India, Ministry of Commerce & Industry, "Special Economic Zones—About."

164 Ibid.

165 A single window facility is a streamlined system that allows all applications to be directed to one single point for review.

166 Industries Commissionerate, Government of Gujarat, *New Initiatives, Special Economic Zones.*

167 Government of India, "SEZ Rules 2006, Chapter 2, Procedure for Establishment of Special Economic Zone."

168 Government of India, Ministry of Commerce & Industry, "Special Economic Zones in India—About."

169 Government of India, Ministry of Commerce & Industry, Department of Commerce, *Annual Report 2005–2006,* 59.

170 Government of India, Ministry of Commerce & Industry, 'Special Economic Zones in India—How to Apply."

171 Embassy of India, "FDI Policy and Procedure." Industries which require an industrial license include alcoholic drinks; cigarettes and tobacco products; electronic aerospace and defense equipment; explosives; hazardous chemicals such as hydrocyanic acid, phosgene, isocynates and di-isocynates of hydrocarbons and their derivatives.

172 Government of India, Ministry of Commerce & Industry, "Special Economic Zones in India—How to Apply."

173 Government of India, Ministry of Commerce & Industry, "Special Economic Zones in India—Criteria for Automatic Approval."

174 EIU, *India Country Commerce Main Report.*

175 Ibid.

176 Ibid.

177 Prior to 1991, all FDI proposals were approved on a case-by-case basis with a 40 percent total foreign equity participation cap. IMF, *India: Selected Issues*, 21.

178 Industrial licenses are regulated under the Industries (Development and Regulation) Act of 1951, and are used to regulate the scale, technology, and location of certain investment projects that may present environmental, safety, or strategic concerns to the government of India. Government of India, Ministry of Commerce & Industry, Department of Industrial Policy and Promotion, *Investing In India: Foreign Direct Investment Policy & Procedures*, 8. Industrial licenses are granted by the Secretariat for Industrial Assistance (SIA) within the Department of Industrial Policy and Promotion, Ministry of Commerce & Industry. Decisions are usually

rendered within 4 to 6 weeks of filing. Government of India, Ministry of Commerce & Industry, Department of Industrial Policy and Promotion, *Investing In India: Foreign Direct Investment Policy & Procedures*, 8.

[179] Ibid., 34.

[180] The FIPB is part of India's Ministry of Finance.

[181] Investments below Rs 10 million (approximately $234,000) in plant and machinery.

[182] Government of India, Ministry of Commerce & Industry, Department of Industrial Policy and Promotion, *Investing In India: Foreign Direct Investment Policy & Procedures*, 1–6.

[183] EIU, *India: Country Commerce 2006*, 22.

[184] Foreign firms may establish as an incorporated or unincorporated entity, an incorporated company, a liaison or representative office, a project or branch office, or a "stand alone" branch office in a special economic zone. Government of India, Ministry of Commerce & Industry, Department of Industrial Policy and Promotion, *Investing In India: Foreign Direct Investment Policy & Procedures*, 14–15.

[185] EIU, *India: Country Commerce 2006*, 21.

[186] Planning Commission, Government of India, *Foreign Investment, India*, 32–3 3.

[187] Government of India, Ministry of Commerce & Industry, Department of Industrial Policy and Promotion, *Investing In India: Foreign Direct Investment Policy & Procedures*, 21.

[188] Government of India, Planning Commission, *Foreign Investment, India*, 71.

[189] Sahoo, "Foreign Direct Investment in South Asia," 10.

[190] World Bank, *The Investment Climate in Brazil, India, and South Africa*, 23–24.

[191] Bhati, *Foreign Direct Investment*, 91.

[192] U.S. Department of Commerce, U.S. Commercial Service, *Doing Business in India*, 113.

[193] Due to the unregulated discretionary power of state and local regulators, corruption has been identified as an additional obstacle to FDI in India. World Bank, *Sustaining India's Services Revolution*, 30.

[194] U.S. Department of Commerce, U.S. Commercial Service, *Doing Business in India*, 113.

[195] Sahoo, "Foreign Direct Investment in South Asia," 11.

[196] IBRD/World Bank, *Doing Business in South Asia 2007*, 31.

[197] EIU, *India: Country Commerce 2006*, 81.

[198] Ibid.

[199] World Bank, *The Investment Climate in Brazil, India, and South Africa*, 19.

[200] IBRD/World Bank, *Doing Business in South Asia 2007*, 31.

[201] World Bank/IFC, *India: Investment Climate and Manufacturing Industry*, 28–29.

[202] Deloitte, *China and India: The Reality Beyond the Hype*, 5.

[203] USTR, *2007 Special 301 Report*, 26; and U.S. Department of Commerce, U.S. Commercial Service, *India Country Commercial Guide*.

[204] U.S. Department of Commerce, U.S. Commercial Service, *India Country Commercial Guide*.

[205] EIU, *Country Commerce 2006*, 45.

[206] ICC, *Global Survey on Counterfeiting and Piracy*, 10.

[207] PhRMA, *PhRMA Survey of Pharmaceutical Counterfeiting Laws and Remedies*, 8.

[208] Ibid., 8–9, 64–65.

[209] Seizure data has inherent limitations; for example, due to resource limitations, the percentage of imports that is inspected is reportedly small. Seizure data thus may not fully and accurately reflect the extent or product and country of origin structure of trade in counterfeits. OECD, *Counterfeiting and Piracy: Measurement Issues*, 9.

[210] USCBP, *FY 2005 Top IPR Commodities Seized*. Similarly, India was the source of 75 percent of all counterfeit medicines seized by European authorities in 2005. EC, *EU 25 Breakdown of Number of Cases Registered*.

[211] U.S. government official, e-mail communication to Commission staff, February 21, 2007.

[212] IIPA, *2003 Special 301 Report: India*, 122.

[213] USTR, *2007 Special 301 Report, 26*. WIPO is a specialized agency of the United Nations responsible for promoting the development and harmonization of international IP laws.

[214] USTR, *2007 National Trade Estimate Report*, "India."

[215] USTR, *2007 Special 301 Report*, 26.

[216] IIPA, *2007 Special 301 Report*, 54.

[217] A product patent grants patent rights—that is the exclusive right to control production and distribution—relating to the product. A process patent grants exclusive rights with respect only to a particular means or process used to make the product.

[218] A compulsory license is one issued by the government that allows the use of a patented invention without consent of the owner, upon payment of a royalty.

[219] USPTO, "U.S. and India Sign Historic Memorandum of Understanding."

[220] PhRMA, *PhRMA Special 301 Submission: India*, 135.

[221] Government of India, Ministry of Commerce & Industry, "2006 Year of Record FDI Inflows."

[222] IBRD/World Bank, *Doing Business in South Asia 2007*, 36.

[223] Ibid., 36.

[224] U.S. Department of Commerce, U.S. Commercial Service, *Doing Business in India*, 111.

[225] EIU, *India: Country Commerce 2006*, 28.
[226] David, "India Sets Semi Subsidy Policy."
[227] Ibid.
[228] Incentives are similar to semiconductor loan rules, except that the minimum investment threshold is $220 million. *BusinessStandard.com*, "Semiconductor Policy Notified."
[229] As of April 2007, no official updates on Intel's investment plans in India have been released. Intel currently operates a product development center in Bangalore. David, "India Sets Semi Subsidy Policy."
[230] AMD is noted to be the most interested in taking an actual investment stake. Singapore-based Flextronics operates a regional manufacturing operation in Bangalore and is currently building an 8 million square foot industrial park in Chennai. Singh, "Analysts Skeptical of Chip Fab in India."
[231] The government of India will allow carriers to share cable-landing station infrastructure. As of February 2007, VSNL/Tata owned the majority of Tippu, "India's Coming Bandwidth Boom."
[232] In 2006, AT&T became the first foreign telecom operator to take advantage of India's FDI revision in 2005, which allows up to 74 percent foreign equity ownership (up from 49 percent) in Indian telecom firms. AT&T has been in partnership with Tata group-owned VSNL since 2000. VSNL, an Indian telecom company, provides international voice services and is a VoIP provider. Tippu, "India's Coming Bandwidth Boom"; and *VoIP Now*, "VoIP in India."
[233] Tippu, "India's Coming Bandwidth Boom."
[234] Ibid.; and *VoIP Now*, "VoIP in India."
[235] Gupta, "India Gears Up For Retail," 28.
[236] These products are seen not to affect small domestic traders or the rural economy. Maddox, "From Single Brand to Open Season."
[237] Ganesh is owned by Mohan Murjani, a non-resident Indian. Bellman, "As Economy Grows, India Goes for Designer Goods."
[238] Ibid.
[239] The joint-venture agreement was approved by the Indian government in January 2007. *Economist.com*, "Indian Retailing: Getting Cheaper and Better."
[240] *Grocer*, "Bharti to Invest $2.5 Billion in Chain."
[241] Gupta, "India Gears Up For Retail," 28.
[242] Ibid., 29.
[243] Law Commission of India, *On Revision of Court Fees Structure* (189th Report); Human Rights Features, *Legal Reform and Investment Prospects in India*; Economic and Social Council, Commission on Human Rights, *Civil and Political Rights, Including the Questions of the Judiciary, Administration of Justice, Impunity*. The Indian court system includes the Indian District Courts, Appellate Courts, and the Supreme Court as well as local or specialized courts.
[244] Human Rights Features, *Legal Reform and Investment Prospects in India*; and Economic and Social Council, *Civil and Political Rights, Including the Questions of the Judiciary, Administration of Justice, Impunity*.
[245] Economic and Social Council, *Civil and Political Rights, Including the Questions of the Judiciary, Administration of Justice, Impunity*.
[246] Ibid..
[247] Government of India, Ministry of Law and Justice, "Civil Procedure Code As Amended Enforced as of Today."
[248] Ibid.
[249] Government of India, Ministry of Law and Justice, "Landmark Legal Reforms in the Social Sector."
[250] Abdullah, Inaugural Address.
[251] Venkatesan, "Trial and Execution."
[252] Rs. 25,000 equals $614.33 at the exchange rate of 40.7 rupees/dollar on May 21, 2007. Venkatesan, "Trial and Execution."
[253] Ibid.
[254] The potential arbitration stipulations are commonly referred to as "arbitration agreements" or "arbitration clauses."
[255] Human Rights Features, *Legal Reform and Investment Prospects in India*.
[256] IACA Part I, Chapter I(1)(f).
[257] Particularly: the requirements and validity of the arbitration agreement, the composition of the arbitral tribunal; the jurisdiction of arbitral tribunals; the conduct of arbitral proceedings; the making of arbitral awards and termination of proceedings; recourse against arbitral awards; finality and enforcement of arbitral awards; and appeals. IACA Chapters II-X.
[258] These three conventions are: (1)The New York Convention of 1958 on the Recognition and Enforcement of Foreign Arbitral Awards (New York Convention); (2)The Geneva Convention on the Execution of Foreign Arbitral Awards of 1927 (Geneva Convention); and (3)The Geneva Protocol on Arbitration Clauses of 1923 (Geneva Protocol). India is not presently signatory to any bilateral conventions regarding arbitration.
[259] Law Commission of India Web site.
[260] United Nations Web site.

[261] Article V of the New York Convention presents a list of defenses to the enforcement of the arbitral award.
[262] *See*: Article VII(2) of the New York Convention.
[263] ICADR Web site.
[264] The Center offers dispute resolution for almost any kind of dispute ranging from commercial to family law disputes as well as ADR guidelines. The panel of arbitrators and conciliators range from retired Indian Supreme Court judges to ICADR-trained arbitrators and conciliators. ICADR offers numerous forms of alternative dispute resolution, including: arbitration, mediation, conciliation, mini-trials, mediation- arbitration, and negotiations.
[265] Committee Report on Reforming Investment Approval & Implementation Procedures, 52, Para. 4.84.
[266] Ibid.
[267] Ibid.
[268] Anderson, "Legal and Practical Protection of U.S. Foreign Investment," 136.
[269] Ibid.
[270] Prasad, and Balan, "Strategies for U.S. Companies to Mitigate Legal Risks," 14–16.
[271] Kantor, "Arbitration Award May Alter Dabhol Debate," 1; and Anderson, "Legal and Practical Protection of U.S. Foreign Investment," 136.
[272] Kantor, "Arbitration Award May Alter Dabhol Debate," 1.
[273] Ibid.
[274] Ibid., 2.
[275] Ibid., 1.
[276] Ibid.
[277] Ibid.., 2.
[278] American Arbitration Association, International Centre for Dispute Resolution, "Bechtel Enterprises International (Bermuda) Ltd."
[279] SAFTA members are Bangladesh, Bhutan, India, Maldives, Nepal, Pakistan, and Sri Lanka. EIU, *India: Country Commerce 2006*, 51.
[280] BITs are bilateral agreements aimed at protecting and promoting foreign investment through legally- binding rights and obligations. OECD, Directorate for Financial and Enterprise Affairs, Investment Committee,"Salient Features of India's Investment Agreements," 3.
[281] Tax treaties serve to prevent the double taxation of income earned in one country by a resident of another country. India Mart, *Taxation - Tax Treaties*.
[282] The most favored nation principle requires that no member country give preferential trade treatment to one WTO member or non-member without giving the same preferential trade treatment to all WTO members. The market access principle requires member countries to open their markets to other members within the limits of the agreement. The national treatment principle requires that no member country give preferential trade treatment to domestic-made products that it does not give to like products from other member countries.
[283] Van den Bossche, *The Law and Policy of the World Trade Organization*, 106. The special status of "developing country" is primarily a matter of self-declaration, that is, a member will declare itself a developing country in order to gain the special treatment afforded developing countries within the WTO.
[284] TRIMS Agreement, Articles 1–2.
[285] Measures that requires certain levels of local procurement by an entity. *See:* Annex to TRIMS Agreement.
[286] Measures that restrict the value or volume of imports a foreign investor can use to produce goods for export. *See*: Annex to TRIMs Agreement.
[287] WTO, *Indonesia—Certain Measures Affecting the Automobile Industry*, 337–42.
[288] Local content. ..requirements in the production of News Print... Rifampicin and Penicillin-G, and [d]ividend balancing requirements in the case of investment in 22 categories [of] consumer goods." U.S. Department of Commerce, *The Agreement on Trade Related Investment Measures*.
[289] U.S. Department of Commerce, *The Agreement on Trade Related Investment Measures*.
[290] TRIMS Article 4.
[291] GATS Article 1(2)(a-d).
[292] Ibid. The other modes are cross-border supply of services, consumption abroad, and the presence of natural persons. For additional information, see WTO, "Understanding the WTO, Services: Rules for Growth and Investment."
[293] India's Schedule of GATS Commitments (as revised by Supplements 1-4).
[294] Ibid.
[295] Sri Lanka will have until 2013 to reduce its tariffs to zero.
[296] South Asian Association for Regional Cooperation, *Agreement on South Asian Free Trade Area*.
[297] Ibid.
[298] Dikshit, "Ban on FDI from Bangladesh May Go."
[299] These bilateral agreements are estimated to cover 65 percent ($4.5 billion) of India's inward FDI and 40 percent ($2 billion) of its outward FDI in 2005. OECD, "Salient Features of India's Investment Agreements." 3.

[300] OECD, Directorate for Financial and Enterprise Affairs, Investment Committee, "Salient Features of India's Investment Agreements," 4.

[301] Ibid., 6.

[302] Ibid., 8.

[303] Ibid., 8.

[304] Ibid., 10.

[305] Fenwick & West LLP, *Structuring Venture Capital and Other Investments in India*, 2.

[306] Ibid., 3.

[307] EIU, *Business India Intelligence,* 3.

[308] Fenwick & West LLP, *Structuring Venture Capital and Other Investments in India*, 3.

[309] To qualify, an offshore company must (1) have two local directors approved by the Mauritian Offshore Business Activities Act Authority, (2) have a bank account in Mauritius, and (3) comply with Mauritian corporate formalities. The full benefits of the treaty would apply even if the Mauritian entity is established primarily for investment into India. Fenwick & West LLP, *Structuring Venture Capital and Other Investments in India*, 3.

[310] Mauritian subsidiaries are usually not deemed to have "permanent establishment" in India as long as the subsidiary does not exercise decision making authority over certain activities. These activities can include making investment decisions, concluding contracts, or securing goods orders on behalf of the parent. Fenwick & West LLP, *Structuring Venture Capital and Other Investments in India*, 2–3.

[311] Ibid.

[312] Government of India, Ministry of Commerce & Industry, "Fact Sheet on Foreign Direct Investment."

[313] Government of India, Ministry of Finance, various press releases of Department of Industrial Policy and Promotion.

[314] Thomas, "Singapore, New Tax Haven for Offshore Investors."

[315] Ibid.

[316] Government of India, Ministry of Commerce & Industry, Department of Commerce, *CECA Between India and Singapore.*

[317] Annual expenditures on operations in Singapore must be at least $132,000 in the 24 months immediately prior to when the tax gains are realized. Fenwick & West LLP, *Structuring Venture Capital and Other Investments in India*, 4.

[318] Swire, "Singapore and Mauritius Vie To Supply India's FDI."

[319] Basu, "India, Singapore Ink Pact."

[320] Ibid.

[321] The largest sector in terms of FDI—"electrical equipments"—totaled $6.9 billion and accounted for 14 percent of the total. Government of India, Ministry of Commerce & Industry, Department of Industrial Policy and Promotion, "Fact Sheet on Foreign Direct Investment."

[322] Licensing refers to the requirement that importers and/or exporters obtain government approval prior to importing or exporting. As of 1993, motor vehicle importers and exporters no longer needed government approval.

[323] The Indian fiscal year runs April 1–March 31.

[324] McKenzie, "2007 Global Outlook."

[325] India Brand Equity Foundation, *Auto Components.*

[326] Fillmore, "Indian Capacity Will Rise," 4.

[327] For example, the two largest Indian automakers, Maruti (majority owned by Suzuki of Japan) and Hyundai of Korea are planning for large scale exports—Suzuki is planning to export one-half of the output at its new plant in Manesar, and Hyundai reportedly plans to export a large percentage of its total Indian capacity, which it is raising to 600,000 vehicles per year. Fillmore, "Indian Capacity Will Rise," 4.

[328] The term OEM refers to original equipment manufacturers (i.e., automakers); the aftermarket refers to replacement parts sold by dealers, retail operations, and service garages, for example.

[329] India Brand Equity Foundation, *Auto Components.*

[330] Just-auto.com editorial team, "ACMA-McKinsey's 'Vision 2015' for the Indian Supplier Industry."

[331] Government of India, Ministry of Heavy Industries and Public Enterprises, *Automotive Mission Plan 2006–2016*, 45.

[332] At least 80 percent of passenger vehicle sales are now financed by loans. KPMG, *Automotive and Components Market in Asia*, 22.

[333] Bissinger, *Dream Machines.*

[334] *newKerala.com*, "India—The New Hub of the Automotive Industry."

[335] Business India Intelligence, "India Automotive: Burning Rubber."

[336] KPMG, *Manufacturing in India*, 40. Taken from Sanjeev Sanyal, *India's Changing Households*, Deutsche Bank, November 2004.

[337] Rathore and Swarup, *A Review of India's Automotive Industry*, 11.

[338] Government of India, Ministry of Heavy Industries and Public Enterprises, *Automotive Mission Plan 2006–2016*, ix.
[339] *Press Trust of India*, "Delphi to Invest $10 Mn in India"; and Doi, "Suzuki Will Build Suppliers Industrial Park," 5.
[340] Government of India, Ministry of Heavy Industries and Public Enterprises, Department of Heavy Industry, *Auto Policy*.
[341] SIAM, "Auto Policy of Government of India."
[342] Government of India, Ministry of Heavy Industries and Public Enterprises, Department of Heavy Industry, *Auto Policy*, art. 8.1.
[343] A CKD is a complete kit needed to assemble a vehicle. It is common practice among automakers to sell knocked down kits to their foreign affiliates; the automaker is typically able to avoid high import taxes, gain market access, and/or receive tax preferences for providing local employment, and the assemblers in developing markets to gain expertise.
[344] Bissinger, *Dream Machines*.
[345] Government of India, Ministry of Heavy Industries and Public Enterprises, *Automotive Mission Plan 2006–2016*, xiii.
[346] Ibid., 13.
[347] Ibid., 26.
[348] Ibid., 10.
[349] Ibid., 25.
[350] Ibid., 26.
[351] KPMG, *Automotive and Components Market in Asia*, 23.
[352] Fillmore, "Short of Engineers at Home," 7.
[353] Mahindra World City Web site.
[354] Adityapur Industrial Area Development Authority Web site.
[355] *Asian Pacific Bulletin*, "Can India Revitalize its Special Economic Zones to Rival Those in China?"; Johnson, "India Lifts Freeze on Enterprise Zones"; and Srinivasan, "China, India and the World Economy."
[356] KPMG, *Manufacturing in India*, 3.
[357] U.S. India Business Council official, interview by Commission staff, January 4, 2007.
[358] KPMG, *Manufacturing in India*, 35.
[359] Ibid.
[360] KPMG, *Manufacturing in India*, 6.
[361] LaReau, "GM Wants More Engineers in India," 6.
[362] *Ward's Automotive Reports*, "Chevy's Spark Key to GM's Growth in India," 7.
[363] Ibid.
[364] Business India Intelligence, "India Automotive: Burning Rubber."
[365] *Ward's Automotive Reports*, "Chevy's Spark Key to GM's Growth in India," 7.
[366] Bhalla and Allen, "GM Says to Buy More Auto Parts from India."
[367] Bureau van Dijk, *Zephyr Mergers and Acquisitions database.* The other M&A deal was a 20 percent stake in International Cars and Motors Ltd., purchased from Sonalika Group of India by Citigroup in 2006. International Cars & Motors Ltd. (ICML) was founded in 2003 with a greenfield plant in Amb to manufacture multi-utility vehicles. Plant capacity is 24,000 multi-utility vehicles (MUV) per year. In 2006, ICML launched the Rhino, an MUV designed in collaboration with MG Rover with engines sourced from Isuzu. 3i Web site.
[368] Business India Intelligence, "India Automotive: Burning Rubber."
[369] Ford Motor Co., "Volvo to Sell Cars in India."
[370] As noted earlier, Mahindra was formerly a joint venture partner with Ford, but was bought out by Ford in 2005.
[371] Bureau van Dijk, *Zephyr Mergers and Acquisitions database*.
[372] OCO Consulting Ltd., *LocoMonitor FDI database*.
[373] Just-auto.com editorial team, "Hyundai Has Ambitious Plans."
[374] Automotive Component Manufacturers Association of India, "Industry Statistics."
[375] OCO Consulting Ltd., *LocoMonitor FDI database*.
[376] Information for mergers and acquisitions compiled from Bureau van Dijk, *Zephyr Mergers and Acquisitions database*.
[377] Of the 44 acquisitions reported in the Zephyr database, the values of 11 deals were not available.
[378] KPMG, *Manufacturing in India.*
[379] Huber, "The Indian Automotive Scenario."
[380] Wells, "Hub or Hubris? Prospects for the AMP to 2016."
[381] Wells and Sadana, "Hub or Hubris? India and the Automotive Mission Plan 2006–16," 29.
[382] Government of India, Ministry of Steel, National Steel Policy 2005.
[383] Wells and Sadana, "Hub or Hubris? India and the Automotive Mission Plan 2006–16," 29.
[384] Ramachandran, "A Grand Plan for Indian Automobiles."
[385] Mueller, "The Tiger Awakens," 16–20.

[386] Ibid., 22–25.
[287] India Patents Act, 1970, § 83.
[388] Chaudhuri, *The WTO and India's Pharmaceuticals Industry,* 37–3 8.
[389] TRIPS Article 65.4.
[390] TRIPS, Arts. 70.8(a) and 70.9.
[391] WTO, "India—Patent Protection for Pharmaceutical and Agricultural Chemical Products."
[392] India Patents Act, § 84 (2005). Domestic "working" requirements are controversial; the United States challenged at the WTO such a requirement in Brazil's patent law, however, the dispute was terminated based on Brazil's agreement to provide advance notice where it intended to issue a compulsory license based on the fact that the patent needed to be domestically worked. USTR, "Brazil."
[393] India Patents Act, §§ 92, 92A (2005).
[394] Mueller, "The Tiger Awakens," 107–09.
[395] U.S. India Business Council, *Recommendations of the Breakout Session on Biotechnology/Life Sciences/Medical Devices Breakout Session*, "Issues Raised by Indian Industry" and Indian industry official, interview by Commission staff, March 28, 2007.
[396] DiMasi, Hansen, and Grabowski, "The Price of Innovation: New Estimates of Drug Development Costs," 151.
[397] See generally, Thomas, *Proprietary Rights in Pharmaceutical Innovation,* CRS-17–19.
[398] PhRMA, *PhRMA, Special 301 Submission: India,* 71–72.
[399] KPMG International, *The Indian Pharmaceutical Industry: Collaboration for Growth,* 18.
[400] India Patents Act, § 3(d).
[401] Mueller, "The Tiger Awakens," 72.
[402] In other countries, this type of evaluation of medical data is typically done by health care regulatory and reimbursement officials, not by patent examiners.
[403] The Group has requested the opportunity to review and resubmit an amended report. Nair, "India: Mashelkar Committee Withdraws Its Report."
[404] *The Business World (India)*, "We Are Not Doing This Out of Spite."
[405] Shared Expertise Forums, "Survey: Pharmaceutical Companies Cautious of Investments in Emerging China and India Markets."
[406] Mueller, "The Tiger Awakens: The Tumultuous Transformation of India's Patent System and the Rise of Indian Pharmaceutical Innovation," 28.
[407] Chaudhuri, *The WTO and India's Pharmaceuticals Industry,* 18.
[408] Mueller, "The Tiger Awakens," 60.
[409] Bureau van Dijk, *Orbis Companies database*.
[410] Sampath, "Indian Pharma within Global Reach," 16–17.
[411] *Pharmabiz.com*, "Pharmabiz Studies of Top Cos."
[412] Sampath, "Indian Pharma within Global Reach," 16.
[413] Mueller, "The Tiger Awakens," 59–60.
[414] Sampath, "Indian Pharma within Global Reach," 19.
[415] *The Economic Times*, "Pharma Tops the FDI Chart in '04 with $340 mn Inflow."
[416] Many global investors in India route their FDI through Mauritius to take advantage of the India- Mauritius bilateral tax treaty. See chaps. 2 and 6 for further discussion of the treaty and its effects.
[417] For overall FDI data, this chapter relies on official statistics of the Indian Ministry of Commerce. For greenfield projects, the chapter cites data reported by OCO Consulting through its LocoMonitor database. Discussions of strategic alliances are based on press releases and M&A data is provided by Bureau Van Dijk through its Zephyr databse. The features and limitations of these data sources are discussed in chapter 1. The projects and deals identified through the company databases and press releases are illustrative of FDI trends rather than identical to the data provided by the Indian Ministry of Commerce.
[418] OCO Consulting Ltd., *LocoMonitor FDI database*.
[419] Ibid.
[420] Biotechmedia, "CRD, Contract Research Organizations."
[421] Ernst & Young, *Unveiling India's Pharmaceutical Future*, 12.
[422] U.S. National Institute of Health, "ClinicalTrials.gov."
[423] Chatterjee, "TCS Wins $35 Mn Eli Lilly Contract."
[424] Singh, "It's Pharmaceutical Giant's Third Drug Development Alliance in India in Six Months."
[425] Jayakumar, "Amgen Opens Subsidiary in India."
[426] Matthew, "GSK Identifies Asia, Eastern Europe as Major Centres for Clinical Research."
[427] Ranbaxy Laboratories Ltd., "Ranbaxy Signs New R&D Agreement with GSK."
[428] *The Hindu Business Line*, "GVK Biosciences to Provide Research Services for Wyeth Pharma."
[429] Biocon, "Biocon Conducts Ground Breaking Ceremony."
[430] Boston Consulting Group, *Harnessing the Power of India*, 5; and Kumar, "How to Protect Data in Outsourcing Deals."
[431] Industry official, interview by Commission staff, Washington, DC, April 24, 2007.

[432] Mueller, "The Tiger Awakens," 52.
[433] *The Economic Times*, "India's on Merck's Outsourcing Radar."
[434] Government of India, Ministry of External Affairs, ITP Division, "Drugs & Pharmaceuticals."
[435] Ernst & Young. *Unveiling India's Pharmaceutical Future*, 10.
[436] IBEF, *Pharmaceuticals*, 13.
[437] Kumar," How to Protect Data in Outsourcing Deals."
[438] Although not addressed in this case study, Indian firms have been extremely active in the last several years in acquiring companies in Europe and the United States, particularly in the generics sector. See Greene, *The Emergence of India's Pharmaceutical Industry and Implications for the U.S. Generic Drug Market*, 8–10.
[439] Roumeliotis, "Mylan in India's Biggest Pharmaceutical Takeover."
[440] Bureau van Dijk, *Zephyr Mergers and Acquisitions database*.
[441] Ibid.
[442] Ibid.

In: Conditions for Foreign Direct Investment in India
Ed: Brent M. Cardenas and Zackary R. Berg
ISBN: 978-1-60456-862-2

Chapter 3

THE ENVIRONMENT FOR AGRICULTURAL AND AGRIBUSINESS INVESTMENT IN INDIA*

Maurice Landes
U.S. Deptarment of Agriculture

ABSTRACT

Despite strong overall economic growth and strengthening food demand, investment in Indian agriculture and agribusiness has remained sluggish, and growth in farm output has slowed, since the early 1990s. An array of policies and regulations affecting agricultural production, marketing, and food processing—along with weak infrastructure and a lack of market services—have discouraged private investment by farmers and large, vertically integrated agribusinesses. The policy environment has grown more investor friendly since the late 1990s and private investment appears to be responding, but significant barriers remain and the pace of future reforms remains uncertain.

Keywords: India, agriculture, agribusiness, investment, trade policy, domestic policy, infrastructure

SUMMARY

Although rising incomes are contributing to expanding and diversifying food demand, investment in Indian agriculture has remained low relative to other sectors and grown slowly since the early 1990s. Lagging private investment in agriculture and agribusiness has corresponded with burden-some regulatory policies, poor infrastructure, and weak institutional support for agricultural markets. Even though India has one of the world's largest agricultural economies, Indian agribusiness is characterized by a multitude of small-scale,

* This is an edited, reformatted and augmented version of a U. S. Department of Agriculture publication dated July 2008.

nonintegrated processing and marketing firms that use mostly outdated technology and are uncompetitive in global markets.

What Is the Issue?

India, with one of the world's fastest growing and most populous economies and one of its largest farm sectors, is emerging as a potentially large market for global agricultural trade and investment. Despite the rapid productivity gains occurring in India's service and manufacturing sectors, average crop yields remain below potential, agricultural markets are underdeveloped, and growth in farm output has slowed. Policymakers are increasingly focused on how to strengthen agricultural investment and growth, raise rural incomes, and help sustain rapid overall gains in income growth and poverty reduction.

What Are the Major Findings?

Both public and private investment in Indian agriculture and agribusiness have remained weak since the early 1990s, despite accelerating growth in the overall economy and a large domestic market for agricultural products. Growth in farm output has slowed since the early 1990s, and although a turnaround is seen as critical for sustained economic growth, consensus on agricultural reforms has proven difficult.

India's numerous domestic policy interventions—along with weak infrastructure and limited institutional support for agricultural markets—have been a deterrent to agricultural investment, particularly in large vertically integrated agribusinesses. Interventions have included restrictions on transporting, storing, and marketing of agricultural commodities, restrictions on the size of agribusiness firms, high taxes on processed products, high-cost credit, and complex food laws. The climate for private investment is also undermined by weak transport and power infrastructure and lack of key services such as market information, risk management tools, and grading/inspection systems.

For farmers, disincentives have included trade and price policies that maintained low domestic prices for many farm commodities, inefficient markets that dampen returns to growers, and few public and private marketing services. Onfarm investment may also be constrained by India's many small and marginal farmers, who account for nearly 40 percent of farmland, and often have limited access to input and output markets and more limited investment options.

Since 2000, the policy environment seems to be improving and investment in agriculture to be strengthening, as evidenced by higher market prices and input subsidies for farmers. Movement and storage restrictions on essential commodities, like wheat and rice, are becoming less common, restrictions on firm size have been largely removed, State marketing laws are evolving to accommodate private marketing channels, and taxes on agricultural products are being reduced and simplified. And although power, transport, and other infrastructure problems will likely be solved only in the longer term, there is evidence that private investment is now on the rise in those sectors. Food marketing ventures oriented toward development of supply chains and retail outlets represent a turnaround in investor confidence.

Recent investment in India's food marketing sector includes a number of ventures by U.S. and other foreign investors, mostly in collaboration with Indian firms. Since India does not permit foreign direct investment by multi-brand retailers, foreign investment has taken the form of wholesale (or "cash and carry") trading enterprises, or partnerships with Indian franchisees who own the retail outlets.

How Was the Study Conducted?

This study was based on analysis of literature and secondary data from published and online sources, together with interviews of representatives from Indian agribusinesses. Data collection and interviews in India were facilitated by Indian Agribusiness Systems, Ltd, of Okhla, Uttar Pradesh. Financial support for this study was provided by the USDA Emerging Markets Program.

INTRODUCTION

Economic growth in India has accelerated since the early 1990s, when a package of market-oriented reforms to domestic, trade, and exchange rate policies sparked investment and productivity gains in the industrial and services sectors. But agricultural investment has lagged investment in the rest of the economy since the 1980s. Output growth has slowed since the early 1990s (table 1), and agreement on reforms to strengthen agricultural performance has proven difficult.[1] With rising incomes, urbanization, and youthful demographics boosting demand for an increasingly diverse array of food and agricultural products, slowed growth in farm output is translating into rising real prices for some foods, as well as more agricultural imports. Although agricultural imports remain low compared with the size of the Indian economy, they have grown about 13 percent annually in real terms since the early 1990s, and India has emerged as a major global importer of edible oils, pulses, and, most recently, wheat.[2]

Despite the robust gains elsewhere in the economy, the poor performance of India's agricultural sector—including both production agriculture and marketing—has become a key concern of Indian policymakers. Agriculture accounts for about 21 percent of economic output (2003/04-2005/06 average; Reserve Bank of India, 2007) and is the primary source of employment and income for about 58 percent the population (Government of India, Ministry of Statistics and Program Implementation, 2005), including a large share of Indians living below the poverty line. Lagging performance in such a large segment of the economy jeopardizes the sustainability of the economy's strong overall growth. It has also prompted political resistance to extending market-oriented domestic and trade policy reforms into a farm sector comprised mostly of small farmers and agribusinesses that are seen as vulnerable and unready to compete in international markets.

The lack of substantive yield growth and the inefficiency of markets in Indian agriculture are correlated with low levels of public and private investment in agriculture and agribusiness. In contrast to the dynamism evident in other sectors, investment in Indian agriculture and agribusiness—public and private, domestic and foreign—has been low and, until very recently, has shown little growth. Public investment has been partially constrained by the large and increasing costs of farm subsidies. Private onfarm investment has been hampered by policies that have historically taxed producers by maintaining relatively low domestic farm prices, inefficient markets that dampen market returns, and weak institutional support for growers, especially small and marginal farmers. Private agribusiness investors, in turn, have faced state and central regulatory policies—including marketing, interstate movement, storage, and taxation policies—that create disincentives for investment, particularly in larger, integrated agribusiness enterprises. Although foreign direct investment is permitted in most agribusiness—the key exception being retailing—the regulatory policies that impede domestic investors have also been a deterrent to foreign investment.

TRENDS IN AGRICULTURAL INVESTMENT

Output and investment in Indian agriculture have not been showing the same robust growth as in the overall economy. For the economy as a whole, real growth in gross domestic product (GDP) and in investment—as captured by gross fixed capital formation (GFCF)—have both been strengthening, particularly since the early 1990s (table 1). In agriculture, however, output growth has been slowing, and investment has continued to lag that in the overall economy. The annual share of GDP that is invested in GFCF averaged a robust 27 percent for the overall economy during 2005-07; by contrast, GFCF in agriculture was only about 7 percent of agricultural GDP during the same period. And while the rate of investment in the overall economy has continued to rise, the rate of investment in agriculture generally declined through 2000 before turning up slightly during 2000-07 (figure 1).

Although overall agricultural investment in India is low and growing slowly compared with investment in the rest of the economy, some categories of investment have shown signs of growth. Among these are investments in agriculture-related infrastructure and services, and in investment by the private as opposed to the public sector.

Investment "In" and "For" Agriculture

The data on capital formation in agriculture (shown in table 1) include primarily onfarm investment in construction, farm equipment, irrigation, and other land improvements. Omitted from these accounts are investments in off-farm agriculture-related infrastructure such as markets, storage facilities, rural roads, and rural electrification. Trends in these off-farm investments— termed investments "for" agriculture—are characterized in table 2 (Ministry of Agriculture, 2003). These data, which are available only through 2000, show that investment for agriculture has been growing much faster than investment in agriculture, though it too lags overall investment in the economy. And investments both in and for agriculture, combined, still represent a small share of agricultural GDP—about 15 percent during 1998-2000—compared with the 26-percent share of investment in the overall economy during that period.

Table 1. Growth of real gross domestic product (GDP) and gross fixed capital formation (GFCF) in India

	Gross domestic product		Gross fixed capital formation	
Period	Total	In agriculture	Total	In agriculture
	Growth rates (percent per year)[1]			
1960s	3.7	2.2	5.9	5.9
1970s	3.2	1.6	4.6	5.1
1980s	5.3	3.4	6.0	0.6
1990-04	5.8	2.9	6.1	2.4
1997-04	5.8	1.8	11.3	3.9

[1] Growth rates between 3-year averages centered on years indicated.

Sources: Government of India, Ministry of Program Planning and Implementation, Central Statistical Organization; Government of India, Ministry of Finance, Economic Survey.

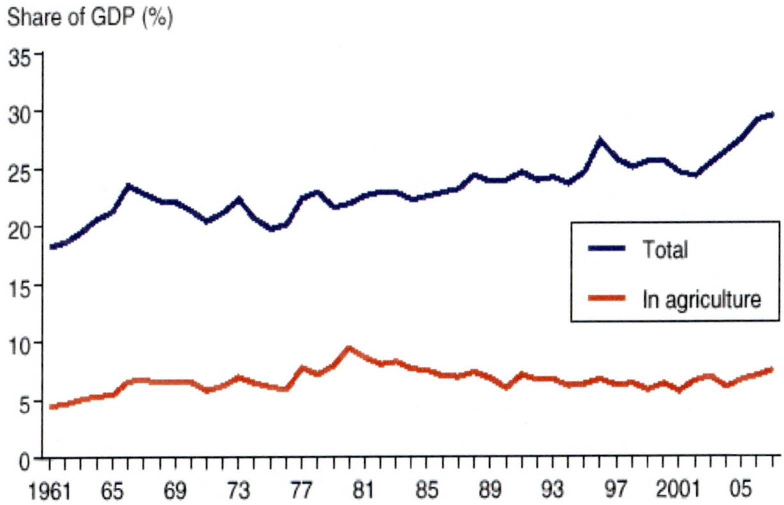

Source: Reserve Bank of India, Handbook of Statistics on Indian Economy.

Figure 1. Gross fixed capital formation in India as share of Gross Domestic Product (GDP)

Table 2. Growth in Public and Private Gross Fixed Capital Formation in and for Agriculture in India

	GFCF in Agriculture			GFCF for Agriculture			GFCF in/for Agriculture		
Period	Public	Private	Total	Public	Private	Total	Public	Private	Total
	Growth rate (percent per year)								
1982-92	-4.3	5.1	1.2	-1.3	5.1	2.0	-2.5	5.2	1.6
1992-99	-0.3	2.4	1.7	1.3	3.0	2.7	0.8	3.5	2.3
1992-97	1.3	2.4	2.0	1.7	3.4	3.2	1.5	4.2	2.8
1997-99	-4.0	2.6	0.7	0.4	2.2	1.3	-1.1	1.8	1.1
	Shares of agricultural GDP (percent)								
1981 -83 avg.	4.3	4.0	8.3	6.0	4.7	10.7	10.3	8.6	19.0
1991 -93 avg.	2.0	4.8	6.8	3.8	5.7	9.5	5.9	10.4	16.3
1996-98 avg.	1.8	4.5	6.4	3.5	5.9	9.4	5.4	10.4	15.8
1998-00 avg.	1.6	4.5	6.1	3.4	5.8	9.1	5.0	10.3	15.3

Source: Government of India, Ministry of Agriculture, Directorate of Economics and Statistics, 2003.

Agricultural Investment in India Compared with Other Countries

Comparing agricultural investment across countries is complicated by limited availability of data and by differences in definitions and methods used to report data. Some data are available for China and Brazil which, like India, are large developing economies with large agricultural sectors. Both China (using a narrow definition of agricultural investment) and India (using either a narrow or broad definition) have substantially lower rates of investment in agriculture than in the overall economy (table 3). By contrast, in Brazil, where the data employ a broad definition of agricultural investment, the rate of agricultural investment is substantially higher than for the economy as a whole.

Agricultural investment averaged 9.6 percent of agricultural GDP in China during 2003-2005. The Chinese data are based on a definition of investment that compares most closely with investment "in" agriculture in India, which averaged 6.6 percent during the same period. Brazilian data, which include investment in rural infrastructure and agribusiness, show investment in agriculture averaging 48 percent of agricultural GDP during 2001-2003 (table 3). By comparison, Indian investment "in" and "for" agriculture, the broadest measure available for India, averaged 15.3 percent of agricultural GDP during 1998-2000, the most recent period for which data are available. While these comparisons suggest that agricultural investment in India is low compared with two other large, developing agricultural countries, definitional differences in the data make it difficult to draw firm conclusions.

Public and Private Investment

Public investment in and for agriculture has averaged roughly half the size of private investment, and grew much more slowly than private investment during both the 1980s and 1990s (table 2). Public investment in agriculture actually declined during the 1980s and showed little growth in the 1990s. Weak public investment in agriculture has corresponded with rapid expansion of public expenditures on price subsidies for the sector (Figure 2), including price supports and subsidized storage and distribution for wheat and rice (the so-called "food grain subsidy"), as well as price subsidies for electricity, irrigation water, and fertilizer (Srinivasan et al., 2007; Landes and Gulati, 2004). No explicit link is apparent between the divergent trends in public outlays on investments versus subsidies in agriculture. However, public investment in irrigation—the major category of public investment in agriculture—has been declining since the mid-1990s. During the same period, political pressure has grown to compensate farmers for rising costs and price instability through input and output price subsidies (Landes and Gulati, 2004).

Studies of investment in Indian agriculture (Chand, 2000; Chand and Kumar, 2004) found that changes in private investment between the early 1980s and the mid-1990s could be explained by the availability of institutional credit for agriculture and improvements in the barter terms of trade—or the ratio of prices received to prices paid—for agriculture. While a significant complementary relationship between public and private investment was evident during the 1960s and 1970s, no such evidence exists since the early 1980s. Further, state-by-state analysis revealed a highly significant positive relationship between private investment and both agricultural output and productivity growth nationally and in most States. Overall, the evidence suggests that since the early 1980s, public investment in agriculture has been less important to overall investment in the sector—and to growth in output and productivity—than has the environment for private investment, defined as profitability and credit availability compared to other sectors.

More recent data indicate that improving terms of trade for agriculture—as determined by the ratio of agricultural product prices to prices of manufactured and other nonagricultural goods—may have been an important factor in expanding private investment in and for agriculture through the end of the 1990s (Figure 3). Improvements in the agricultural terms of trade during the 1990s were driven by two key factors (Landes and Gulati, 2004). First, liberalizing reforms to industrial and manufacturing sector policies in the early 1990s led to declining real prices for many nonagricultural goods. Second, agricultural commodity prices tended to strengthen during the late 1990s when the Government implemented large increases in support prices for wheat and rice—India's major farm products and food staples (Srinivasan et al., 2007).

Table 3. Comparisons of Total and Agricultural Investment in Brazil, China, and India

Country/year	Total	Agriculture
	Percent of GDP	
Brazil (2001-03 average)	16.2	48.4[1]
China (2003-05 average)	42.8	9.6[2]
India (1 998-00 average)	25.7	15.3[1]
India (2003-05 average)	27.3	6.6[2]

[1] Includes onfarm and rural infrastructure investment.

[2] Includes primarily onfarm investments.

Sources: Banco Central do Brasil; National Bureau of Statistics of China; Reserve Bank of India; Government of India, Ministry of Agriculture, Directorate of Economics and Statistics, 2003.

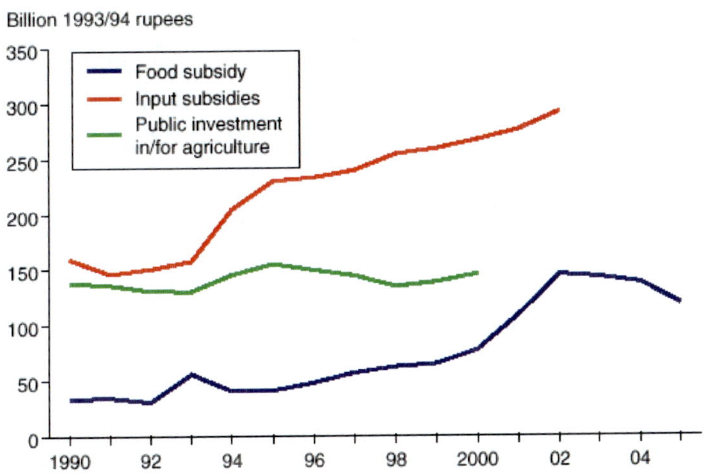

Source: Government of India, Ministry of Agriculture, Directorate of Economics and Statistics, 2003; Government of India, Ministry of Finance, Economic Survey; Mullen, Orden, and Gulatia, 2006.

Figure 2. Public investment and subsidies in Indian agriculture

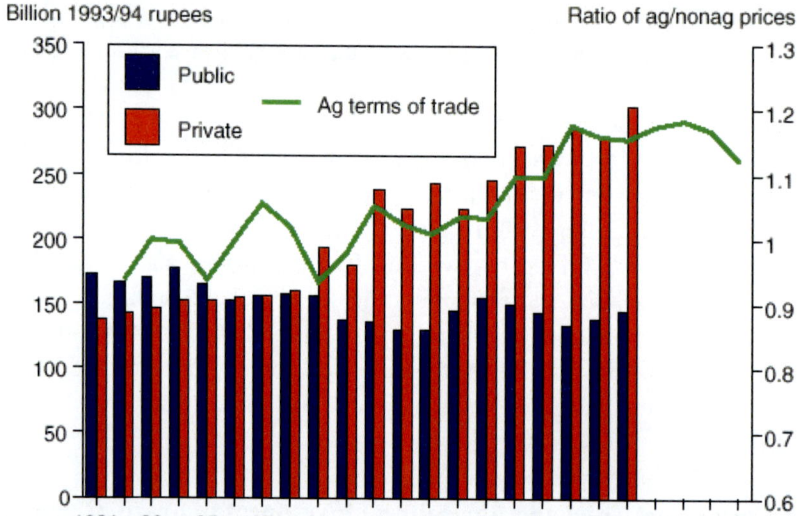

Source: Government of India, Ministry of Agriculture, Directorate of Economics and Statistics, 2003; Government of India, Ministry of Finance, Economic Survey.

Figure 3. Public and private gross fixed capital formation in and for Indian agriculture

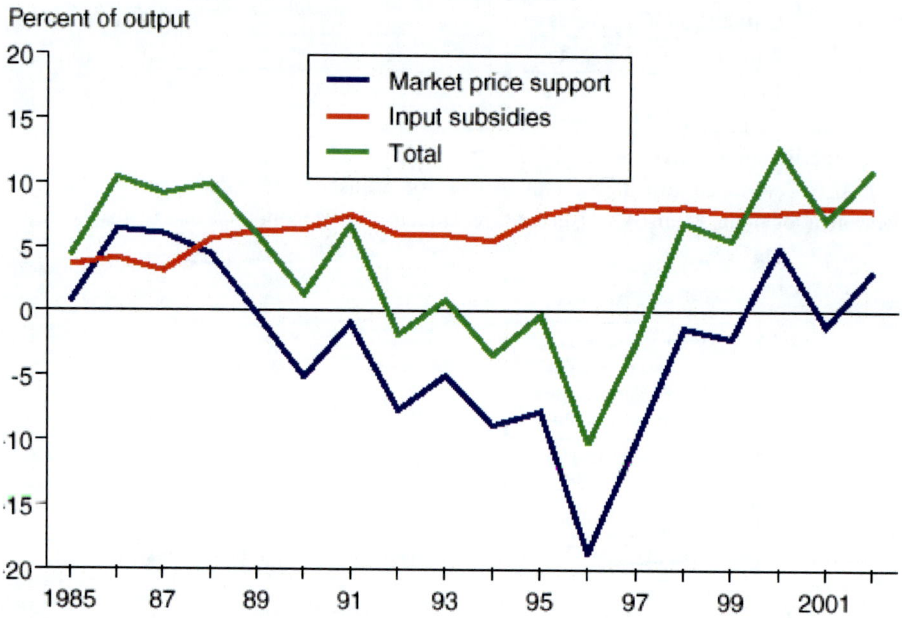

Source: Mullen, Orden, and Gulati, 2004.

Figure 4. Producer support estimates for India Percent of output

Strengthening terms of trade for agriculture are also reflected in producer support estimates (PSEs) for Indian agriculture (Figure 4). These estimates, which account for input subsidies and policy-induced differentials between domestic and international reference prices (termed market price support), indicate that India transitioned from taxing agriculture during the early and mid-1990s to supporting it during 1997-2002. This trend was driven by steadily increasing support of farmers through input subsidies and, particularly, by substantial increases in market price support in the late 1990s.

Increased producer support and strengthening terms of trade for agriculture suggest improved incentives for private investment by farmers and agribusinesses during the late 1990s and early 2000s. Although the most recent available data on the terms of trade for agriculture indicate some weakening during 2004-2005, more recent increases in world and domestic agricultural commodity prices have likely sustained price incentives for domestic producers.

Foreign Direct Investment

Prior to 1991, foreign direct investment (FDI) was negligible in the Indian economy because of highly restrictive policies regarding the permissible types of projects and foreign ownership shares, and the repatriation of earnings. In 1991, the Government began to liberalize FDI policies, initially giving automatic approval for up to 51 percent foreign ownership in 34 industries, including food processing, but with continued restrictions on imports and earnings repatriation.

FDI began to flow into India immediately following the 1991 reforms, growing about 36 percent annually in real terms between 1990-92 and 2003-05, but with only small amounts flowing into agriculture. Overall FDI growth has been aided by the implementation of additional reforms that have further eased the approval process, increased permissible sectors and foreign ownership shares, and loosened foreign exchange balancing restrictions. Still, FDI continues to make only a small contribution to annual fixed capital formation in India—now averaging about 4 percent (figure 5).

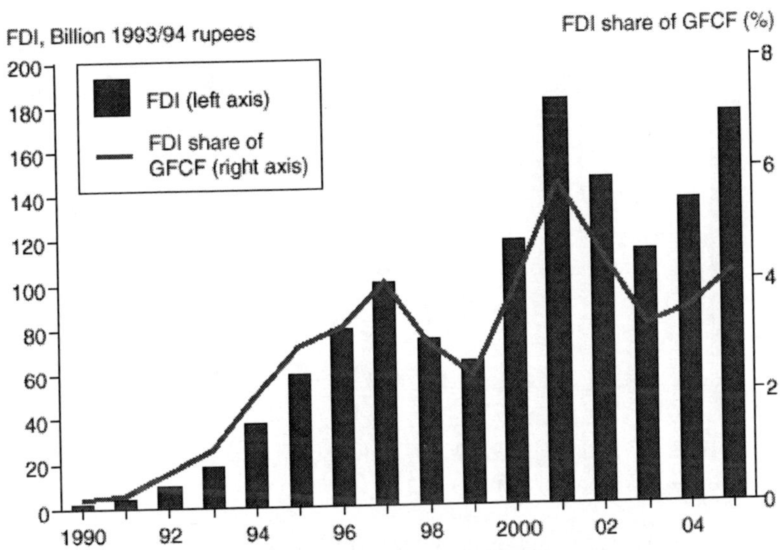

Source: Reserve Bank of India, Handbook of Statistics on Indian Economy.

Figure 5. Foreign direct investment (FDI) in India and share of gross fixed capital formation (GFCF

Although many agricultural sectors have been open to FDI since the early 1990s, FDI in Indian agriculture has not been significant. Leading sectors for FDI in India have been electrical equipment (17 percent of total FDI during 1991-2006), telecommunications (11 percent), transport (10 percent), services (9 percent), and power/petroleum refining (8 percent). Of the $38.9 billion in total FDI inflows during 1991-2006, about $1.7 billion—or 4 percent—has been in industries that can be identified as specific to agriculture. Food processing accounted for $1.2 billion of FDI, with agricultural machinery ($166 million), timber products ($107 million), and fertilizers ($78 million) accounting for most of the remainder. Some additional FDI that is classified in general activities, such as trading and services, might also be attributed to the agricultural sector.

Sources of Foreign Direct Investment

The United States has been the second largest single-country source of FDI in India, accounting for about 15 percent of Indian FDI during 199 1-2006 (figure 6). The largest source of FDI to India, accounting for 37 percent of the total during 1991-2006, has been the island nation of Mauritius. A bilateral double taxation treaty affords favorable treatment to funds that move through Mauritius, a situation that likely disguises the true origin of much of the FDI flows to India. Other major sources are the European Union, collectively accounting for about 24 percent of FDI into India during 199 1- 2006, and the countries of East Asia (13 percent).

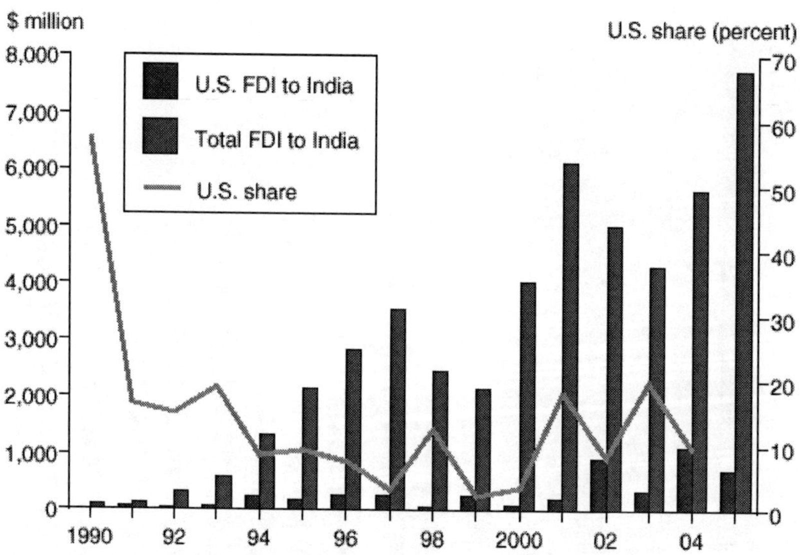

Source: Reserve Bank of India, Handbook of Statistics on Indian Economy; U.S. Department of Commerce, Bureau of Economic Analysis.

Figure 6. Total and U.S. foreign domestic investment (FDI) in India

Indian data on inward FDI by industry and country of origin are not available, but U.S. sources suggest that U.S. FDI in food-related industries there has been minor—about $18 million over 1990-2005. However, data for several years are not reported in order to protect the confidentiality of the small number of firms investing.

THE PRIVATE INVESTMENT CLIMATE

Prospects for agricultural investment hinge largely on the environment for private investment by farmers and agribusinesses. Private investment accounts for the bulk of total investment in agriculture, while fiscal constraints—including growing subsidy outlays—may continue to restrict public investment. Key factors likely to shape the climate for private investment by farmers and agribusinesses include (1) the extent to which domestic demand for agricultural products makes investment potentially profitable; (2) a range of government regulatory, credit, tax, and other policies that affect incentives for domestic and foreign investment in Indian agriculture; and (3) infrastructure constraints.

Consumer Demand

Consumer demand for food products in India has registered significant growth and diversification since the early 1990s, when a package of reforms to industrial, trade, and exchange rate policies launched India on a path of relatively strong income growth. India's youthful demographics and rapid urbanization also bode well for further growth and diversification of food demand (Joshi et al., 2007; Pingali and Khwaja, 2004).

Income growth in India, as measured by growth in real gross domestic product (GDP), has averaged more than 6 percent annually since the early 1990s, and more than 8 percent since 2003, establishing India as one of the fastest growing economies in the world. Rising incomes have contributed to a steady decline in the share of the population living in poverty, with poverty defined as the level of per capita income needed to purchase a nutritionally adequate diet (Figure 7). Although growth has been strong, India's per capita income remains at a level—about $588 annually in 2006—where most households continue to spend a large share of new income on food, both to increase caloric intake and to diversify and upgrade diets (World Bank, 2007).

India's youthful demographics—about 34 percent of the population was age 14 or under in 2001 compared with 25 percent in China—is also a driver of food demand (figure 8). Not only can average levels of daily food intake be expected to rise as more children grow to adulthood, but young adults are often more likely to try new foods and diversify their diets beyond traditional foods. Urbanization is another force that typically contributes to dietary change, through more intense exposure to foods from other cultures and increased demand for convenience foods to accommodate the schedules of two-earner households. The urban share of India's population was 27.8 percent (285 million) in 2001 and is rising steadily. In 2001, India had 35 cities with a population of 1 million or more, with these larger urban areas accounting for more than 10 percent of India's total population of more than 1 billion.

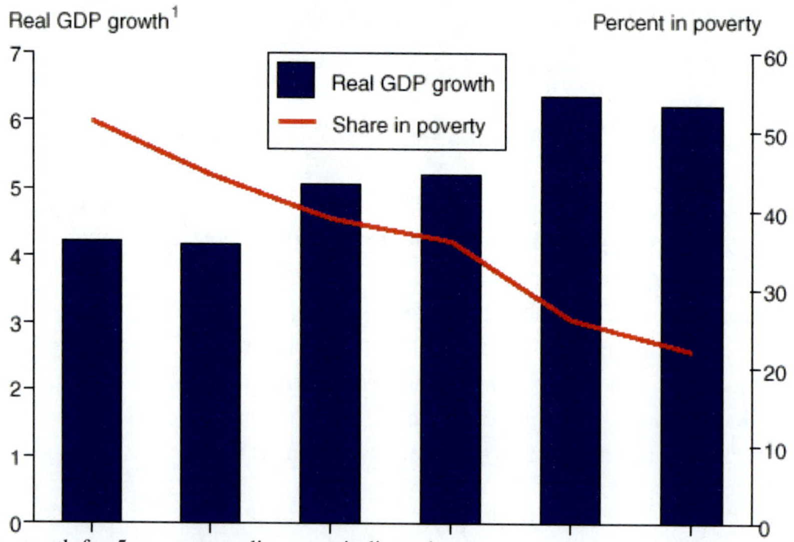

[1]Real GDP growth for 5 years preceding year indicated.
Source: Government of India, Ministry of Finance, Economic Survey.

Figure 7. Income growth and poverty reduction in India

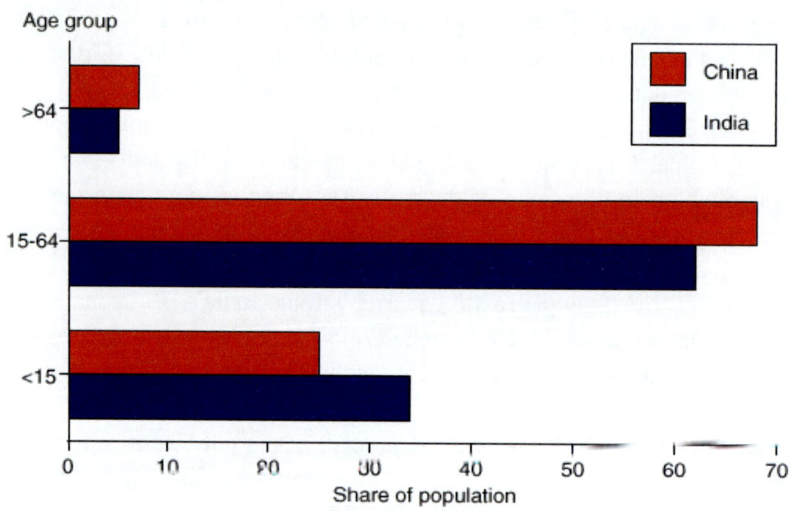

Source: Census of India, 2001.

Figure 8. Age composition of India's and China's populations

Data on food consumption by major food groups demonstrate the impact of rising incomes, demographics, and urbanization on the growth and diversification of food demand since the early 1990s (figure 9). While consumption of traditional items such as cereals and pulses continues to expand, other food categories—including vegetable oils, eggs, fruit, vegetables, milk, and meats—have been exhibiting substantially more rapid growth in demand.[3] These patterns are also evident from Indian consumer surveys that provide expenditure data by food group and expenditure class. Expenditures on cereals—the traditional food staples that still account for the bulk of average consumer food expenditure—tend to decline among higher income consumers (figure 10). For higher valued foods groups, however, consumer expenditure tends to accelerate as incomes rise. Foods in greater demand as incomes rise include not only fruit, vegetables, and edible oils, but also animal-based products such as milk, eggs, and meat (figures 11-13).

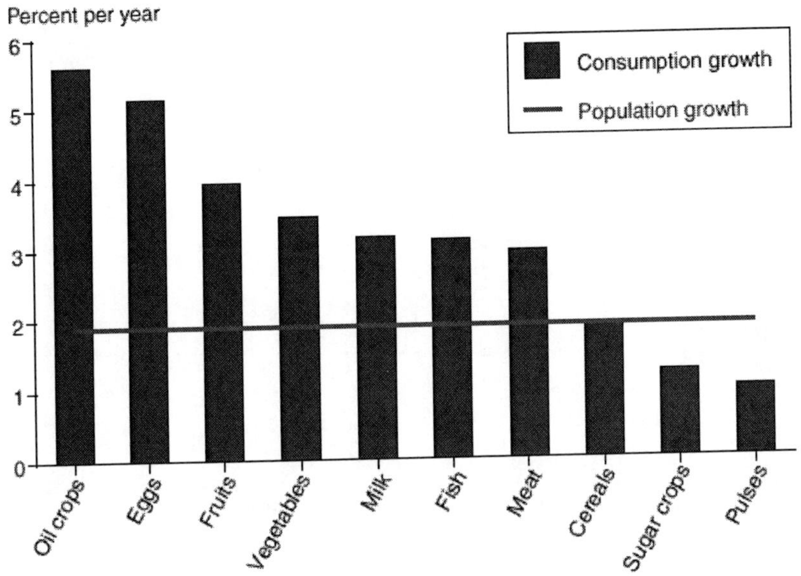

[1] Endpoints based on 3-year year averages centered on middle year; 1991 = 1990-92 average.
Source: Food and Agriculture Organization, FAOSTAT database.

Figure 9. Consumption growth by food group in India, 1991-2004[1]

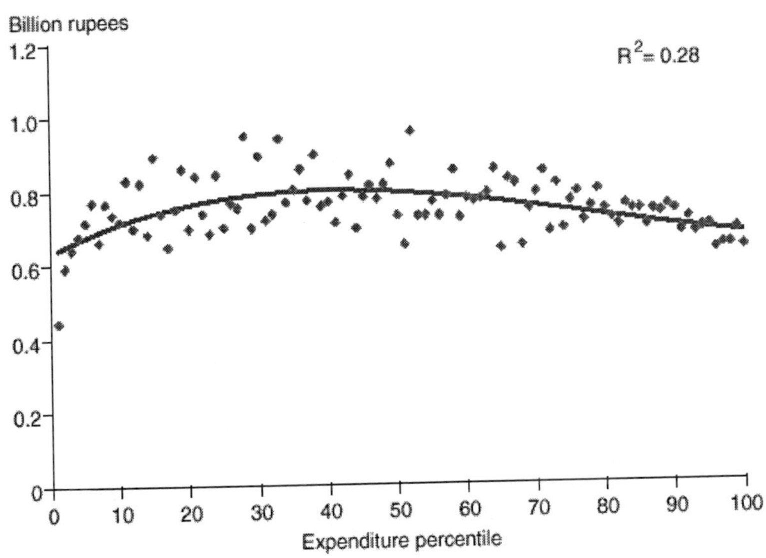

Source: National Samply Survey, 1999/2000.

Figure 10. Consumer expenditures on cereals by expenditure percentile in India

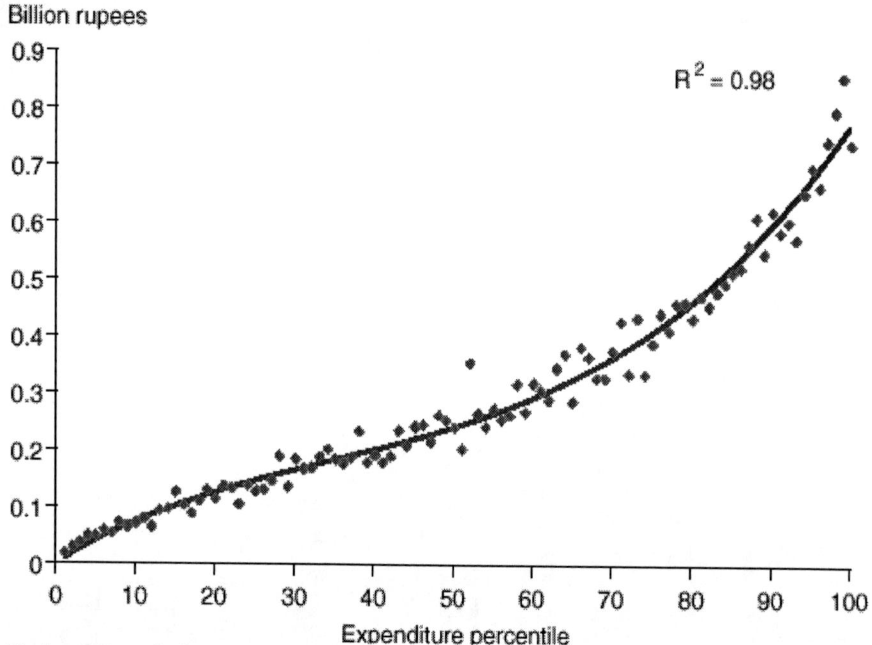

Source: National Samply Survey, 1999/2000.

Figure 11. Consumer expenditures on milk products by expenditure percentile in India

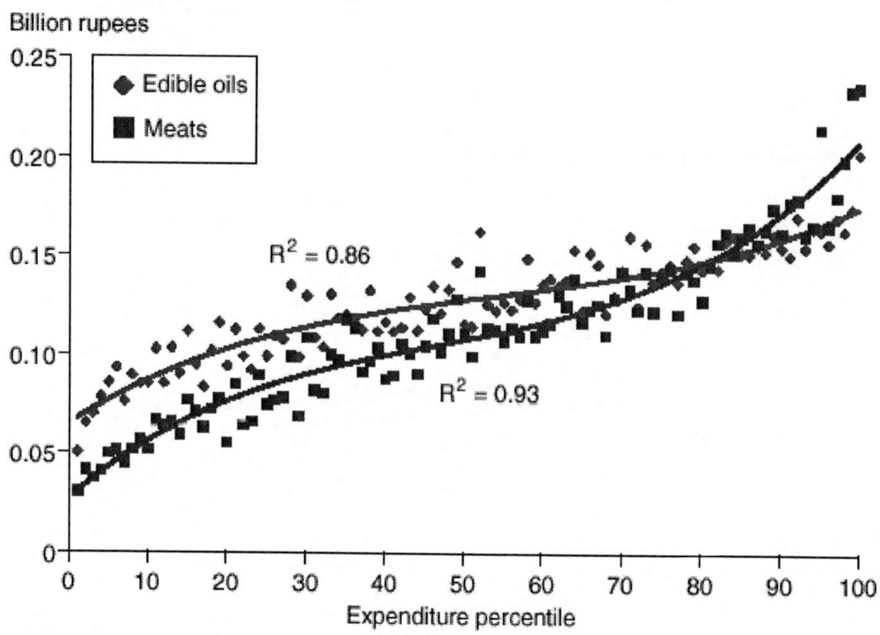

Source: National Samply Survey, 1999/2000.

Figure 12. Consumer expenditures on edible oils and meats by expenditure percentile in India

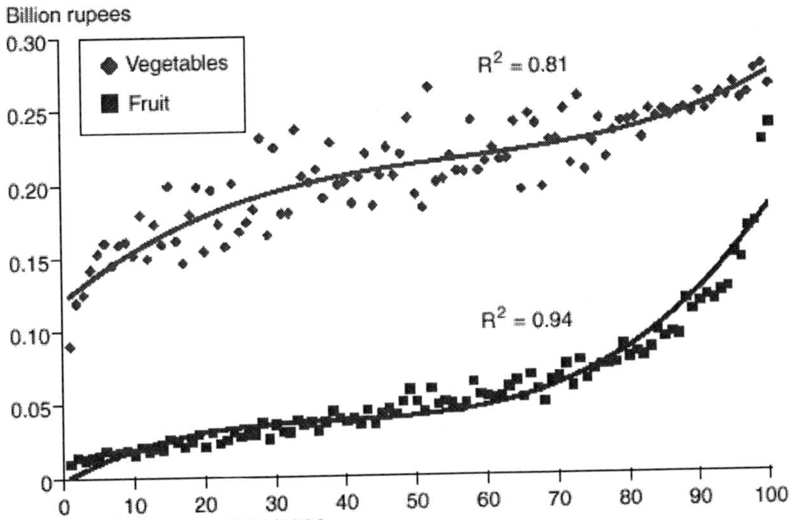

Source: National Samply Survey, 1999/2000.

Figure 13. Consumer expenditures on fruit and vegetables by expenditure percentile in India

Overall, the robust prospects for growth and diversification of food demand in India contrast sharply with sluggish agricultural investment. Constraining new investment in and for agriculture are policies that diminish incentives for both domestic and foreign investors, as well as infrastructure constraints that increase costs.

Policy Factors Affecting Investment

India's agricultural sector—including most aspects of agricultural production, marketing, processing, and trade—has traditionally been heavily regulated. Although an earlier study (Chand and Kumar, 2004) identified the importance of credit availability in driving private investment, a broader range of Indian policies and regulatory interventions is at play in shaping the environment for private investment by farmers and agribusiness. To the extent that regulatory and institutional disincentives for investment have resulted in inefficient markets, they can also limit the potential for farmers—including India's many small farmers—to benefit from and respond to signals from India's expanding and diversifying consumer markets.

The primary goals of regulation have been to enhance food security by ensuring adequate supplies of food staples at affordable prices and to support employment growth through labor-intensive import substitution. Historically, regulation of agriculture has included strict controls on foreign trade, domestic marketing and interstate movement of agricultural produce, the scale of agricultural processing firms, and land ownership (in addition to the taxation, labor, and investment measures that applied to all areas of the economy). While regulation has eased since the early 1990s, there has been less reform in agriculture than in the manufacturing or service sectors of the Indian economy.

India's Constitution vests the governments of India's 35 States and Union Territories with most of the authority to make and implement regulations and policies affecting the agricultural sector. Central government influence over the regulations and policies promulgated by the States stems largely from the extent to which States are dependent on the central government for funds. Many States tend to have unique regulations and policies, which complicates the regulatory climate facing agribusinesses when operating across State lines. The necessity for obtaining State-by-State legislation and implementation can also slow the process of reform.

India has made progress in reforming market interventions and improving the climate for private investment by farmers and agribusiness since the late 1990s. Plant-scale restrictions have been eliminated for most agribusinesses. Regulation of private movement and storage of farm produce is now less restrictive in many States, and restrictions on the private marketing of farm produce are undergoing reform in most States. Farmers and agribusiness face an improved credit environment. Business taxes are being reduced, food laws are being simplified, and tariff barriers, though high, are declining for some commodities. However, most reforms are being implemented gradually and the lack of a clear political consensus on reducing government intervention in agriculture is likely to continue to slow progress and create risk for investors. In addition, political sensitivity has prevented real progress in several key areas of concern to domestic and foreign investors, including easing restrictive labor laws and developing legal systems to support equitable and efficient rental and sale markets for agricultural land.

Overall, the analysis of individual factors below indicates that the regulatory and policy climate is becoming more supportive of new investment by farmers and agribusiness, but it is not clear if the completed reforms will be adequate to stimulate rapid growth in investment, or if the process of implementing reforms will be sustained.

The Essential Commodities Act

The Essential Commodities Regulation & Enforcement Act of 1955 (or ECA) authorizes the Central and State Governments to make broad ranging interventions in the markets for essential food products to ensure their availability and to protect consumers from possible exploitation by commercial traders (Government of India, Ministry of Consumer Affairs, Food, and Public Distribution, 2007). Under the ECA, Ministries and Departments of the Central Government may issue rules for regulating production, distribution, quality standards, movement, and pricing of essential commodities, including cereals, pulses, edible oils, and sugar. Regulations are implemented through "control orders" issued by State Governments, with monitoring and oversight by the Central Government.

The ECA gives authority to the Central and State Governments to intervene at any level of the supply chain, including:

- Regulating production or manufacture of essential commodities;
- Controlling the price at which essential commodities are bought or sold ;
- Prohibiting the withholding from sale of any essential commodity ordinarily kept for sale (stock holding limits);
- Restricting or preventing private movement of essential commodities across district or State borders.

Control orders under the ECA can be issued by State authorities at any time without Central or State legislative action. State governments may, for example, issue control orders when local prices of essential commodities rise sharply, or if there is suspicion of "hoarding" or black market activities by traders.

Although there is evidence that the imposition of ECA-related restrictions has been declining over time—perhaps because of improved local supplies of cereals and other foods—all States continue to have ECA laws and many have some operative controls over commodity storage and movement (World Bank, 1999). Examples include ongoing controls on the storage, sale, and movement of rice in the State of Tamil Nadu, and recent restrictions on wheat and pulse storage in the State of Maharashtra (Government of Tamil Nadu, 2007; Government of Maharashtra, 2007). Even with declining use, the continued existence of the legal authority to restrict commercial trading and movement of commodities is a source of risk for private investors.

Small-scale industry reservations

The small-scale industry (SSI) sector is a major component of the Indian economy, with about 3.6 million firms accounting for about 39 percent of total industrial value added, 20 million jobs, and 45 percent of total exports. From shortly after independence in 1947 until the late 1990s, most of the food processing sector was, by law, reserved for small-scale firms with a prescribed maximum investment. According to the Industries (Development and Regulation) Act of 1951, this policy was intended to promote the small- scale sector with two objectives: (1) ensuring increased production of consumer goods in the small-scale sector, and (2) expanding employment opportunities through small-scale industries (Government of India, Ministry of Micro, Small, and Medium Enterprises, 2007).

The limit for fixed capital assets for small-scale industries (SSIs) has been increased over time and is currently set at Rs 10 million (about $247,000). These limits effectively prevented the establishment of large-scale or vertically integrated food processing firms in the past, and continue to do so in the sectors that remain reserved for SSIs. Additionally, the manufacture of most agricultural machinery and many types of food processing machinery was reserved for SSIs before being "dereserved" during 1997-2007. These constraints limited the availability of modern farm equipment and food processing technology. Although some firms received waivers of SSI restrictions to operate larger enterprises, these special licenses have mostly been made available to firms exporting at least 50 percent of their output (Government of India, Ministry of Micro, Small, and Medium Enterprises, 2007).

Since 1997, when rice and wheat milling were removed from the SSI list, food processing industries reserved for the small-scale sector have grown fewer. At present, just six food processing industries remain on the reserved list (Government of India, Ministry of Micro, Small, and Medium Enterprises, 2007):

- Pickles and chutneys
- Bread
- Pastry
- Hard-boiled sugar candy
- Rapeseed, mustard, sesame, and groundnut oil (except solvent extracted)
- Ground and processed spices (other than spice oil and oleoresin spices).

Perhaps as important as SSI policies to the structure of Indian food processing and marketing are the very small-scale, "unorganized sector" firms. These small enterprises operate outside the legal, tax, and regulatory systems that are pervasive in agricultural processing and marketing, and account for about 75 percent of food processing industry output (Government of India, Ministry of Food Processing, 2007). The unorganized sector firms—which the State, local, and Central governments generally choose not to try to control—benefit from avoidance of taxes and regulations and are often competitive with both SSIs and larger firms in supplying small volumes of relatively low-quality goods.

Although only a few food processing industries continue to be reserved for the small-scale sector, the legacy of the SSI policy is an agricultural processing and marketing industry characterized by small, nonintegrated firms and a generally low level of technology. While this structure is beginning to change—with some former SSIs either supplying larger firms, expanding themselves, or closing—agribusiness investors currently face a general lack of competitive suppliers of intermediate goods and services, which may also discourage new investment.

State Agricultural Produce Marketing Committee Acts

Under the authority of India's Agricultural Produce Marketing Act of 1972 (and its amendments), most Indian States have similar acts (Agricultural Produce Marketing Committee, or APMC, Acts) that regulate the establishment of markets and the marketing of agricultural produce. These acts are intended to ensure that all (or most) trade between farmers and initial buyers occurs through a regulated market, primarily to protect farmers from unfair or exploitative trading practices. But the requirement to market all produce through the regulated markets also facilitates the collection of marketing taxes and fees for State and local governments.

The APMC policies have led to the establishment of more than 7,500 regulated markets in India, each operated by a local marketing committee and supported by the marketing fees collected on each transaction. Marketing fees typically range from 1 to 2 percent, on top of which a market levy is often imposed to support State or local investments in market infrastructure. In general, the quality of marketing infrastructure and services—including roads, marketing floor, weighing, storage, grading, and market information—is poor (Patnaik, 2006). Studies have also found that transactions in regulated markets, where licensed traders can have significant market power, often lack transparency and lead to exploitation of farmers (World Bank, 2006)

The Indian Government has acknowledged that policies established under the APMC Acts have hampered the development of India's agricultural markets and is now promoting reforms by the State governments (Government of India, Ministry of Agriculture, 2000). In addition to the cost, quality, and performance issues already noted, the policies have prevented private investment in agricultural markets and infrastructure, and have largely prevented development of coordinated or integrated market structures, such as contracting, that more directly connect farmers and buyers. Although some States have permitted contracts between growers and buyers for specific products, the APMC requirement to trade in regulated markets tended to prevent the emergence of contract farming. Although views differ, some analysts and policymakers have noted the potential advantages of contract farming in India, both in helping growers manage risk and in engaging the private sector in the delivery of inputs and technology (Birthal, 2007; Singh, 2007).

The Ministry of Agriculture is currently promoting the reform of State APMC regulations, including those impeding contract farming and private investment in primary markets, by urging States to conform to a new "model" agricultural marketing act (Government of India, Ministry of Agriculture, Department of Agriculture and Cooperation. 2007). Significant progress has been made in implementing the suggested policy changes, with 25 of India's 35 States and Union Territories having completed or partially completed the suggested reforms as of January 2007 (table 4). With these reforms and past waivers granted by States to specific enterprises, contract farming activities, particularly for horticultural crops and poultry, are becoming increasingly common. In addition, the recent initiatives by central and State governments to build new terminal markets in Punjab, Haryana, Chandigarh, and Madhya Pradesh, and by the National Dairy Development Board to build the new Safal fruit and vegetable market in Bangalore—all with majority private-sector ownership—indicate an improved climate for private investment (Sharma, 2007; Patnaik, 2006).

Table 4. Status of State Agricultural Produce Marketing Act reforms (as of January 2007)

Stage of reform	Number	States and Union Territories
Reforms completed as suggested by the model act.	12	Andhra Pradesh, Arunachal Pradesh, Chandigarh, Chattisgarh, Himachal Pradesh, Madhya Pradesh, Maharashtra, Nagaland, Orissa, Punjab, Rajasthan, Sikkim
Reforms suggested by the model act partially completed.	5	Delhi, Gujarat, Haryana, Karnataka, Uttar Pradesh
Existing act already provides for reforms suggested by the model act.	1	Tamil Nadu
No existing act; no reforms required.	7	Andaman & Nicobar Islands, Bihar, Dadra & Nagar Haveli, Daman & Diu, Kerala, Lakshadweep, Manipur
Reforms suggested by the model act initiated but not completed.	10	Assam, Goa, Jammu & Kashmir, Jharkhand, Meghalaya, Mizoram, Pondicherry, Tripura, Uttaranchal, West Bengal

Source: Ministry of Agriculture, Government of India, 2007.

Land tenure policies

Operational holdings of agricultural land in India are small and fragmented, reflecting the pressure of a large rural population on available cultivable land, as well as laws that set landownership ceilings and weak legal frameworks to support the sale and rental markets for farmland. About 63 percent of India's land is farmed in operational holdings of less than 4 hectares, and holdings are becoming more fragmented as farms are divided through inheritance (table 5). India's average operational holding of just 1.3 hectares is larger than in China and some other developing countries, but small relative to holdings in other major agricultural regions such as the United States, the EU, Brazil, Argentina, Canada, and Australia.

Such small operational holdings discourage agribusiness investment by complicating vertical coordination or integration by traders and processors because of the need to assemble produce from so many farmers. Throughout India, national and State laws prevent private companies, as opposed to individuals, from owning agricultural land except for specific approved purposes, such as producing seed or conducting scientific research. It is unclear whether Indian marketing firms and processors will be able to work successfully with large numbers of small farmers. If unsuccessful, this factor could limit the economic viability or scale of vertically integrated food marketing and processing enterprises.

Table 5. Distribution of Operational Agricultural Landholdings in India

Size	1995/96 Share of holdings	1995/96 Share of area	2000/01 Share of holdings	2000/01 Share of area
	Percent			
Marginal (< 1 hectare)	61.6	17.2	63.0	18.8
Small (1-2 hectares)	18.7	18.8	18.9	20.2
Semi-medium (2-4 hectares)	12.3	23.8	11.7	24.0
Medium (4-10 hectares)	6.1	25.3	5.4	23.8
Large (>10 hectares)	1.2	14.8	1.0	13.2

Source: Ministry of Agriculture, Directorate of Economics and Statistics, *Agricultural Statistics at a Glance 2006.*

With laws typically capping landholdings at 15-20 hectares, far above the current average holding size, progress in improving land rental markets may be an important step in allowing operational holdings to grow to more efficient scales. Land rental and tenancy laws vary by State, with relative freedom of land rental in some States (Assam, Punjab and Haryana), and a total ban on rentals in others (Bihar, Gujarat, Karnataka, Kerala, Manipur, Orissa, Rajasthan, Jammu & Kashmir and Uttar Pradesh). Lack of clear landownership records is often a key impediment to reform, although a number of States have made progress in land registration and computerization of land records. Also, legal frameworks often place landowners at risk by giving tenants ownership rights after land is rented and operated for several years. This precedent reportedly discourages the rental of farmland and results in near-term rentals that discourage investment in land improvement.

Some States, including West Bengal, have achieved success in improving tenant registration and strengthening land rental and sales markets. Recent policy statements—including the National Agricultural Policy, 2002, and 10th Five-Year Plan document—urge the reformulation of tenancy laws to encourage advanced commercialization of agriculture.

Credit policies

India's agricultural credit system—an extensive network of cooperative, public sector, and commercial banks—has significantly improved both the availability and terms of credit for agriculture and allied activities since the late 1990s. Following sluggish growth in availability during most of the 1990s, institutional agricultural credit has expanded about 19 percent annually in real terms since 2000, with private commercial banks accounting for most of the expansion (Figure 14). The surge in credit availability has been particularly strong since the announcement of a "Farm Credit Package" in 2004 that aimed at doubling farm credit within 3 years, but has exceeded its annual targets with increases of 37 percent and 40 percent in the first 2 years of implementation.

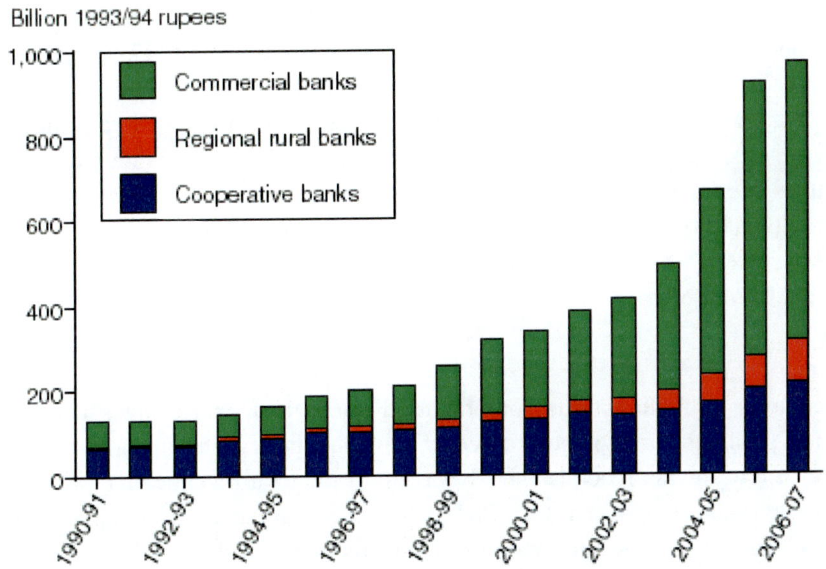

Source: Reserve Bank of India; Government of India, Ministry of Agriculture, Statistics at a Glance, 2006.

Figure 14. Direct institutional credit for agriculture and allied activities in India

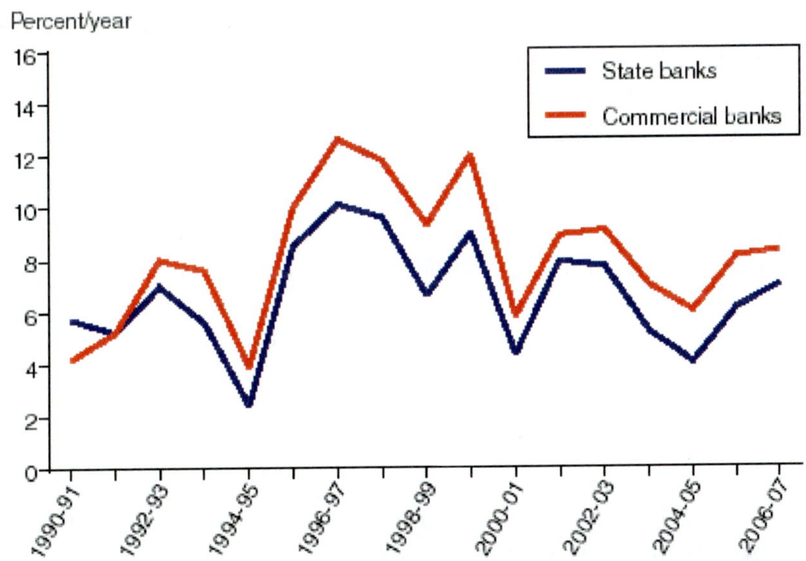

Source: Reserve Bank of India; Government of India, Ministry of Agriculture, Statistics at a Glance, 2006.

Figure 15. Prime real lending rates in India

An important mechanism for expanding the availability and use of credit by producers has been "Kisan (Farmer) Credit Cards." The cards were introduced in 1998 and, by 2006, were available to about 64.5 million farmers (Government of India, Ministry of Finance, Economic Survey, 2008). Despite the improved availability of institutional credit, about 41 percent of Indian farmers, often those with smaller landholdings, remain dependent on traditional moneylenders at other noninstitutional sources of credit (Government of India, Ministry of Statistics and Program Implementation, 2005).

Credit availability has also improved—and interest rates have generally declined—for business investors. Ensuring a supportive monetary and interest rate environment for investment has been a top policy priority of the Indian Government. Despite rapid economic growth, inflation has averaged about 5 percent and interest rates have generally declined since the late 1990s. Overall, business investors have enjoyed relatively low and stable real interest rates since 2000 (figure 15).

Tax policies

Indirect taxes, including tariffs on imported goods and excise taxes on domestically manufactured products, are a major source of government revenue in India, accounting for about 52 percent of the tax receipts and 41 percent of the total revenue receipts of the central government. Agricultural marketing and retail sales taxes are also important sources of State revenue. Declining excise tax rates and tariffs have reduced the share of indirect taxes in total government revenues since the early 1990s, while direct taxes on personal and business income have accounted for an increasing share of revenues.

In 2005, the Central and State governments began implementing a central value-added tax (VAT) system that will eventually unify the central excise and State sales tax systems across all States. The VAT system imposes taxes only on the value added at each step of the supply chain through a system of firm credits for taxes paid on purchased intermediate inputs, thus preventing the cascading of taxes on final products. Introduction of the VAT, together with simplification and reduction of State sales and marketing taxes and indirect taxes, will lower business costs, particularly for larger and integrated firms operating across multiple States.

Excise taxes. India's traditionally high excise taxes have been reduced significantly since economywide reform began in the early 1990s (Figure 16). The excise tax system has been steadily simplified with fewer basic rates, and peak tax rates have been reduced from 110 percent (ad valorem) in 1991 to 24 percent by 2004. However, despite declining rates, excise tax revenues have remained buoyant—growing more than 9 percent annually in real terms since 1999/2000—due to rising demand and improved tax compliance (Government of India, Ministry of Finance, *Economic Survey*, various issues).

Traditionally high excise tax rates for many processed agricultural products have also been reduced (table 6), stimulating demand through lower consumer prices and improving the investment climate for food processors. For "organized" sector firms—those that pay taxes—lower excise taxes will also improve their competitiveness with firms qualifying as small-scale industries, which receive concessional tax treatment, and with unorganized sector firms, which often pay little or no taxes.

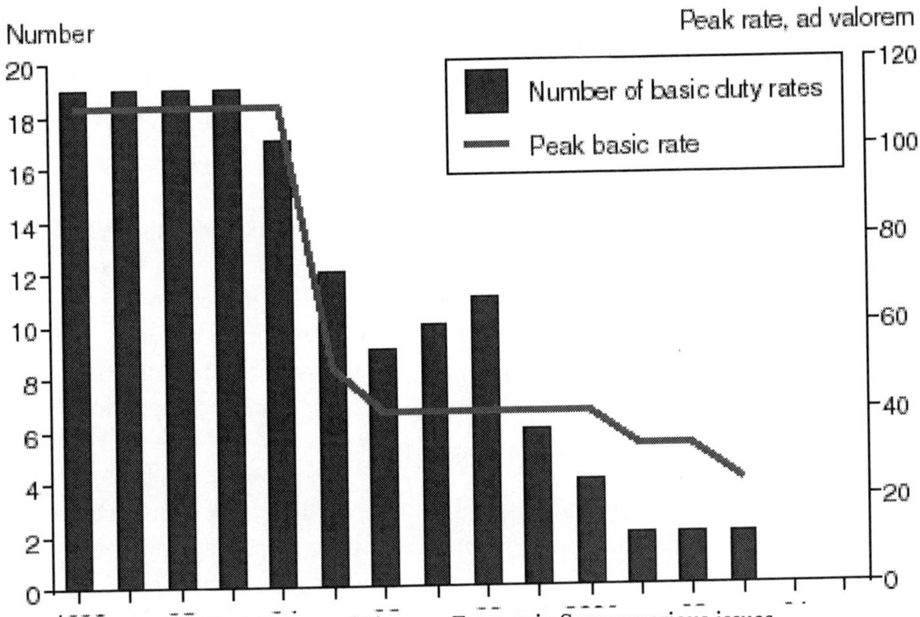

Source: Government of India, Ministry of Finance, Economic Survey various issues.

Figure 16. Trend in central excise taxation in India

Table 6. Changes in India's excise taxation of food products since 2001

Year and product	From	To
2001/02:		
Fruit & vegetable preps	16%	0
2002/03:		
Tea	2 rupees/kg	1 rupee/kg
2003/04:		
Branded, packed refined edible oils	0	8%
2004/05:		
Processed meat, fish, and poultry prod.	16%	8%
Cakes and pastries	8%	16%
2005/06:		
Surcharge on refined edible oils	1 rupee/kg	0
2006/07:		
Condensed milk	16%	0
Ice cream	16%	0
Processed meat, fish, and poultry prod.	8%	0
Pasta	16%	0
Ready-to-eat processed foods	16%	8%
2007/08		
Packed biscuits	16%	0

Source: Government of India, Ministry of Finance, Economic Survey, various issues.

State sales and agricultural marketing taxes. State taxes on retail sales and transactions in regulated agricultural markets are typically major sources of State revenue. Tax rates vary by State as well as by product. In 2005, prior to introduction of the value added tax (VAT) system, sales tax rates for processed agricultural products ranged from 8 to 23 percent, with most of the largest States imposing taxes of 12-16 percent. With the VAT, these rates will likely decline and converge across States, although it is not clear how quickly this will happen (World Bank, 2005).

Agricultural marketing taxes imposed on all agricultural produce at the first point of sale also vary significantly by State. These taxes typically include marketing fees of 1-2 percent and development or infrastructure "cesses" (fees) as high as 5 percent, on top of mandatory commissions and fees for cleaning, weighing, bagging, and other services paid to private agents in the market (World Bank, 2005). The reform of State Agricultural Produce Marketing Committee laws—already underway—may create more competition with private markets and eventually reduce these fees.

Direct taxes. India has also taken steps to extend direct tax incentives to the food processing industry. In 2004/05, the Government announced a package of incentives for new firms that process, preserve, and package fruits and vegetables, including a 5-year waiver of direct taxes plus a 25- percent reduction in taxes for the next 5 years. In 2005, India also increased tax incentives for the development of Special Economic Zones (SEZs) and for firms, including agro-processing firms, operating in SEZs, among them:

- Duty-free import of goods for development, operation, and maintenance of SEZ units;
- 100-percent income tax exemption on exports from SEZ units for the first 5 years, 50-percent exemption for years 6-10, and a 50-percent exemption of reinvested export profits for years 11-15;
- External commercial borrowing by SEZ units up to $500 million/year, without restriction, through recognized banking channels;
- Exemption from central Government sales and service taxes;
- Exemption from State sales taxes and other State levies.

As of April 2008, six new food and agri-processing SEZs have been approved. How quickly the SEZ policy will improve investment in these sectors is uncertain due to ongoing disputes over the acquisition of land— particularly agricultural land—to accommodate the SEZs.

Tariff policy

Import tariffs have also been simplified and reduced since the early 1990s (Figure 17). Peak tariffs—the rates charged for the most highly protected products—for nonagricultural goods dropped from 300 percent in 1991 to 12.5 percent by 2006. In agriculture, import access has improved due to the removal of quantitative restrictions in 2001 and some reductions in applied tariffs, but bound agricultural tariffs remain high relative to other sectors of the Indian economy, and relative to most other countries. Although the Government has been reluctant to reduce agricultural tariffs that protect India's many small farmers and small-scale agribusinesses, many agricultural tariffs are now set well below World Trade Organization bound rates (table 7). There has been a tendency in recent years to reduce tariffs when domestic shortages lead to significantly higher consumer prices for essential food commodities. Setting applied tariffs well below bound rates has led to India's emergence as a major importer of pulses and vegetable oils since the 1990s. More recently, India has reduced its applied tariffs for wheat and corn to zero and sharply lowered its tariffs on palm oil products to help augment domestic supplies and stabilize prices.

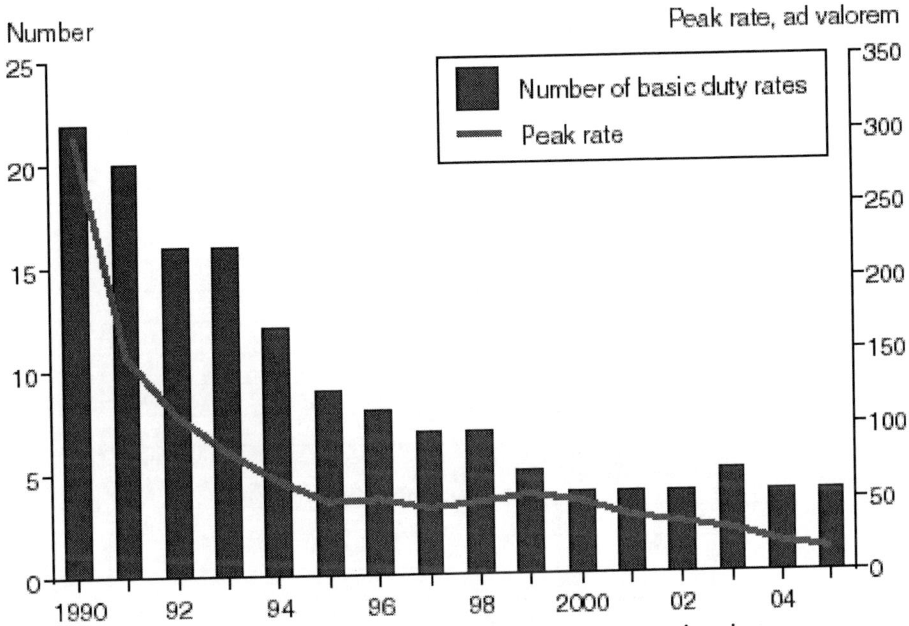

Source: Government of India, Ministry of Finance, Economic Survey various issues.

Figure 17. Trend in nonagricultural tariffs in India

Reduced tariff protection presents both challenges and opportunities for investors in agriculture and agribusiness. On the challenge side, lower tariffs imply more competitive pressure to reduce costs and improve quality through increased scale, improved technology, and vertical integration. Reduced agricultural tariffs may tend to discourage some new investment aimed at serving rising domestic demand. However, competitive pressure could foster gains in efficiency and quality that allow agriculture and agribusinesses to expand in both domestic and global markets. Some agribusinesses may benefit from freer trade in raw materials and intermediate products. For example, greater access to imported oilseeds could benefit producers and consumers by allowing greater oilseed processing efficiency (Persaud and Landes, 2006). And, access to competitively priced feed can be critical to contain production costs and maintain growth in consumption and production of poultry meat and eggs (Landes et al., 2004).

Table 7. India's bound and applied tariffs for selected agricultural products

	Bound rate	Applied rate[1]
	Percent	
Grain and oilseeds		
Pulses	100	0
Wheat	100	0
Rice	70	70
Corn	70	0
Oilseeds	100	30
Horticulture		
Apples	50	50
Oranges, lemons, grapes	100	30
Potato	100	30
Onions	100	5
Meats		
Poultry, whole	100	30
Chicken, leg	150	100
Processed products		
Wheat flour	150	0
Milk powder	60	60
Cheese	40	30
Sugar	150	60
Frozen vegetables	150	30
Oilcake	100	15
Crude soybean oil	45	40
Crude palm oil	300	45
Refined soybean oil	45	45
RBD palm olein	300	52.5

[1]As of January 2008.
Source: Ministry of Agriculture, Directorate of Economics and Statistics, *Statistics at a Glance, 2007.*

Labor policies

Under the Indian constitution, labor law is on the "concurrent list," giving both the Central and State governments the authority to enact legislation on most labor matters. India's comprehensive labor laws—aimed primarily at protecting the rights of employees—are often seen as a disincentive to new investments by larger, organized sector firms. For example, firms with more than 100 employees are required to obtain government permission before laying off workers and can remain obligated to pay workers even after a unit has gone out of business. There are approximately 45 central government laws addressing labor practices and roughly four times that number of additional laws enacted by States (Basu, 2006). Some of the major central government laws are:

- Workmen's Compensation Act, 1923: Specifies compensation to be paid in case of injury or death of a worker.
- Payment of Wages Act, 1936: Specifies when and how wages must be paid and what deductions are permitted.
- Industrial Employment (Standing orders) Act, 1946: Requires employers to clearly define the conditions of employment in conformance with model "standing orders"

dealing with worker classification, holidays, shifts, payment of wages, leaves, termination etc.

- Industrial Disputes Act, 1947: Provides for investigation and settlement of disputes; sets conditions for laying off workers.
- Minimum Wages Act, 1948: Sets minimum wages for all employees.
- Employees Provident Fund and Miscellaneous Provisions Act, 1952: Requires minimum employee and employer contributions to "Provident Fund" or retirement accounts.
- Maternity Benefit Act, 1961: Requires payment of maternity benefits and/or medical bonus and maternity leave for women employees.
- Payment of Bonus Act, 1965: Requires payment of specified bonuses to employees of firms with 20 or more employees.
- Payment of Gratuity Act, 1972: Requires payment of specified gratuity, or separation allowance, to employees of firms with 10 or more employees, (Embassy of India, 2007).

Significant reform to India's labor laws to give employers more flexibility in hiring and laying off workers has proven difficult at the central government level, but several States have made changes to support growth in the information technology industry or to attract foreign investment. To avoid falling under the purview of these laws, many larger firms prefer hiring contract labor or organizing into a number of units small enough to avoid the regulations. Locating within an SEZ, where labor laws are sometimes less restrictive, may also be increasingly attractive to new investors.

Food laws

Until the new Food Safety and Standards Bill was passed in August 2006, India's food processing industry was subject to regulation by eight government ministries administering more than a dozen legislative acts dating as far back as 1954. The complex, overlapping, and sometimes contradictory regulatory environment was seen as a deterrent to investment and innovation in food processing.

The 2006 bill, which awaits implementation, consolidates the laws relating to food and establishes a Food Safety and Standards Authority of India to set science-based food standards and regulate the manufacture, import, processing, distribution, and sale of food. The "Food Authority" is to be established in the Ministry of Health and supported by scientific committees and panels in setting standards. According to the legislation, the goal is to have an effective and transparent regulatory framework that will allow the food industry to work efficiently and attract investment. The new legislation is to be enforced by State Governments, State Commissioners for Food Safety, and local government bodies.

Foreign direct investment policy

Indian investment rules currently permit FDI up to 100 percent ownership in most sectors, and in most cases with automatic approval. This includes investment in India's Export Oriented Units and, more recently, in India's planned Special Economic Zones. Key agricultural areas where FDI is currently not permitted (Government of India, Ministry of Finance, Union Budget, various issues) are:

- Retail trading, except for wholesale trading and single-brand retailing.
- Agricultural production, except for floriculture, horticulture, development of seeds, animal husbandry, fisheries, cultivation of vegetables under controlled conditions, tea plantations, and services related to agriculture and allied sectors.
- Housing and real estate.

Foreign investors and firms can enter India as either incorporated or unincorporated entities. Incorporated firms can be established through joint ventures with existing firms, or as wholly owned subsidiaries of foreign companies. Unincorporated entities can take the form of liaison, project, or branch offices of foreign firms. All profits, dividends, and foreign investment may be freely repatriated, except for special cases where nonresident Indians invest in specific schemes that do not permit repatriation (Government of India, Ministry of Commerce and Industry).

Restrictions on agricultural production and, particularly, multi-brand retailing likely deter some foreign firms from investing in Indian agribusiness. In the absence of a competitive and efficient domestic food retailing industry, the inability to integrate forward into retailing likely reduces the potential profitability of investments in food supply chains by multinational retailers. However, it is likely that foreign investors are as discouraged— and perhaps even more so—by the same regulatory and policy disincentives faced by domestic firms investing in agribusiness.

Infrastructure Factors Affecting Investment

The climate for agribusiness investment in India is also shaped by the availability, quality, and costs of various infrastructural services required by agricultural producers, traders, and processors. In general, India's transport, power and water infrastructure, while often available at low cost, is of poor quality. Similarly, the institutions that provide important agricultural services, such as market information and grading/inspection services, are generally considered to be weak, while the agricultural research and extension system is criticized for being unresponsive to emerging needs of the farm sector. These infrastructural and institutional deficiencies impose additional costs and risks for new investors.

Power

India's economy labors under a chronic shortage of electrical power. During 2003-2005, the average energy deficit was more than 7 percent and the average peak shortage was about 11 percent, gaps that have not been closed significantly in the last decade. About 64 percent of India's power is generated by thermal plants, 25 percent from hydroelectric facilities, 8 percent from wind and other renewable sources, and 3 percent from nuclear plants (Ministry of Power, 2008). Plans to reduce the energy deficit by expanding public and private investment in power generation and transmission are ambitious, but have generally fallen below target.

Low cost recovery is a fundamental problem of the power sector, leading to underinvestment in new generation and transmission capacity, as well as poor maintenance of existing capacity. Large subsidies on household and agricultural power use, together with significant theft, are key sources of low cost recovery. Power rates for agricultural uses are heavily subsidized throughout India, while industrial users are charged high power rates that cross-subsidize agricultural and household users. Overall, however, the average power tariff accounts for only about 70 percent of the costs of generation and transmission (table 8).

Power costs for both agricultural and household (domestic) uses in India are low by international standards (figure 18). This cost advantage for farmers and farm households is at least partially offset by power rationing, frequent power interruptions, and voltage fluctuations that damage pumps and make water supplies unreliable. In addition, India's power subsidies are hastening the depletion of groundwater resources due to the low cost of operating electric irrigation pumps (Gulati and Narayanan, 2003).

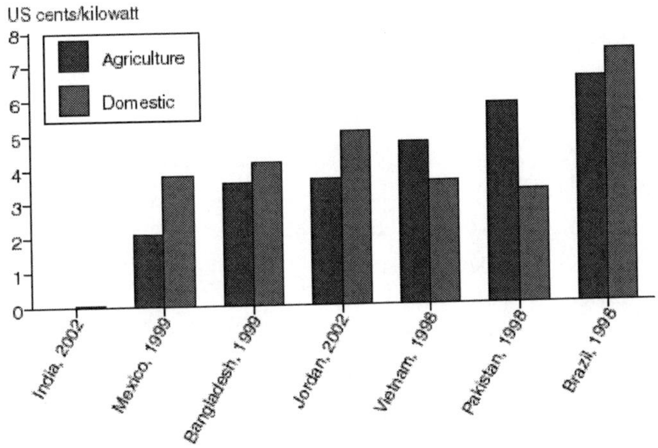

Source: Kapoor and Barnes, 2003.

Figure 18. Agricultural and domestic (household) power tariffs, selected countries

Table 8. Estimated average power tariffs and costs in Indian States, 2001-02

Category	India average	Andhra Pradesh	Uttar Pradesh	Rajasthan	Tamil Nadu	Haryana
	Rupees per kilowatt-hour					
Agriculture	0.42	0.14	1.19	0.46	0.01	0.48
Domestic	1.95	1.74	1.81	1.90	1.81	2.80
Industry	3.79	4.41	4.82	3.95	3.95	4.51
Overall	2.40	2.22	2.59	2.21	2.37	2.25
Cost of supply	3.50	3.61	3.83	3.68	3.09	4.12

Source: Planning Commission, May 2002.

The industrial and commercial sectors account for about 36 percent of India's power use, compared with 29 percent by agriculture, 21 percent by households, and 14 percent by other users. However, because of problems with power availability and quality and the high cost of power to industrial users, a growing number of firms (and households) are investing in their own "captive" power generation facilities to supplement supplies from the power grid. Captive power capacity is estimated to be about 20,000MW, or 16 percent of the total capacity operated by public utilities (Hindu Business Line, 2005; Government of India, Ministry of Power, 2008).

In June 2003, the Government of India enacted the Electricity Act, which provides a framework for comprehensive power sector reforms. The act authorizes the Central Government to harmonize central and State laws, enforce national policies, and establish a competitive environment for the power sector. Power generation no longer requires a license, and new rules are established to strengthen transmission and support private investment in power generation and distribution. The act progressively reduces cross-subsidies and moves tariffs toward the actual cost of supply. Progress on power reform has been mixed. Additions to generating capacity are expected to meet only 57 percent of the current 5-year planning target, while the weighted-average power tariff increased 13.4 percent between 2003 and 2007, led by large hikes in agricultural tariffs (Government of India, Ministry of Finance, Economic Survey, 2006/07).

Transportation

More than two-thirds of India's domestic freight is transported by road, with the remainder shipped primarily by rail. Although India has an extensive rail transport system, the use of road transport grew from 51 percent of all freight in 1991 to 67 percent by 1998. Users have grown to regard road transport as more readily available, reliable, and cost-effective than rail transport (Cook et al., 1999; World Bank, 2005a).

India's road freight transport sector, while competitive and low-cost compared with other countries (Figure 19), tends to be slow and unreliable. For example, average transit time for the 1,408-kilometer (875 mile) trip between Delhi and Mumbai is 3 days, and for the 2,019-kilometer (1,255 mile) trip from Delhi to Bangalore it is 4-5 days, both about twice the time that would be expected in the United States. Slow and unreliable transit times stem from low speeds associated with poor roads and mixed traffic, lack of urban bypasses, and delays for inspection and fee collection at internal border checkpoints. Checkpoint delays alone typically account for 15-25 percent of the transit time (World Bank, 2005a).

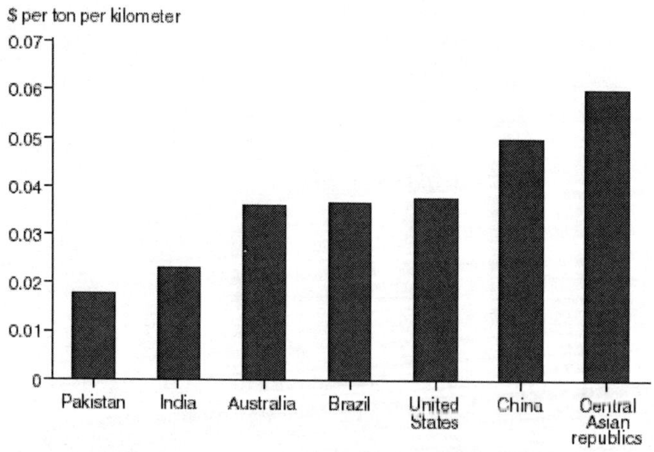

Source: World Bank, India Road Transport Service Efficiency Study, Energy and Infrastructure Operations Division, South Asia Regional Office, November 1, 2005.

Figure 19. Average truckload freight rates in selected countries, 2002

Both road and rail transport systems have very limited capacity for bulk handling and transport of agricultural commodities. With a few exceptions, cereals, oilseeds, and other basic agricultural commodities in India are handled and transported in gunny sacks via standard, multi-purpose trucks or railway wagons. Refrigerated rail or road transport of perishable agricultural products is also limited. However, private investment in refrigerated road transport is growing, with subsidized financing available through government programs.

Water

Growth in irrigated area has boosted Indian farm output through both higher yields and increased cropping intensity. About 54 million hectares—or 30 percent of all agricultural land—is now irrigated, making India second only to China in irrigated area (figure 20). The largest share of and most of the growth in irrigated area is associated with private investment in wells and diesel/electric pumps for groundwater irrigation. Power subsidies have prompted the expansion of groundwater irrigation. Surface-water irrigation—which is dependent on public investment in dams, reservoirs, and canals—accounts for about a third of irrigated area, a share that has been declining. Rising public investment costs for new surface-water projects, together with the cost of subsidies for canal water, are contributing to the slowed growth of surface irrigation. In some areas, particularly in north India where intensively irrigated wheat and rice have become common, agriculture is increasingly threatened by water logging and salinity problems associated with high rates of canal irrigation and extraction of groundwater (Gulati and Narayanan, 2003; Gulati et al., 2005).

With the expansion of irrigation, agriculture now accounts for 84 percent of total water use in India (Government of India, Planning Commission, 2002). Many regions face a growing challenge as agricultural, industrial, and household uses compete for water resources. Industrial uses now account for 3-5 percent of water use, about half from surface-water and half from groundwater sources. While most States promise adequate water supplies as part of their industrial policies, highly water-dependent industries tend to locate facilities only in water-surplus areas. Water demand by domestic and industrial users is projected to grow 27 percent and 14 percent, respectively, between 2010 and 2025 (Rosegrant et al., 2002), necessitating more government emphasis on water use regulation, pricing of water, and water resource development.

Agricultural research and extension

India has one of the largest public sector agricultural research and extension systems in the world, as well as a growing private sector research and extension industry. Both public and private research and extension have been important factors in agricultural productivity growth in India, with public research accounting for about 30 percent of total factor productivity growth between 1956 and 1987 and private sector research accounting for about 11 percent (Evenson et al., 1999).

The public agricultural research system—governed by the Indian Council for Agricultural Research (ICAR)—includes 47 central research institutes, 32 national research centers, and 37 State agricultural universities with more than 30,000 research staff (Government of India, Ministry of Agriculture, Indian Council of Agricultural Research, 2007). ICAR and the public research system have been criticized for failing to adapt research priorities to the changing economic and scientific environment for agriculture (Government of India, Planning

Commission, 2005; World Bank, 2004). Key issues include making research more demand based to meet the needs of an increasingly diverse agricultural consumption basket, adapting research and extension to new agricultural technologies, and developing more effective public-private research partnerships. A new multi-year National Agricultural Innovation Project funded by the World Bank seeks to address these issues through research capacity building and the formation of public-private consortia focusing on research questions across agricultural supply chains.

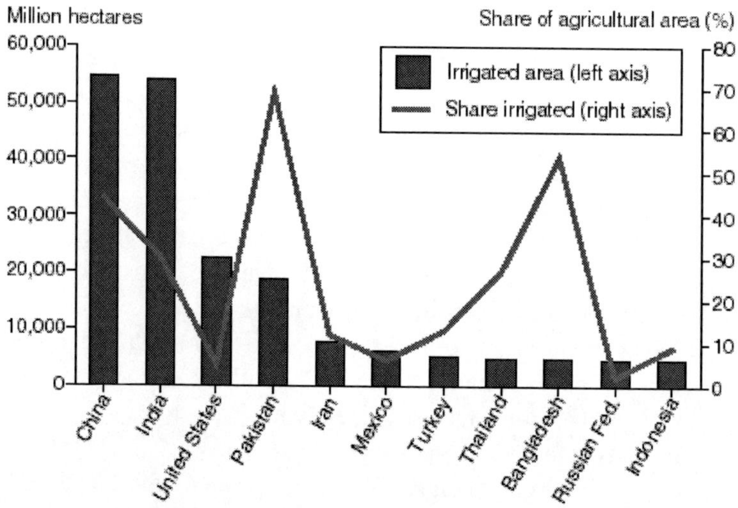

Source: Food and Agriculture Organization, FAOSTAT database.

Figure 20. Countries with the largest irrigated area

Private sector participation in agricultural research is increasing. Government efforts to promote biotechnology research and recent steps to strengthen and clarify intellectual property protections—including passage of the Plant Variety Protection and Farmers' Rights Act (2002) and formulation of the National Seed Policy (2002) and the National Seed Act (in draft)—provide an impetus for private sector involvement in research. At present, private sector research tends to focus on higher value crops (Bt cotton, Bt eggplant, etc.) and on plant types (hybrid seeds) with high expected returns to private investment.

Historically, public investment in agricultural research in India has been low relative to many other countries (Figure 21), but investment has increased since the late 1990s (figure 22). During 2000-2007, available data indicate that public investment grew about 6 percent annually in real terms, implying a continued increase in investment as a share of agricultural output.

Public agricultural extension is primarily the responsibility of State governments, and has been much criticized for lack of effectiveness (Government of India, Ministry of Agriculture, Department of Agriculture and Cooperation, 2002; Planning Commission, 2005). Key problems include under-staffing, lack of coordination, and difficulty in shifting from the historical focus on food grain production to a more diverse set of crop and marketing issues. The Government's New Policy Framework for Agricultural Extension (2002) seeks to instill a new approach that concentrates on increasing farm household income through agricultural diversification. The goal is to make the extension system more market-oriented and farmers more competitive in domestic and international markets.

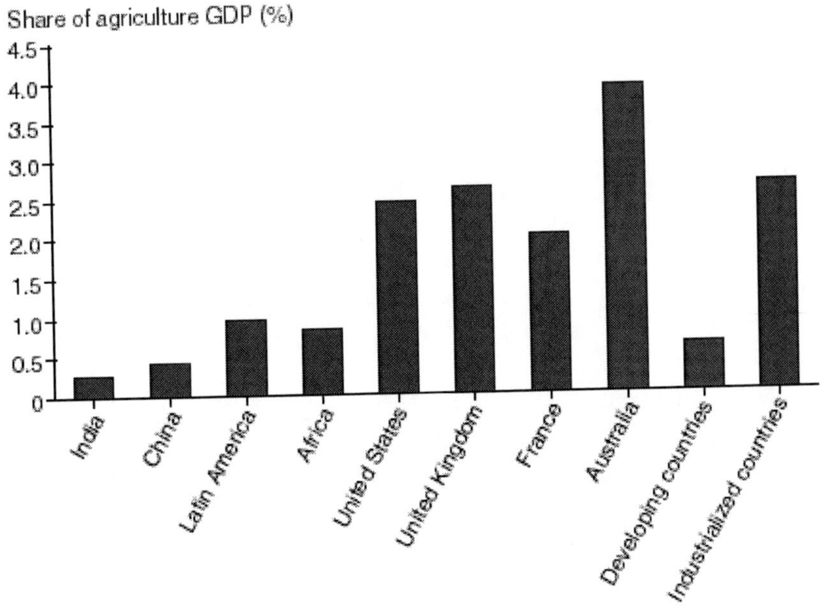

[1] 1995 data for all countries except the United States (1993) and Australia (1994).
Source: Pal and Byerlee, 2003.

Figure 21. Public agricultural research expenditures in selected countries and regions[1]

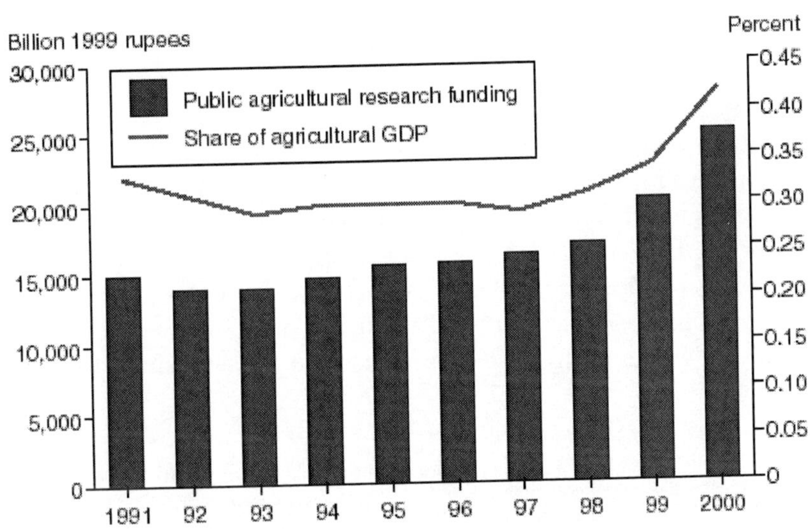

Source: Pay and Byerlee, 2003.

Figure 22. Public agricultural research funding in India

Along with the government effort to strengthen and improve funding for public extension services, private companies and nongovernmental organizations (NGOs) are becoming more active in providing extension services. Models employed by private firms and NGOs include fee-for-service extension, extension linked to input supply or marketing services, and extension linked to contract farming or vertical coordination (World Bank, 2004).

Cold chain capacity

Although cold chain capacity is expanding due to public and private investments, India's capacity for cold storage and refrigerated transport of perishable food products is limited. Cold storage capacity in 2006 was 21.7 million tons, reflecting growth of about 11 percent since 2004 (Government of India, Ministry of Food Processing, 2007). As of 2003, approximately 90 percent of total cold storage capacity was used to store potatoes, with other fruit and vegetable products accounting for about 7 percent and dairy products about 1 percent.

Only a few integrated cold chains are established in India, including two serving the dairy industry (Gujarat Cooperative Milk Marketing Federation, and Mother Dairy Foods Processing Ltd), one serving the franchises of McDonald's India, and Snowman Frozen Foods Ltd, which operates the only countrywide cold storage and refrigerated transport network. Most cold storage and refrigerated transport capacity is operated by small, nonintegrated firms that do not make use of state-of the-art technology or management practices (U.S. Trade and Development Agency, 2006).

A number of programs now aim at expanding investment in cold chain capacity:

- A capital investment subsidy scheme for construction, expansion, and modernization of cold storage for produce is being implemented by the National Horticulture Board of the Ministry of Agriculture. Between 2001 and 2004, this scheme facilitated private investment in about 4.7 million tons of new cold storage capacity (Government of India, Ministry of Agriculture, Department of Agriculture and Cooperation, 2005).
- The Central Warehousing Corporation (CWC), the largest owner of warehouse capacity in India, is developing a large cold storage facility near Delhi, with plans to develop other modern cold storage facilities throughout the country.
- The Agricultural Processed Food Products Export Development Authority (APEDA), part of the Ministry of Commerce and Industry, is promoting the development of world-class perishable cargo facilities at air cargo terminals.
- The Container Corporation of India Ltd is building cold storage units across the country, as well as refrigerated containers, to support agricultural exports.

Institutional services for agriculture

Many of the institutional services needed to support agricultural markets are in the early stages of development in India. In some cases—such as grades/standards and market information—the services have been the responsibility of government agencies that have not adapted to provide the services needed by expanding and diversifying markets. In other cases— such as futures trading—government policies that have regulated markets to protect consumers or farmers have prevented or slowed the evolution of market services.

Grades and standards. The Agricultural Produce (Grading and Marketing) Act of 1937 empowers the Government to fix quality grades, authorize commodity grading, specify labeling and packaging requirements, and confiscate substandard produce. In practice, government decisions on grades and standards issues are seldom rendered in cooperation with the private sector. Although government agencies establish and revise grades and standards for many commodities, there are generally no inspection services in Indian markets and commodities are seldom bought and sold based on these grades and standards. Most Indian grain, for example, is traded based on the broad standard of "fair-to-average quality (FAQ)" with no formal grading, although some private buyers and sellers trade grains at premiums or discounts to the FAQ price based on their independent quality assessments.

Market information. There is a critical shortage of objective, reliable, and timely public information on most major Indian commodity markets, including traded volumes and prices, production, consumption, and stock levels. Although public market reporting by the Ministry of Agriculture and State governments is improving, current reporting includes a limited range of variables—mostly wholesale prices and production estimates—of uncertain quality. The lack of adequate public market information tends to raise the transaction costs and price risk faced by market participants, creates the potential for information asymmetry between large and small players in the market, likely reduces marketing efficiency, and limits information available to support policy formulation. Several private sector firms now sell market information based on their proprietary data collection, and others provide marketing data through their village-level agricultural service centers.

Futures trading. The Government removed its longstanding prohibition on futures trading in most agricultural commodities in 2003/04, leading to the immediate formation of several exchanges to trade futures contracts in major farm commodities (Government of India, Ministry of Finance, Union Budget, 2004/05). However, except for a few commodities that have had a longer history of futures trading—most importantly soybean oil, which has been traded since 2000—traded volumes remain small compared with overall market size and contracts often lack liquidity, thus limiting the utility of the markets for hedging risk.

While the availability of futures contracts and traded volumes have tended to increase, there continues to be concern over the impact of speculators and unscrupulous traders on the stability of consumer prices for essential commodities. In 2006/07, a government panel determined that futures market activity was contributing to a runup in consumer wheat and rice prices, leading the Government to announce a cessation of wheat and rice trading in February 2007, which remains in effect (U.S. Department of Agriculture, Foreign Agricultural Service, 2007). As a result of limited contract liquidity and uncertain government policy, prospective investors in agricultural production, marketing, and processing enterprises continue to face limited and uncertain access to risk management tools.

PROSPECTS FOR AGRICULTURAL INVESTMENT

Continued sluggish private investment in Indian agriculture and agribusiness since the early 1990s, despite sustained high growth in consumer incomes and food demand, suggests that policy and infrastructure factors have been a deterrent to new investment. Historically, extensive policy intervention in markets and industries has created disincentives and risks for investments in agriculture, including farmers and agribusinesses, and particularly large-scale vertically integrated agribusinesses.

During much of the 1990s, agricultural trade and price policies resulted in taxation of agricultural production despite substantial and rising farm subsidies. At the same time, movement, storage, and private marketing restrictions for agricultural commodities, scale restrictions on agribusinesses, high taxes on processed products, the high cost of credit, and complex food laws were among the disincentives and risk factors facing investors. This uncertainty was compounded by weak transport and power infrastructure and lack of key market services such as market information, risk management tools, and grading/inspection systems. Through the late 1990s, public investment in agriculture remained sluggish despite rising food demand, while more public funds went to meet the rising cost of subsidies on food grains and farm inputs.

Since 2000, however, there is evidence that the policy environment is improving and that investment in agriculture and agribusiness is beginning to strengthen. Movement and storage restrictions on essential commodities are less common, plant scale limitations have been largely removed, State marketing laws are beginning to permit development of private marketing channels, and taxes on agricultural products are being reduced and simplified. And, although power, transport, and other infrastructure problems will likely be solved only in the longer term, private investment is seemingly on the rise. Private investment in food marketing ventures has increased noticeably in the last several years (table 9). These new ventures collectively amount to $ 10-$20 billion over the next 5-7 years to develop supply chains and "front-end" retail outlets. This activity represents a turnaround in investor confidence.

Recent investment in India's food marketing sector includes a number of ventures by foreign investors, including a Wal-Mart collaboration with the Indian conglomerate Bharti. Since India does not permit foreign direct investment (FDI) by multi-brand retailers, foreign investment has taken the form of wholesale (or "cash and carry") trading enterprises, or partnerships with Indian "franchisees" who own the retail outlets. Other than multi- brand retailing, all other areas of agricultural processing and marketing are open to FDI. While the FDI restrictions on retailing may be deterring some foreign investment in agricultural marketing, the increased activity in chain food retailing by many of India's largest domestic companies indicates their confidence in a supportive policy environment.

While there is evidence that the investment climate is improving for agriculture and agribusiness and that private investment is beginning to respond, it is unclear how quickly or how much agricultural productivity and marketing efficiency will respond. If rapid income growth is sustained, the growth and diversification of food demand will likely continue to outpace production for the next several years, leading to continued pressure on domestic food prices and demand for imports. However, given India's extensive land and water resources and low current farm yields, there is scope to expand output of many farm products and become more globally competitive in the longer term.

Table 10. Growth of India's chain food retailing industry, 2007

Retailer	Year entered	Ownership	Formats	Outlets/plans	Locations
Nilgiri's	1971	Local (Part ownership by Actis, UK)	Supermarkets, convenience stores	40; plans for 500 stores by 2010	Major cities in south India
Trinethra & Fabmill	1986	Local (Aditya Birla Group)	Supermarkets, convenience stores	170	Major cities in Andhra Pradesh, Tamil Nadu, Karnataka, and Kerala
Margin Free	1994	Local Cooperative (Consumer Protection and Guidance Society)	Discount stores, supermarkets	350	Major cities in Kerala, Tamil Nadu and Karnataka
Spencers	1996	Local (RPG Group)	Hypermarkets, supermarkets, convenience stores	97; plans to add 50 hypermarkets by 2008	Major cities in South India
Subhiksha	1997	Local (Subiksha Trading Services Pvt. Ltd.)	Discount stores	520; plans for 1,200 stores all over the country by 2007/08	Major cities in Tamil Nadu, Andhra Pradesh, and Pondicherry, and Delhi region
Foodworld	1999	Local (Subsidiary of Dairy Farm International)	Supermarkets	55; plans to expand in south India	Bangalore, Hyderabad
Trumart	2001	Local (Pyramid Retail)	Supermarkets, convenience stores	29; plans for 90 stores by end of 2007	Maharashtra and Gujarat; Bangalore, Chennai, Hyderabad, and Kolkata
Food Bazaar	2002	Local (Future Group)	Hypermarkets, supermarkets	90; Plans for 250 stores by 2010	National (major met-ros and large cities)
Metro Cash & Carry*	2003	Foreign (Metro AG, Germany)	Wholesale "cash & carry"	3; plans to add 15-18 new outlets by 2009	Bangalore, Hyderabad, Mumbai, Kolkata, Chennai

Table 10. (Continued)

Retailer	Year entered	Ownership	Formats	Outlets/plans	Locations
My Dollar Store	2004	Local (Franchisee of My Dollar Store of the U.S.)	Convenience stores	50; plans for 400 stores by 2010	Nationwide
Shoprite	2004	Local (Subsidiary of Shoprite (PTY) Ltd., South Africa)	Hypermarket	1; plans to add 2-3 new outlets by 2007	Mumbai
Star India Bazaar	2004	Local (Trent; division of Tata Group)	Hypermarket	3; plans to add 23-	Nationwide
Reliance Retail	2006	Local (Reliance Industries Ltd.)	Hypermarkets, supermarkets, convenience stores	230; plans for 3,000 stores, 2,500 super-markets and 500 hypermarkets by 2010	Nationwide
Spinch	2006	Local (Wadhawan Retail)	Supermarkets	89; plans to add 1,500 stores in 90 cities by 2010	Nationwide
Max Hypermarkets	2007	Local-foreign joint venture (Spar International, Neth.)	Hypermarkets	Plans to develop 7 stores by 2009	Nationwide
Bharti[1]	2007	Local (Bharti Enterprises)	Hypermarkets, supermarkets	Plans to invest $2.5 billion by 2014	Nationwide
Bharti Walmart	2007	Local-foreign joint venture (Wal-Mart USA)	Wholesale "cash & carry"	Plans for 15 stores by 2014	Nationwide

[1]Retail partner of Walmart.

Source: U.S. Department of Agriculture. Foreign Agricultural Service. 2006; updated from various press reports.

REFERENCES

Banco Central do Brasil: Anuário Estatístico do Crédito Rural, 2007. http://www.agricultura.gov.br/images

Basu, K. (2006). "*Why India's Labour Laws Are a Problem*," BBC News, 18 May. http://news.bbc.co.uk/2/hi/south_asia/4984256.stm

Birthal, Pratap. (2007). "Conditions for Success of Contract Farming," NCAP-USDA-IFPRI Workshop on *Contract Farming: Methods and Experiences,* New Delhi, May 5-6.

Chand, R. & Kumar, P. (2004). "Determinants of Capital Formation and Agriculture Growth: Some New Explorations," *Economic and Political Weekly, V.39 (52)*: 5611-5616.

Chand, R. (2000). "*Emerging Trends and Regional Variations in Agricultural Investments and Their Implications for Growth and Equity*," NCAP Policy Paper No. 11, New Delhi.

Cook, P. D., Das, S. Aeppli A. & Martland, C. (1999). "Key Factors in Road-Rail Mode Choice in India: Applying the Logistics Cost Approach," in *Proceedings of the 31st Winter Simulation Conference, Vol. 2*, ACM Press (NY), pp. 1280-1286.

Evenson, R. E., Pray, C. & Rosegrant, M. W. (1999). *Agricultural Research and Productivity Growth in India*. Research Report 109. International Food Policy Research Institute, Washington, DC.

Government of India. Embassy of India (Washington, DC). (2007). *Labour Laws.* http://www.indianembassy.org/newsite//Doing_business_In_India/ Labor_Laws . asp

Government of India, Ministry of Agriculture. 2007. "Status of Market Reforms in Agriculture (APMC Act amendments) as of 3 1st January, 2007." http://agricoop.nic.in/PolicyIncentives/progress.pdf

Government of India, Ministry of Agriculture, Department of Agriculture and Cooperation, (2005). http://agricoop.nic.in/ncpm.htm

Government of India. Ministry of Agriculture. Directorate of Economics and Statistics. (2003). *Report of the Committee on Capital Formation in Agriculture*, March. http://agricoop.nic.in/Capital%20Formation/FinalReport.doc

Government of India, Ministry of Agriculture. (2003). *Report of the High- Level Expert Committee on Cold Storage and Storage*, Nov.

Government of India, Ministry of Agriculture, 2002. *Report of Inter- Ministerial Task Force on Agricultural Marketing Reforms*. May 27. http://agmarknet.nic.in/taskrep.htm

Government of India, Ministry of Agriculture, (2000). *National Agricultural Policy.* http://agricoop.nic.in/agpolicy02.htm

Government of India, Ministry of Agriculture, Department of Agricultural Research and Education, Indian Council of Agricultural Research. (2004). *Annual Report, 2003/04.*

Government of India, Ministry of Agriculture, Department of Agriculture and Cooperation. (2007). *Model Rules*, http://agricoop.nic.in/FINAL%20Model%20Rule%20as%20 corrected%20on%2007%20 11 %20 07.pdf

Government of India, Ministry of Agriculture, Department of Agriculture and Cooperation, Extension Division. 2002. *Policy Framework for Agricultural Extension.*

Government of India, Ministry of Commerce and Industry. Department of Industrial Policy and Promotion. (2003). *Foreign Direct Investment in India—Policy and Procedures*, New Delhi, May. http://dipp.nic.in/manual/manual_0403 .pdf

Government of India, Ministry of Finance. *Economic Survey*, various issues. Government of India, Ministry of Finance. *Union Budget*, various issues.

Government of India, Ministry of Consumer Affairs, Food, and Public Distribution, Department of Consumer Affairs. (2007). *Essential Commodities Act, 1955*, http://fcamin.nic.in/Events/EventDetails.asp?EventId=600&Section=Acts%20and%20Rules&ParentID=0&Parent= 1&c heck=0#

Government of India, Ministry of Food Processing. (2007). Answer to parliamentary question, August 21.

Government of India, Ministry of Micro, Small, and Medium Enterprises. 2007. http://www.laghu-udyog.com/ssiindia/statistics

Government of India, Ministry of Power. 2006. *Annual Report 2005/06*.

Government of India, Ministry of Statistics and Program Implementation, 2005. *National Sample Survey, 59th Round; (2005), Situation Assessment Survey of Farmers: Indebtedness of Farmer Households*, May. http://mospi.nic.in/rept%20_%20pubn/ftest.asp?rept_id=498&type=NSSO

Government of India, Ministry of Statistics and Program Implementation, (2005). *National Sample Survey, 61st Round; 2004-2005*. http://mospi.gov.in/mospi_nsso_rept_pubn.htm

Government of India, Planning Commission. *Annual Reports*, various issues.

Government of India, Planning Commission, Agriculture Division. (2005). *Report of the Task Group on Revamping and Refocusing of National Agricultural Research*, Jan.

Government of India, Planning Commission, Power and Energy Division. (2002). *Annual Report (2001-02)*, May.

Government of Maharashtra; Food, Civil Supplies and Consumer Protection Department. (2007). Mantralaya, Mumbai, India, March 7. http://fcs.maharashtra.gov.in/data/gr/marathi/2007/03/07/20070309103540001.pdf

Government of Tamil Nadu. (2007). http://www.tn.gov.in/rti/proactive/cfcp/control_essential_trade_articles_regulation.pdf

Gulati, A., Meinzen-Dick, R. & Raju, K. V. (2005). *Institutional Reforms in Indian Irrigation*. International Food Policy Research Institute, Sage Publications, New Delhi.

Gulati, A., & Narayanan, S. (2003). *The Subsidy Syndrome in Indian Agriculture*. Oxford University Press, New Delhi, 297 pages.

Hindu Business Line. (2005). "*Govt to Tap India Inc's Captive Power Capacity*," May 16. http://www.thehindubusinessline.com/2005/05/16/stories/200505 160 1950300.htm

Joshi, P. K., Gulati, A. & Birthal, P. S. (2007). "Agricultural Diversification in India: Status, Nature and Pattern," in *Agricultural Diversification and Smallholders in South Asia*, P.K. Joshi, A. Gulati, and R. Cummings Jr (eds.), Academic Foundation, New Delhi, pp. 219-242.

Kapoor, S. & Barnes, D. (2003). "*Agricultural Pricing and Rural Electrification in India: Some International Comparisons*." Draft Paper, World Bank, Washington, DC.

Landes, M.R. (2004). "The Elephant Is Jogging: New Pressures for Agricultural Reform in India," *Amber Waves 2(1)*, 28-35, Feb., U.S. Department of Agriculture, Economic Research Service, http://www.ers.usda.gov/AmberWaves/February04/pdf/features_elephant.pdf

Landes, R., & Gulati, A. (2004). "Farm Sector Performance and Reform Agenda," *Economic and Political Weekly* (Mumbai), Aug. 7-13, pp. 3611- 3619.

Landes, M., Persaud, S. & Dyck, J. (2004). *India's Poultry Sector: Development and Prospects,* Agriculture and Trade Report No. WRS04- 03, U.S. Department of Agriculture, Economic Research Service, Feb. http://ers.usda.gov/publications/WRS0403/

Mullen, K., Orden, D. & Gulati, A. (2005). *"Agricultural Policies in India: Producer Support Estimates, 1985-2002."* MTID Discussion Paper No. 82, International Food Policy Research Institute, Feb.

National Bureau of Statistics of China. 2006. *China Statistical Yearbook,* http://www.stats.gov.cn/tjsj/ndsj/2006/indexeh.htm

Pal, S., & Byerlee, D. (2003). *"The Funding and Organization of Agricultural Research in India: Evolution and Emerging Policy Issues,"* Policy Paper 16, National Centre for Agricultural Economics and Policy Research (ICAR), New Delhi, India, February.

Patnaik, G. (2006). *"State Level Marketing Reforms: A Status Report, Federation of Indian Chambers of Commerce and Industry,"* Oct. www.ficci.com/media agri/SessionI/GokulPatnaik.pdf

Persaud, S., and M. Landes. 2006. *The Role of Policy and Industry Structure in India's Oilseed Markets,* Economic Research Report No. 17, U.S. Department of Agriculture, Economic Research Service, April. http://ers.usda.gov/publications/err17/

Pingali, P. & Y. Khwaja. (2004). *"Globalization of Indian Diets and the Transformation of Food Supply Systems,"* Keynote Address, 17th Annual Conference, Indian Society of Agricultural Marketing, Hyderabad, Feb. 5-7.

Reserve Bank of India. (2007). *Handbook of Statistics on Indian Economy*, Sept.

Sharma, Ashok B. (2007). "Punjab, Haryana, Madhya Pradesh Likely to Have Modern Terminal Markets," *Financial Express* (India), Aug. 26. http://www.financialexpress.com/news/Punjab-Haryana-Madhya-Pradeshlikely-to-have-modern-terminal-mkts/2 12766/).

Singh, Sukpal. (2007). "*Understanding Contract Farming in India: Models and Learnings*," NCAP-USDA-IFPRI Workshop on Contract Farming: Methods and Experiences, New Delhi, May 5-6.

Srinivasan, P. V., Jha, S. & Landes, M. (2007). *Indian Wheat and Rice Sector Policies and the Implications of Reform*, ERR-41, Economic Research Service, U.S. Department of Agriculture, May.

U.S. Department of Agriculture, Foreign Agricultural Service. (2007). *India: Agricultural Situation, Weekly Highlights and Hot Bites*, #9 Gain Report IN- 7018, March 2. http://www.fas.usda.gov/gainfiles/200703/146280326.pdf

U.S. Department of Agriculture. Foreign Agricultural Service. (2006). *India Report: Retail Food Sector*, Gain Report IN- 6111, Dec. 12, http://www.fas.usda.gov/gainfiles/200612/146269832.pdf

U.S. Trade and Development Agency. (2006). *India Cold Chain Improvement Program: Definitional Mission Report*, USTDA-06-Q-21-143, Arlington, VA.

World Bank. (2007). World Development Indicators Database.

World Bank. (2005a). *India Road Transport Service Efficiency Study*. Energy and Infrastructure Operations Division, South Asia Regional Office, Nov.

World Bank, (2005b), *Review of India Agricultural Marketing*. WB0262, Programme of Advisory Support Services for Rural Livelihoods, Department for International

Development, Final Technical Output, Nov. http://www.passlivelihoods.org.uk/default.asp?project_id=254

World Bank. (2004). *Re-energizing the Agricultural Sector to Sustain Growth and Reduce Poverty*. Report No. 27889-IN, Rural Development Unit, South Asia Region, Washington, DC, July 30.

World Bank. (1999). *India Foodgrain Marketing Policies: Reforming to Meet Food Security Needs, Vols I & II*. Rural Development Sector Unit, South Asia Region, Washington, DC, Aug. 17.

World Bank. (1998). *India*: *Water Resources Management Sector Review*; *Groundwater Regulation and Management Report*. Washington, DC.

End Notes

[1] Calculation of representative growth rates in Indian agriculture is complicated by weather-induced fluctuations in annual performance. To minimize the influence of these fluctuations, growth rates are calculated between endpoints based on 3-year average levels of agricultural GDP (see table 1).

[2] Agricultural exports grew just 8 percent annually during the same period, but agricultural exports continue to average about double the size of agricultural imports.

[3] The same pattern of growth across food groups is reflected in consumer survey data collected for selected years by India's National Sample Survey Organization (Government of India, Ministry of Statistics and Program Implementation). The FAO data used here provide broader commodity coverage within food groups and allow use of more stable 3-year average endpoints when computing annual growth rates.

In: Conditions for Foreign Direct Investment in India
Ed: Brent M. Cardenas and Zackary R. Berg
ISBN: 978-1-60456-862-2

Chapter 4

OPENNESS TO FOREIGN INVESTMENT - 2009 INVESTMENT CLIMATE STATEMENT - INDIA

Bureau of Economic, Energy and Business Affairs

OPENNESS TO FOREIGN INVESTMENT

India continues controlling foreign investment with limits on equity and voting rights, mandatory government approvals, and capital controls. Since 1991, as it has slowly implemented a program of economic reform, the GOI has gradually relaxed many of these constraints. Nonetheless, a complex array of restrictions remains, along with an undercurrent of resentment towards foreign investment from some quarters. Foreign direct investment (FDI) is still prohibited in some sectors or sub-sectors.

Since the mid 1990s, India has allowed "automatic" FDI approvals in many sectors, gradually expanding the list over time. Where applicable, foreign investors do not need government licenses or approvals and simply notify the Reserve Bank of India (RBI) of their investments. Other sectors require approval by either the Foreign Investment Promotion Board (FIPB) or the Cabinet Committee on Foreign Investment. Under the Government approval route, applications for FDI proposals, other than by Non-Resident Indians and proposals for FDI in Single Brand product retailing, are received in the Department of Economic Affairs of the Ministry of Finance. Proposals for FDI in Single Brand product retailing and by NRIs are received in the Department of Industrial Policy and Promotion, Ministry of Commerce and Industry. The rules vary from industry to industry and are frequently changed.

Although the changes have tended toward greater liberalization, the investment process is not always transparent or straightforward. In January 2005, for example, the GOI relaxed restrictions on new FDI in India by foreign partners of joint ventures. The previous rules, issued in Press Note 18 in 1998, had required a release by the Indian partner and GOI approval for any new investment, a provision often subject to abuse. The new rules maintain restrictions on the majority of existing joint ventures, but leave new ones to negotiate their own terms on a commercial basis. A local firm's ability to restrict its foreign partner's business strategy has been reduced, but exit strategies and dissolution procedures for existing joint ventures remain uncertain.

Equity caps for foreign portfolio investment are sometimes included in FDI caps. There are no universal rules specifying the combination of FDI and foreign portfolio investment allowed in share holding of a particular company. In some cases, the portfolio investment is included within the FDI cap; in others, foreign portfolio investment is not subject to the FDI cap, although the government of India does spell out where different caps are in place. The GOI is planning to formulate uniform guidelines on FDI across all sectors. An amendment to the Companies Act denies voting rights to foreign investors holding preferred stock in Indian companies if their holdings exceed the FDI limit.

Foreign investment is prohibited in many areas or subsectors of real estate, multi-brand retailing, legal services, security services, nuclear energy, and railways. Some forms of realty development, such as integrated townships, are permitted FDI. Non-Resident Indians (NRIs), however, are allowed to invest in housing and real estate development. They are also allowed to hold up to 100 per cent equity in civil aviation companies, where foreign equity is otherwise limited to 49 percent. NRIs are allowed to claim dual citizenship and enjoy new investment opportunities in India as citizens. Capital outflow restrictions for Indian citizens are incrementally being relaxed.

To curb the flow of funds by Indian residents through their NRI counterparts overseas, the Indian government in 2003 banned all investments by Overseas Corporate Bodies (OCBs -- a company or other entity owned by NRIs directly or indirectly to the extent of at least 60 percent) in Indian companies through the portfolio as well as FDI routes. The GOI also withdrew the facility of opening and maintaining new Non-Resident External accounts, foreign currency non-resident accounts and non-resident ordinary accounts in India by OCBs. A ban on OCB investment in the stock market under the portfolio investment scheme remains in place.

The GOI's privatization policy permits foreign investors to bid for the sale of the state-owned units. Its privatization program, however, stalled after a change in government in May 2004. Foreign investors are given national treatment at the time of initial investment or after the investment are made. In sectors where licensing is required, procedures do not discriminate against foreign companies. However, in certain consumer goods industries export obligations and local content requirements are imposed on foreign investors.

Existing companies can also use automatic FDI approval to obtain foreign equity for FDI/NRI investment, provided the sector falls under the "automatic" route. Requirements are (i) the equity increase must accompany an expansion of the company's equity base (i.e., the NRI/foreign investors cannot simply acquire existing shares); (ii) the investment must involve a foreign currency remittance; and (iii) the Indian company's Board of Directors must give its approval.

Sector-Specific Guidelines for FDI in key industries (alphabetical order):

Advertising and Films: 100 percent FDI with automatic approval is allowed, but certain conditions apply in film industry.

Agriculture: No FDI is permitted in farming, nor may foreigners own farmland. FDI in the seed industry/ floriculture, horticulture, animal husbandry, aquaculture and cultivation of vegetables and mushrooms is permitted without any limits under the automatic route. 100

percent FDI is also permitted in tea plantations, but proposals require prior government approval. However, there is compulsory divestment of 26 percent equity of the company in favor of an Indian partner or the Indian public within five years. In Floriculture/Horticulture/ Aquaculture/Seed Development/Services related to agro and allied products, 100 percent FDI is allowed through the automatic approval process without any condition.

Airport Infrastructure: 100 percent FDI allowed for fresh projects through automatic route. FDI up to 74 percent is allowed in existing projects through the automatic route; for higher FDI in existing projects FIPB approval is required. To participate in a ground handling business at the airports, foreign companies can hold up to a 74 percent share. NRIs are allowed 100 percent FDI in ground handling services. 100-percent FDI is allowed on automatic route for maintenance and repair organizations, flying training institutes and technical training institutes.

Alcoholic Distillation and Brewing: No FDI limit is applicable. The automatic approval route is available in this area but a license from the GOI is required.

Asset Reconstruction Companies: FDI is limited to 49 percent. Prior government approval is required. No portfolio investments are allowed. Where any individual investment exceeds 10 percent of the equity, the approval is subject to Securitization and Reconstruction of Financial Assets and Enforcement of Security Interest Act, 2002.

Nuclear energy: FDI is limited to 74 percent for mining and mineral separation, integration, and value addition in mining and mineral separation. FIPB approval is subject to guidelines issued by Department of Atomic Energy.

Automobiles: No FDI caps or local content requirements or export obligations are applicable. FDI in automobile manufacturing is allowed under the automatic approval route.

Banking: The FDI limit for private banks is 74 percent, including all foreign portfolio investments. Automatic approvals are granted, however, no individual foreign bank may own more than 5 percent in an Indian bank, and no non-bank, foreign or otherwise, may own more than 10 percent without prior approval of the Reserve Bank of India. For state-owned banks, the FDI limit remains at 20 percent. At all times, at least 26 percent of the paid up capital must be held by residents. Wholly owned subsidiaries of foreign banks are exempt from this requirement. The Foreign Institutional Investment (FII) limit remains at 49 percent. Foreign banks in India have the option to operate as branches of their parent banks or as subsidiaries. Shareholders of banking companies may exercise their voting rights to a maximum of 10 percent of equity, even if they hold more equity. Legislation to remove this voting rights cap is stalled in Parliament.

Broadcasting: FDI (including portfolio investments) is limited to 20 percent in FM terrestrial broadcasting, with prior government approval, subject to guidelines issued by Ministry of Information and Broadcasting. For direct-to-home broadcasting and up-linking hubs, foreign investment from all sources is limited to 49 percent (with a maximum FDI component of 20 percent), again with prior government approval. In satellite broadcasting also, FDI is limited to 49 percent with prior government approvals. TV channels, irrespective of the ownership or management control, have to up-link from India provided they comply with the broadcast code. FDI is limited to 26 percent (including portfolio investment) in news and current affairs channels up-linking from India. 100 percent FDI is permitted in entertainment and general interest channels. Under the revised Up-linking policy announced by the GOI in December 2005, FDI up to 49 percent is permitted with prior approval of the Government for setting up Up-linking HUB/Teleports.

Cable Network: FDI is limited to 49 percent (inclusive of both FDI and portfolio). Prior approval is required and the approval is subject to Cable Television Networks Rules, 1994.

Cigars/cigarettes of tobacco: There is no FDI limit but prior government approval and an industrial license is required.

Civil Aviation (domestic airlines): FDI is limited to 49 percent under the automatic route for air transport services including domestic scheduled passenger airlines. For non-scheduled/chartered/cargo airlines, the FDI limit is 74 percent. Helicopter services are allowed 100 percent FDI on automatic approval basis. Foreign airlines are allowed to own the equity of companies operating helicopter services/cargo services, however, they may not make either a direct or indirect investment in an Indian domestic airline. NRIs and domestic companies may own 100 percent of a domestic airline. Although frequently debated, India has yet to open its state-run international airlines to outside investment. The US-India "Open Skies" agreement, signed in April 2005, allows unrestricted access by U.S. carriers to the Indian market, and by India carriers to the U.S. market. 100 percent FDI is permitted to new and existing airport construction projects under the automatic route subject to Ministry of Civil Aviation regulations. Existing projects, however, have to seek FIPB approval beyond 74 percent FDI.

Coal/Lignite: FDI is allowed up to 100 percent in coal processing plant/power projects, but limited to 74 percent for exploration and mining for captive consumption. Proposals in private sector companies are approved automatically. FDI is limited to 49 percent in state-owned units.

Coffee Processing and Warehousing: 100 percent FDI is permitted under the automatic route without any condition.

Commodity exchanges: Overall FDI of up to 49 percent (including FII) is allowed with prior government approval, however, FDI equity limit is 26 percent. FII purchases are restricted to secondary market subject to certain conditions.

Construction Development Projects: Construction and maintenance of roads, highways, vehicular bridges, tunnels, ports and harbors, housing, commercial premises, resorts, educational institutions, infrastructure and township is allowed at 100 percent FDI, with automatic approval subject to certain minimum capitalization, minimum area of development conditions issued under Press Note 2 of 2005.

Courier Services other than distribution of letters: 100 per cent FDI is permitted; however, FIPB approval is required.

Defense and strategic industries: FDI is limited to 26 percent, subject to a license from the Defense Ministry and guidelines on FDI in production of arms and ammunition. There are no automatic approvals.

Drugs/Pharmaceuticals: FDI is allowed up to 100 percent for drug manufacturing on automatic approval route

E-commerce: FDI up to 100 percent is allowed in business-to-business e-commerce with no divestment requirements. FDI is limited to 49 percent under the automatic approval route. No FDI is allowed in retail e-commerce.

Hazardous chemicals: 100 percent FDI is allowed through the automatic approval route. However, a license is needed.

Food Processing: 100 percent FDI is allowed with automatic approval for most products with the exception of malted foods, alcoholic beverages including beer, and in a protected category reserved for "small scale industries" where foreign equity ownership up to 24 percent is allowed. FDI up to 74 percent is allowed with automatic approval for cold storage facilities.

Health and Education Services: FDI is limited to 51 percent with automatic approval. Higher equity proposals need FIPB approval.

Hotels, Tourism and Restaurants: FDI at 100 percent is allowed with automatic approval.

Housing/Real Estate: No FDI is permitted in the retail housing sector. NRIs, however, may invest up to 100 percent. FDI up to 100 percent, on prior government approval, is permitted for projects such as the manufacture of building materials and the development of integrated townships, including housing, commercial premises, resorts, and hotels.

Industrial explosives: FDI at 100 percent on automatic route is allowed subject to obtaining license from appropriate authorities.

Information Technology: FDI at 100 percent is allowed with automatic approval in software and electronics, except in the aerospace and defense sectors.

Insurance: FDI is limited to 26 percent in the insurance and insurance brokering. While FDI approval is automatic, a license must first be obtained from the Insurance Regulatory and Development Authority. In July 2004, the GOI announced its intention to increase the FDI cap to 49 percent, but this change first requires parliamentary approval of an amendment to the Insurance Regulatory and Development Authority (IRDA) Act. In December 2008, the GOI introduced this amendment bill in the upper House of the Parliament (Rajya Sabha).

However, the introduction of the bill is the first step in a lengthy process and an increase in the FDI limit to 49 percent would take effect only after approval from both Houses of Parliament.

Investing companies in infrastructure sector other than telecommunication sector: FDI at 100 percent is allowed with prior government approval subject to sector-specific conditions.

Legal services: No FDI is allowed. The GOI is currently engaged in consultation with local law associations for exploring possibilities of opening up the sector to foreign lawyers.

Lottery, Gambling, Betting: No FDI in any form is allowed.

Manufacturing: FDI at 100 percent is allowed, with automatic approval, in the manufacture of textiles, paper, basic chemicals, rubber, plastic, non-metallic mineral products, metal products, ship building, machinery and equipment. FDI had been limited to 24 percent in a protected category reserved for "small scale industries" (SSI), but the government announced in December 2007 that it intended to remove that cap and allow SSI FDI caps to be governed by the overall FDI policies in their sectors. The FDI change had not yet been made effective as of December 2008. The government has been steadily decreasing the number of industry sectors reserved under the SSI policy - from a peak of 800 industries in the late 1990s - and currently reserves just 35 specific goods/services for SSIs with a capital investment of less than $250,000. A higher percentage of foreign equity may also be approved if the company obtains a license and undertakes to export 50 percent or more of its product.

Mining: 100 percent FDI is allowed, with automatic approval, for diamond and precious stone, gold/silver and other mineral mining.

Non-Banking Financial Companies (NBFCs - Merchant banking, underwriting, portfolio management, financial consulting, stock-brokerage, asset management, venture capital, credit rating, housing finance, leasing & finance, credit card business, foreign exchange brokerage, factoring and custodial services, investment advisory services): FDI is allowed up to 100 percent with automatic approval. For joint venture operating NBFCs, subsidiaries for undertaking other NBFC activities are allowed. Foreign investors can set up 100 percent operating subsidiaries without any conditions if they bring in $50 million in capital. Capital norms are as follows: if FDI is less than 51 percent, $500,000 needs to be provided up front; if FDI is between 51 percent and 75 percent, $5 million must be invested up front; and if FDI exceeds 75 percent, $50 million is needed, out of which $7.5 million must be fronted and the balance invested in two years. Approvals may not be used to undertake holding company operations pertaining to downstream investments.

Petroleum: FDI limits (along with tax incentives, production sharing and other terms and conditions) vary according to the sub-sector. Foreign Investment Promotion Board (FIPB) approval is required for refining with public sector unit; automatic approval is granted to all other activities.

- Discovered small fields 100 percent
- Unincorporated joint venture 60 percent
- Incorporated joint venture 51 percent
- Refining with domestic private 100 percent
- Refining with public company 49 percent
- Petroleum product/pipeline 100 percent
- Marketing and marketing infrastructure 100 percent
- LNG Pipeline 100 percent
- Exploration 100 percent
- Investment Financing 100 percent
- Market study and formulation 100 percent

Pollution Control: FDI up to 100 percent is allowed with automatic approval for equipment manufacture and for consulting and management services.

Ports and harbors: FDI up to 100 percent with automatic approval is allowed in construction and manufacturing of ports and harbors.

Power: FDI up to 100 percent is permitted with automatic approval in projects relating to electricity generation, transmission, distribution, and power trading other than nuclear reactor power plants.

Print Media: Foreign investment is restricted to 26 percent for news publications with editorial/management control in the hands of resident Indians. 74 percent cap is applied to non-news publications. FDI is permitted up to 100 percent in printing Science and Technology magazines/journals, subject to prior government approval and guidelines issued by Ministry of Information and Broadcasting.

Professional services: FDI is limited to 51 percent in most consulting and professional services, with automatic approval. Legal services, however, are not open to foreign investment.

Railways: FDI is not allowed in train operations, although 100 percent FDI is permitted in auxiliary areas such as rail track construction, ownership of rolling stock, provision of container services, and container depots.

Retailing: The government allows 51 percent FDI for retail trade in Single Brand products, subject to Government approval. FDI is still not allowed in any other retail activities, including in retailing of goods of multiple brands where the same manufacturer produces such branded products. However, large multinational retailers are exploring franchise-like joint venture deals with Indian partners that do not violate the FDI bar.

Roads, Highways, and Mass Rapid Transport Systems: FDI up to 100 percent is allowed with automatic approval for construction and maintenance.

Satellites: FDI is limited to 74 percent for the establishment and operation of satellites with prior government approval.

Shipping: FDI is limited to 74 percent with automatic approval for water transport services.

Special Economic Zones: For setting up the Zones and for setting up individual units in the SEZs, 100 percent FDI is allowed through the automatic route, subject to Special Economic Zones Act, 2005 and India's Foreign Trade Policy.

Stock Exchanges: FDI including FII up to 49 percent is allowed in stock exchanges through FIPB approval. FDI limit is 26 percent and FII ceiling is 23 percent. No single foreign investor can hold more than 5 percent stake.

Telecommunications: FDI limits are listed below. FDI can be made directly or indirectly in the operating company or through a holding company subject to licensing and security requirements. FDI up to 74 per cent is allowed under the automatic route in all telecom services; higher FDI needs FIPB approval. All FDI limits are inclusive of portfolio investments. The revised GOI guidelines on telecom services mandate Indian shareholding not less than 26 percent in any case. The Department of Industrial Policy and Promotion's Press Note No. 3 of 2007 sets out new security conditions which have to be adhered to by prospective investors in the telecom sector.

- National and International 74 percent
- Long Distance 74 percent
- Equipment manufacturing 100 percent (automatic approval)
- Global Mobile Communication 49 percent
- Radio paging, Internet Service 74 percent Providers (ISP) with international
- gateways and end-to-end bandwidth

ISP without international 100 percent gateways, voice-mail and e-mail (FDI proposals above 49 percent require GOI approval, 26 percent divestment within 5 years)

Trading/Wholesale: FDI at 100 percent is allowed through automatic route, for activities like exports, bulk imports with export warehouse sales, as well as cash and carry wholesale trading. However, in case of test marketing or if the items are sourced from the small scale sector, then FIPB approval is required. Single brand retailing is allowed subject to the FIPB approval and FDI limited to 51 percent.

Venture Capital: FDI is allowed up to 100 percent in venture capital funds (VCF) and venture capital companies (VCC) through the automatic route, subject to Securities and Exchange Board of India (SEBI) regulations and sector specific FDI limits. VCFs and VCCs may own up to 40 percent of unlisted Indian companies. Investment in a single company by a VCF or VCC may not exceed five percent of the paid up corpus of a domestic VCF or VCC.

CONVERSION AND TRANSFER POLICIES

There are no restrictions on remittances for debt service or payments for imported inputs. In some sectors, investments in the development of integrated townships and NRI investment in real estate may be subject to a "lock-in" period. Profits and dividend remittances are permitted without approval from the Reserve Bank of India (RBI). Income tax payment clearance is required, but there are generally no delays beyond 60 days. RBI approval is required to remit funds from asset liquidation. Foreign partners may sell their shares to resident Indian investors without approval of RBI, provided shares were held on a repatriation basis. GDR/ADR proceeds from abroad may be retained without restrictions except for an end-use ban on investment in real estate and stock markets. FIPB approval is required for converting non-repatriable shares to repatriable ones. Up to $1 million may be remitted for transfer of assets into India. Individual professionals including journalists and lawyers are allowed to keep 100 percent of their earnings from consultancy services rendered abroad in foreign currency accounts.

The Indian rupee is fully convertible for current account transactions. Current account transactions are regulated under the Foreign Exchange Management Rules, 2000. Prior RBI approval is required for acquiring foreign currency above certain limits for specific purposes (foreign travel, consulting services, foreign studies). Capital account transactions are open for foreign investors, subject to various clearances. In recent years, with growing foreign exchange reserves, the Indian government has taken additional steps to relax foreign exchange and capital account controls for Indian companies and individuals. For example, individuals are now permitted to transfer abroad for any purpose up to $200,000 a year without approval. The GOI now allows all NRI proposals for conversion of non-patriable equity into repatriable equity under the automatic approval route. At the end of 2008, the exchange rate was Rs.47.10 to $1, compared to Rs.39.80 at the end of 2007.

Foreign Institutional Investors (FIIs) may transfer funds from rupee to foreign currency accounts and vice versa at the market exchange rate. They may also repatriate capital, capital gains, dividends, interest income, and any compensation from the sale of rights offerings, net of all taxes without approval.

The RBI accords automatic approval to Indian industries for foreign collaboration agreements up to 400 per cent of the net worth of the Indian company. For technology-transfer agreements with foreign companies, Indian firms may remit royalties up to 5 percent for domestic sales and 8 percent for exports without approval; but recurring royalty payments, such as patent licensing, are normally limited to eight percent of the selling price over a ten-year period. Royalties and lump sum payments are taxed at 20 to 30 percent. Where technology transfer is not involved, royalty payments for the use of trademarks and brand names are limited to 2 percent on exports and 1 percent on domestic sales. In case of technology transfer, payment of royalty includes the payment of royalty for use of trademark and brand name of the foreign collaborator.

Foreign banks may remit profits and surpluses to their headquarters, subject to the banks compliance with the Banking Regulation Act, 1949. Banks may also issue credit cards without RBI approval. Banks are permitted to offer foreign currency-rupee swaps without any limits to enable customers to hedge their foreign currency liabilities. They may also offer forward cover to non-resident entities on FDI deployed after 1993.

Expropriation and Compensation

There have been few instances of direct expropriation since the 1970s. While a program of privatization of state-owned enterprises stalled since 2004 with a change in the ruling government, there has been no reversal in the overall movement away from public ownership of industry.

After years of negotiation, the Government of India in 2005 persuaded state-owned financial institutions and the State of Maharashtra to reach a settlement with U.S. investors, the Overseas Private Investment Corporation, and other foreign lenders on the investment dispute surrounding the Dabhol power project. A comprehensive commercial settlement was subsequently achieved in 2006. There has been significant progress in resolving several payment disputes that American power sector investors have with the State of Tamil Nadu. The GOI, which has limited jurisdiction over commercial disputes involving matters under state jurisdiction, has been helpful in convincing Tamil Nadu to settle these commercial disputes. The United States continues to urge the GOI that to create an attractive and reliable investment climate, India and its political subdivisions need to provide a secure legal and regulatory framework for the private sector, as well as institutionalized dispute resolution mechanisms to expedite resolution of ccmmercial issues.

At least two U.S. pharmaceutical companies with production and distribution facilities in India have yet to resolve long-standing disputes with the GOI (dating from the 1980s) resulting from India's drug price-control regime.

Dispute Settlement

Foreign investors frequently complain about a lack of "sanctity of contracts." Although Indian courts are independent, they are backlogged with unsettled dispute cases. Critics say that liquidating a bankrupt company may take as long as 20 years. In an attempt to unify its adjudication of disputes over commercial contracts with the rest of the world, India enacted the Arbitration and Conciliation Act of 1996, based on the UNCITRAL (United Nations Commission on International Trade Law) Model Law. Foreign awards are enforceable under multilateral conventions like the Geneva Convention. The International Center for Alternative Dispute Resolution (ICADR) has been established as an autonomous organization under the Ministry of Law and Justice and Company Affairs to promote settlement of domestic and international disputes through different modes of alternate dispute resolution. India is not a member of the International Center for the Settlement of Investment Disputes, but is a member of the New York Convention of 1958. The Permanent Court of Arbitration (PCA, Hague) and the Indian Law Ministry have agreed to establish the regional office of the PCA in New Delhi to make available an arbitration forum to match the facilities offered at The Hague at a far lower cost. The work to set up the court in New Delhi is progressing.

PERFORMANCE REQUIREMENTS AND INCENTIVES

Local sourcing is generally not required, but has been mandated for certain sectors in the past. In some consumer goods industries, the GOI requires the foreign party to ensure that the inflow of foreign exchange and foreign equity covers the foreign exchange requirement for imported goods. In 2002, the GOI removed measures previously requiring local content and foreign exchange balancing in the automobile industry.

Plant Location: Industrial undertakings are free to select the location of a project. The earlier restriction prohibiting location of factories near urban settlements was lifted in July 2008. However, projects will still need clearance by the concerned state pollution board and the environment ministry.

Employment: There is no requirement to employ Indian nationals. Restrictions on employing foreign technicians and managers have been eliminated, though companies complain that hiring and compensating expatriates is time-consuming and expensive. The RBI permits remittance of a per-diem rate up to $1000, with an annual ceiling of $200,000 for services provided by foreign workers payable to a foreign firm. Employment of foreigners in excess of 12 months requires approval from the Ministry of Home Affairs. In addition, there are certain employment restrictions in the telecommunications industry. Majority directors on the boards of telecom companies including the Chairman, Managing Director and Chief Executive Officer, should be resident Indians. The Chief Technical Officer and the Chief Finance Officer should also be resident Indian citizens. The chief officer in charge of the technical network operations and the chief security officer for all telecom companies have to be resident Indian citizens.

Taxes: The GOI provides a 10-year tax holiday for knowledge-based start-ups. Most state governments also offer fiscal concessions. Large state and central government fiscal deficits, along with attempts to reform both the direct and indirect tax regimes throughout India, have increased uncertainty over tax liability for investors. The general trend, however, has been toward simplification of the tax code, a reduction in tax rates and exceptions, and greater transparency in tax administration.

The 2008 annual supplement to the FTP announced some incentives for the export community, including a duty reduction to 3 percent from 5 percent for capital goods imported under the Export Promotion Capital Goods scheme (EPCG is an export incentive scheme that seeks to modernize production facilities); and sector-specific incentives in farm products, toys/sports goods, gems/jewelry, IT hardware and telecommunication sectors. India's Foreign Trade Policy exempts exporters from service tax, and provides for duty-free import of inputs and capital goods, exemption from excise taxes on capital goods, textile machinery, components and raw materials, as well as exemption on sales tax at the federal and state level. Import of consumables, professional equipment, and spare parts in the service sector are allowed duty-free up to 10 percent of the average foreign exchange export earnings in the preceding three years. Tax holidays are available in the form of deductions for priority sectors. Deduction of 100 percent of the profits from business for a period of 10 years is available for infrastructure industries. Income by way of dividend, interest, or long term capital gains in respect of infrastructure companies is 100 percent tax exempt.

Right to Private Ownership and Establishment

Subject to certain sector-specific restrictions, foreign and domestic private entities may establish and own businesses in trading companies, subsidiaries, joint ventures, branch offices, project offices and liaison offices. The GOI does not permit investment in real estate by foreign investors, except for company property used to do business and the development of most types of new commercial and residential properties. NRIs are permitted 100 percent equity investment in real estate. FIIs can now invest in real estate Initial Public Offerings (IPOs). They can also participate in pre-IPO placements undertaken by such real estate companies without regard to the FDI stipulations.

To establish a business, various approvals and clearances are required such as: incorporation of the company; registration and allotment of land; permission for land use in case of industry located outside an industrial area; environmental site approval; sanction of power and finance; approval for construction activity and building plan; registration under State Sales Tax Act and Central and State Excise Acts; and consent under Water and Air Pollution Control Acts. Industries such as petrochemicals complexes, petroleum refineries, cement thermal power plants, bulk drugs, fertilizers, dyes, and paper (among others) need to obtain environment clearance from the Ministry of Environment and Forest.

The GOI passed the Securitization Act in 2002 to introduce bankruptcy laws. The requirement to obtain government permission before shutting down some businesses, however, makes it difficult to dispose of company assets.

Protection of Property Rights

The legal system puts a number of restrictions and imposes a stamp tax on the transfer of land, making title unclear, often making buying and selling transactions difficult. There is no reliable system for recording secured interests in property, making it difficult to use property as collateral or to foreclose against such property.

India has generally adequate copyright laws, but enforcement is weak and piracy of copyrighted materials is widespread. India is a party to the Geneva Convention for the Protection of Rights of Producers of Phonograms and the Universal Copyright Convention, and a member of the World Intellectual Property Organization (WIPO) and UNESCO. India has not yet ratified and incorporated into domestic law the WIPO Internet treaties. The nodal ministry has reportedly prepared the draft amendments to update the Copyright Act, which still need intra-agency approval before they can be approved by the Cabinet.

Trademark protection is good and meets international standards. The Trade Marks Act (1999) and implementing regulations accord national treatment for trademark owners and statutory protection of service marks. Although U.S. firms report few trademark related problems, India's weak judicial system can make it difficult to exercise rights established by the law. India is currently working on amending its Trademark Laws to make them compliant with the Madrid Protocol. The Indian government in November 2008 approved modification of the Trade Marks (Amendment) Bill, 2007 to ensure better protection for Indian trademarks in designated member countries and afford reciprocal protection to trade marks from member countries abroad. The amendment Bill is expected to be passed by the Parliament.

In 2005, India expanded product patent coverage to include pharmaceuticals and agro-chemicals, sectors of significant interest to U.S. firms. Embedded software may also now be patented. The GOI introduced these changes through presidential ordinance in order to meet on time India's commitments under the Agreement on Trade Related Aspects of Intellectual Property Rights (TRIPS). On March 23, 2005, the Indian Parliament approved legislation to make permanent the change to India's patent law that the GOI had introduced by temporary ordinance. The new law extends product patent protection to pharmaceuticals and agricultural chemicals. However, the new law lacks specificity in several important areas such as compulsory license triggers, pre-grant opposition provisions, and defining the scope of patentable inventions. India also provides protection for plant varieties through the Plant Varieties and Farmers' Rights Act.

Indian law does not provide for protection against unfair commercial use of test or other data that companies submit to the government in order to obtain marketing approval for their pharmaceutical or agricultural chemical products. The GOI is working on legislative changes based on recommendations made by the GOI data protection inter-ministerial group, also known as the Reddy report. A small but growing domestic constituency of Indian pharmaceutical companies, technology firms, and educational institutions favors improved patent protection.

Indian law provides no protection of trade secrets. The GOI in October 2008 put forth draft legislation for public comment. In 2000, India passed legislation (Designs Act 2000) to meet its obligations under the TRIPS Agreement for industrial designs. The Indian government in September 2008 announced Design Rules 2008 detailing classification of design to conform to the international system and to take care of the proliferation of design related activities in various fields. India's semiconductor Integrated Circuits Layout Designs Act 2000 is based on standards developed by WIPO. However, this law remains inoperative due to the lack of implementing regulations.

TRANSPARENCY OF THE REGULATORY SYSTEM

Even though India has made much progress on economic reform since 1991, the economy is still constrained by excessive rules and a powerful bureaucracy with broad discretionary powers. Moreover, India has a decentralized federal system of government in which the state governments possess broad regulatory powers. Regulatory decisions governing important issues such as zoning, land-use and environment can vary from one state to another. Opposition from labor unions and political constituencies has slowed reform in such areas as exit policy, bankruptcy, and labor law reform.

Despite these shortcomings, central government efforts to establish independent and effective regulators in some sectors, such as telecommunications, securities, and insurance, have shown positive results. In December 2004, the GOI also created an independent pension regulator as part of its larger program to reform India's pension system. It also established a

Competition Commission and has indicated its intention to strengthen the commodities futures markets. SEBI enforces corporate governance, which is considered better than in many other emerging markets by foreign institutional investors. Financial disclosures are strict though there is scope for improvement.

EFFICIENCY OF CAPITAL MARKETS AND PORTFOLIO INVESTMENT

The Indian capital market has grown rapidly in recent years, with market capitalization on the Bombay Stock Exchange hitting new highs before the 2008 financial crisis battered stock markets around the world. Spot prices for index stocks are usually market-driven and settlement mechanisms are close to international standards. India's debt and currency markets lag behind its equity markets. Although private placements of corporate debt have been increasing, the daily trading volume remains low. The Indian stock markets lack broad liquidity, although high transaction costs and systemic risk have come down with recent regulatory and administrative improvements. Institutional improvements and better regulations have helped to reduce episodes of market manipulation, which had caused a lack of confidence by retail investors who invested primarily in public sector debt instruments and debt-oriented mutual funds. SEBI has initiated further policy changes such as allowing all investors to short sell, introducing borrowing and lending of shares, and introducing Real Estate Investment Trusts that would be listed in the market. These measures add depth and breadth to the market making it more liquid than before.

In 2004, the GOI announced its intentions to integrate the commodities and securities markets and to revamp taxes on securities transactions, although this is still being debated. The GOI eliminated the tax on long-term capital gains on stocks and this year increased the tax on short-term capital gains to 15 percent from 10 percent. The GOI imposes a securities transaction tax of 0.075-0.012 percent.

Foreign Institutional Investors (FIIs) have a relatively small (compared to their global portfolios) but growing presence in India. However, after 11 consecutive years of net inflows, FIIs made net sales of about $13 billion in the Indian capital markets as of year-end 2008. The 2008 net outflow contrasts with net inflows of approximately $17 billion in 2007. While FIIs are allowed to invest in all securities traded on India's primary and secondary markets, in unlisted domestic debt securities, and in commercial paper issued by Indian companies, the GOI imposes several restrictions that vary by type of investment. For example, the GOI has hiked the amount of FII investment in government securities and corporate debt by taking the total investment to $8 billion. The FII limit in corporate debt was raised in 2008 and again in early 2009 in light of reduced capital inflows. The new limit is $15 billion in a single fiscal year on a first-come, first-serve basis subject to a ceiling of $200 million per registered entity. FII equity holdings in a single company are also capped at a level below the overall sector-specific foreign investment limits unless specifically authorized by that company's board of directors.

FIIs investing in India's capital markets must register with the Securities and Exchange Board of India (SEBI). They are divided into two categories: (a) Regular FIIs - those which are required to invest not less than 70 per cent of their Indian exposure in equity-related instruments, and (b) 100 percent debt-fund FIIs -- those which are permitted to invest only in debt instruments. The list of eligible FIIs has been expanded to include endowment and university funds, foundations, charitable trusts, and hedge funds. SEBI allows foreign brokers to work on behalf of registered FIIs. The FIIs can also bypass brokers and deal directly with companies in open offers. FII bank deposits are fully convertible and their capital, capital gains, dividends, interest income, and any compensation from the sale of rights offerings, net of all taxes, may be repatriated without prior approval.

Non-resident Indians (NRIs) are subject to separate investment limitations. They can repatriate dividends, rents and interest earned in India and their specially designated bank deposits are fully convertible.

The National Stock Exchange (NSE) and the Bombay Stock Exchange (BSE), both based in Mumbai, use screen-based trading systems. Computers and telecommunications links permit automated buy/sell transactions. Other regional exchanges and the National Over-the-Counter Exchange in Delhi also have computer-trading systems. The efficiency of the capital market has improved because of the compulsory depository system for most stocks, abolition of the traditional speculative "badla" system of carry forward trades, and introduction of derivatives trading by way of stock options and index trading. SEBI regulates all market intermediaries. Securities can be transferred through electronic book entry. The National Securities Depository Limited, which is promoted by the NSE, commenced operation in 1996. The BSE, the other market with national reach, has also set up a depository system. Together, the NSE and BSE account for 96 percent of total turnover in the stock markets. The NSE and BSE are the world's fourth and fifth largest stock exchanges in terms of volume of transactions, although they are smaller in terms of market capitalization compared to the world's largest markets.

Companies incorporated outside India can raise resources in India's capital market through the issuance of Indian Depository Receipts (IDRs), subject to certain conditions established and monitored by SEBI. Companies are required to have pre-issue paid-up capital and free reserves of least $100 million, as well as an average turnover of $500 million during the three financial years preceding the issuance.

India's banking industry (with total assets of about $1082 billion in March 2008) is split into three categories - - 28 public sector banks (70 percent of total assets in the banking system), 23 private banks (21 percent), and 28 foreign banks (about 8.4 percent). According to official figures, the ratio of non-performing loans to total assets for public sector banks was 2.3 percent in 2007-08 compared to 2.7 percent the previous year. A Board for Financial Supervision ensures compliance with guidelines on loan management, capital adequacy, and asset classification. All banks operating in India are regulated through the Reserve Bank of India (RBI) whose authority the GOI has limited gradually as part of the economic reform process.

Domestic banks are mandated to extend 40 percent of their loans to "priority" borrowers (agriculturists, exporters, and small businesses). A similar requirement for foreign banks is 32 percent of loans to exporters and small businesses. In April 2003, the lending commitment for regional rural banks in priority sectors was raised to 60 (from 40) percent. In addition to imposing sector lending requirements, the dominance of state-owned banks in the market also allows the GOI to exert influence over individual lending decisions.

The GOI has been slowly liberalizing external commercial borrowings (ECBs) in the last few years, although in the last two years it has treated it as a source of foreign capital to turn on and off in response to currency and balance of payment needs. It currently allows ECBs under the automatic route up to $500 million for meeting rupee expenditure/foreign currency expenditure for permissible end-uses for all borrowers. In October 2008, the requirement of a minimum average maturity period of seven years for ECBs of more than US$ 100 million for rupee capital expenditure by the borrowers in the infrastructure sector was abolished. In August 2007, the GOI had permitted ECBs of more than US$ 20 million per borrower per financial year only for foreign currency expenditure for permissible end-uses and those up to US$ 20 million were permitted under the automatic route. In June 2008, hotels, hospitals and software companies were allowed to use ECBs of up to US$ 100 million per fiscal year, for the purpose of import of capital goods under the approval route. The definition of infrastructure for the purpose of utilizing ECBs was expanded in October 2008 to include mining, exploration and refining while payments for obtaining licenses/permits for 3G spectrum by telecom companies were classified as eligible end-uses for the purpose of ECB. The central bank also authorizes an additional $250 million in ECBs with an average maturity of at least 10 years, under the approval route. All companies except banks, financial institutions and non-banking financial companies (NBFCs) are eligible to pursue ECB or provide guarantees for such loans. In January 2009, in order to enable more ECBs, the GOI removed interest rate ceiling caps on ECBs and allowed NBFCs to access multilateral or bilateral official ECB loans for infrastructure. ECB funds cannot be used for investment in the stock market or real estate.

Takeover regulations require disclosure on acquisition of shares exceeding five percent of total capitalization. Acquisition of 15 percent or more of the voting rights in a listed company triggers a public offer for an additional 20 percent stake as per SEBI's Substantial Acquisition of Shares & Takeovers Regulations. Companies may buy back their shares in the market to make inter-corporate investments. From October 2008 consolidation through creeping acquisition up to 5percent has been allowed to persons holding 55 percent and above but below 75 percent, subject to the condition that such acquisition can only be via open market purchases in the normal segment, and no consolidation via bulk/ block/ negotiated deal or through preferential allotment would be permitted. RBI and FIPB clearances are required to acquire a controlling stake in Indian companies. Cross shareholding and stable shareholding are not prevalent in the Indian market. The Hostile Takeover Code and the SEBI Takeover Committee regulate hostile takeovers. The Committee makes ad hoc decisions on takeovers, and tends to protect the target firm when takeover bids come from foreign entities.

POLITICAL VIOLENCE

In general, there have been few incidents of politically motivated attacks on foreign projects or installations in recent years. There were no politically motivated attacks on U.S. companies operating in India in 2008. There are some violent insurgent movements in Kashmir and some northeastern states, as well as a Maoist guerilla movement in some eastern states. In addition, India has been the target of Islamist terrorist attacks, including bombings in 2008 in Jaipur, New Delhi, Bangalore, Hyderabad, Guwahati, and Ahmedabad, as well as the November 2008 sea-borne terrorist attacks on Mumbai, which killed six Americans and other foreigners. Prior to Mumbai, major terrorist attacks had not specifically targeted hotels and facilities frequented by American travelers.

CORRUPTION

Corruption is a major concern. In the past, the government procurement system, especially for telecommunications, power and defense, has been particularly subjected to allegations of corruption. Several government employees and public figures have been indicted or convicted under anti-corruption laws over the last eight years.

The legal framework for fighting corruption is provided in the following laws: the Prevention of Corruption Act, 1988; the Code of Criminal Procedures, 1973; the Companies Act, 1956; and the Indian Contract Act, 1872. Amended anti-corruption laws since 2004 have given additional powers to vigilance departments in government bodies and made the Central Vigilance Commission (CVC) a statutory body. The GOI intends to amend the Prevention of Corruption Act (PCA), 1988 through an inter-ministerial group to prescribe a sanction-granting authority for prosecution of Members of Parliament, Members of State Legislatures and local bodies.

U.S. firms have identified corruption as one obstacle to foreign direct investment. Indian businessmen agree that red tape and wide-ranging administrative discretion serve as a pretext to extort money. According to some foreign business representatives in India, corruption lies in the lack of transparency in the rules of governance, extremely cumbersome official procedures, and excessive and unregulated discretionary power in the hands of politicians and bureaucrats. Clusters have developed, however, such as in the New Delhi suburb of Gurgaon, where the business climate is relatively free of corruption. Officials of foreign businesses in these areas say that local political and bureaucratic machinery generally leaves them alone.

BILATERAL INVESTMENT AGREEMENTS

The GOI states that it has concluded 57 bilateral investment promotion agreements (BIPAs). These included agreements with the United Kingdom, France, Germany, Malaysia, and Mauritius. Negotiations are also underway with other countries. The United States does not have a bilateral investment treaty (BIT) with India as yet, but the two countries launched BIT exploratory discussions in 2008, with formal negotiations scheduled to commence in early 2009. India and the US already have a double taxation avoidance treaty. Several tax disputes are pending which are addressed during regular meetings between the two countries' Competent Authorities.

OPIC AND OTHER INVESTMENT INSURANCE PROGRAMS

The U.S. and India signed an Investment Incentive Agreement in 1987 that covers the Overseas Private Investment Corporation (OPIC) programs. OPIC is currently open in India for all its programs, specifically supporting three regional private equity funds and five global funds. OPIC projects in India are in the following sectors: energy and power, telecommunications, manufacturing, and services. India is a member of the World Banks Multilateral Investment Guarantee Agency (MIGA).

LABOR

Although there are more than 7 million unionized workers, unions represent less than one-seventh of the workers in the organized sector (primarily in state-owned concerns), and less than two percent of the total work force. Most unions are linked to political parties. Worker-days lost to strikes and lockouts dropped 50 percent during the decade 1991-2000 from the previous decade.

The payment of wages is governed by the Payment of Wages Act 1936, and the Minimum Wages Act, 1948. Industrial wages range from about $3.50 per day for unskilled workers, to over $150 per month for skilled production workers. Retrenchment, closure and layoffs are governed by the Industrial Disputes Act, which requires prior government permission to layoff workers or close businesses employing 100 or more workers. Permission is not easily obtained. Private firms have successfully downsized using voluntary retirement schemes. Foreign banks are also required to get the RBI's approval for closing branches.

Comprehensive Legislation on Labor Reforms was introduced several years ago but is still stalled in the Parliament Consultative Committee. The prospect of a new government in 2009 will require the reintroduction of this legislation. The proposed law contains stringent provisions for strikes and lockouts. The Comprehensive legislation was meant to integrate both the Trade Unions Act and the Industrial Disputes Act in a single piece of legislation. In addition, a key amendment to the Industrial Disputes Act would increase the threshold limit to 300 employees for seeking government approval before laying-off workers.

FOREIGN TRADE ZONES/FREE TRADE ZONES

The GOI has established several foreign trade zone schemes to encourage export-oriented production. These provide a means to bypass many of the domestic economy's fiscal and infrastructural obstacles that otherwise make Indian goods and services less competitive in international markets. The most recent of the schemes is the Special Economic Zone (SEZ), a duty-free enclave with separately developed industrial infrastructure. Other schemes include the Export Processing Zone (EPZ) and the Software Technology Park (STP), both of which are designated areas for export-oriented activities. In addition, India allows an individual firm to be designated an Export Oriented Unit (EOU). All of these schemes are governed by separate rules and granted different benefits. In May 2005, the GOI passed new legislation called the "Special Economic Zones (SEZ) Bill 2005" endorsing its commitment to a long-term and stable policy for the SEZ structure which had previously been only an administrative construct. Pursuant to certain controversies over land acquisition for SEZ development projects, the GOI issued new guidelines for SEZ in 2006. Although legislative changes have been introduced through a new Land Acquisition and Rehabilitation Act, some political unrest over SEZ development projects continue.

SEZs are regarded as foreign territory for the purpose of duties and taxes, and operate outside the domain of the custom authorities. SEZ units are allowed to retain 100 percent of their foreign exchange earnings in special Export Earners Foreign Currency Exchange accounts. They are free to sell goods in the domestic tariff area (DTA) on payment of applicable duties. Sales from DTA firms to SEZ units are on par with regular trade transactions and hence eligible to benefit from all export incentive and foreign currency exemption schemes. In addition, many state governments have granted a sales-tax exemption for DTA-SEZ sales. SEZ units are also exempt from the central government's service and excise tax regimes.

SEZ businesses are expected to be a positive foreign exchange earner within five years from the commencement of production. None of the FDI equity caps are applicable to units in SEZs, including those sectors reserved for small-scale industries. SEZs are exempted from the requirements of industrial licensing.

The new law increased the tax holiday period (phased out over time) from 10 years to 15-years for both SEZ developers and SEZ production units. The SEZ legislation also provides for the establishment of an International Financial Services Centre to facilitate financial services for SEZ units. Offshore banking units (OBUs) are permitted to operate in SEZs, virtually like a foreign branch of a bank, to make available financing at international rates. The OBUs enjoy some exemptions from Reserve Bank (central bank) of India requirements, but other limitations have constrained their popularity.

Subsequent to the first and main promulgation of SEZ Rules in February, 2006, 531 SEZ projects have been approved so far, and formal notifications for 260 SEZs have been issued. Land acquisition for SEZs has become a controversial issue because of the alleged allocation of large blocks of agricultural lands to upcoming SEZs. This has prompted the government to issue guidelines that only uncultivable land can be acquired for SEZ development or if fertile land is involved then it should not be more than 10 percent of the total area and adequate compensation and rehabilitation need to be provided. However, the compensation and rehabilitation provisions are not transparent. There is also land ceiling of 5000 hectares on large SEZs which has become a contentious issue for many SEZ developers.

EPZs are industrial parks with incentives for foreign investors in export-oriented business. STPs are special zones with similar incentives for software exports. EPZ/STP units may import intermediate goods duty-free. The minimum net foreign exchange earning as a percentage of exports by EPZ/STP units is required to be at least 3 percent. EPZ/STP units may sell up to 50 percent of their level of exports on the domestic market after payment of taxes, with the exception of motor cars, alcoholic beverages, tea, books, and refrigeration units.

EOUs are industrial companies established anywhere in India that export their entire production. There are approximately 2300 fully operational EOUs in India. They are granted: duty-free import of intermediate goods duty- free; income tax holiday up to 2009; exemption from excise tax on capital goods, components, and raw materials; and waiver of sales taxes. EOUs may sell up to five percent of "seconds" on the domestic market after paying appropriate taxes.

Foreign Direct Investment Statistics

Table A. Inflow of FDI by top 5 countries ($ million)

(IFY) Year	2000-05	2005-06	2006-07	2007-08	2008-09*
--------	-------	-------	-------	-------	-------
Total	16,657	5,546	15,726	24,579	17,211
Of which Mauritius	5,606	2,570	6,363	11,096	7,014
Singapore	431	275	578	3,073	1,751
U.S.A.	2,086	502	856	1,089	1,229
U.K.	1,043	266	1,878	1,176	695
Netherlands	1,290	76	644	695	714
FDI/GDP(%)	0.9	0.9	2.5	N/A	N/A

Note: Indian Fiscal Year (IFY) is from April to March.

* FDI inflows for April 2008-September 2008 only.

Source: Secretariat for Industrial Assistance Newsletters, Ministry of Commerce and Industry, GOI

Table B. Top 10 New FDI proposals approved in IFY 2008-09 (April-September)

Company	Project	Equity ($ million)
DE Shaw Composite Investments, Mauritius	Construction	385
Fiat Automobiles, Italy	Auto Manufacturing	288
New Opportunities Ltd. Mauritius Construction	Real Estate	197
Holdrind Investments, Mauritius	Cement Manufacturing	189
BNP Paribas Leasing Group, France	Financial Services	184
Lehman Brothers, Singapore	Other Banking Services	141
BOC Group Plc. U.K.	Industrial Gas Manufacturing	139
Morgan Stanley, Mauritius	Financial Services	132
CRH India Investments, Netherlands	Cement Manufacturing	121
Cisco Systems Capital, Mauritius	Credit Services	118

Note: The Indo-Mauritius investment agreement provides tax advantages that have attracted U.S. and businesses of other countries to make FDI into India from Mauritius, rather than the headquarter country.

Table C. FDI Inflows by Sector - Top 5

Sector	FDI (US millions)	
IFY	April 2000-Sept 2008	2008-09*
All Services (fin and non-fin)	15,634	2,576
Computers/Software	8,678	1,400
Telecommunication	5,796	1,954
Construction Activities(roads/hwys)	4,885	1,722
Housing and Real Estate	4,335	1,624

Note: * data is for April - September 2008 only

Source: Secretariat for Industrial Assistance, Ministry of Commerce and Industry, GOI.

INDEX

A

accountability, 41
accounting, 20, 31, 36, 51, 63, 67, 74, 111, 130, 133, 137, 141, 142, 152, 154
accounting standards, 111
acid, 113
acquisitions, 10, 13, 16, 17, 28, 74, 81, 86, 109, 118
ADC, 17
adult literacy, 2, 4
adulthood, 133
aerospace, 113, 167
age, 2, 7, 133
agricultural exports, 155, 162
agricultural market, 122, 139, 144, 155, 159
agricultural sector, 41, 123, 126, 130, 136
airports, 4, 30, 38, 39, 45, 46, 100, 165
alcohol, 47
alternatives, 48
aluminum, 21, 31
animal husbandry, 101, 148, 164
annual rate, 20
apparel, 2, 54
arbitration, 55, 56, 57, 58, 61, 115, 116, 172
assets, 5, 26, 98, 138, 171, 174, 177
asymmetry, 155
attacks, 30, 178
attractiveness, 111
auditing, 111
authority, 37, 77, 100, 117, 136, 137, 138, 147, 177, 179
automobile, 64, 66, 97, 99, 116
automotive sector, 21, 63, 65
availability, 2, 44, 51, 52, 75, 78, 111, 126, 127, 136, 137, 138, 141, 148, 150, 156
averaging, 126, 130
avoidance, 5, 62, 138, 179
awareness, 36, 57

B

backward integration, 86
balance of payments, 13, 26
bandwidth, 53, 170
banking, 5, 17, 41, 44, 60, 74, 145, 165, 168, 177, 178, 181
banking industry, 177
bankruptcy, 53, 174, 175
banks, 5, 6, 41, 45, 141, 165, 171, 177, 178, 180
barriers, viii, 1, 6, 13, 44, 50, 121, 136
barter, 127
beer, 167
beverages, 2, 167, 181
binding, 56, 116
biochemistry, 85
biotechnology, 81, 82, 83, 153
black market, 137
blocks, 181
bonds, 42
borrowers, 177, 178
borrowing, 145, 176
breaches, 57
breakdown, 25, 57, 110
breeding, 43
bribes, 49
broadband, 54
bureaucracy, 33, 37, 41, 43, 175
business costs, 143
business environment, 68, 111
by-products, 47

C

call centers, 12, 23
caloric intake, 132
canals, 151
cancer, 78

capacity building, 152
capital account, 171
capital controls, viii, 163
capital expenditure, 53, 178
capital flows, 11, 14, 109
capital gains, 24, 48, 109, 110, 171, 174, 176, 177
capital goods, 2, 173, 178, 181
capital inflow, 41, 176
capital intensive, 30, 31
capital markets, 41, 176
capital productivity, 68
capitalism, 7
carbon, 113
case study, 51, 52, 63, 75, 84, 120
catalyst, 56
category a, 110
cell phones, 31, 35, 40
central bank, 178, 181
central planning, 1
certification, 60, 85
channels, 44, 123, 145, 156, 166
child labor, 49
children, 2, 4, 133
citizenship, 61, 164
classification, 50, 147, 175, 177
classrooms, 41
cleaning, 144
clinical trials, 75, 77, 83
closure, 37, 180
clusters, 29, 30, 32, 69
coal, 75, 166
coffee, 36
collaboration, 30, 48, 60, 68, 118, 123, 159, 171
collateral, 174
collective bargaining, 5
colleges, 2, 39, 41
commerce, 46, 81, 91, 98, 167
commercial bank, 141
commodity, 86, 127, 129, 137, 155, 162
commodity markets, 155
communication, 20, 60, 70, 114
community, 173
comparative advantage, 2
compensation, 49, 50, 147, 171, 177, 181
competence, 86
competition, 7, 12, 13, 66, 144
competitive advantage, 46
competitiveness, 33, 37, 41, 42, 67, 68, 111, 143
competitor, 34
competitors, 3, 76, 85
compliance, 1, 49, 51, 76, 83, 86, 87, 143, 171, 177
components, 10, 11, 21, 63, 65, 66, 67, 68, 70, 74, 89, 110, 173, 181
composition, 66, 79, 115, 132
computer software, 10, 109, 110
computer systems, 25
computerization, 141
computing, 40, 162
concentrates, 153
concentration, 21
conciliation, 56, 116
confidence, 33, 123, 156, 159
confidentiality, 14, 83, 131
congestion, 4, 38, 45
connectivity, 38
consensus, 122, 136
consent, 114, 174
consolidation, 178
constitution, 136
construction, 4, 20, 30, 35, 39, 42, 47, 54, 57, 60, 62, 72, 124, 154, 166, 169, 174
consultants, 36
consulting, 32, 33, 112, 168, 169, 171
consumer expenditure, 133
consumer goods, 116, 137, 164, 173
consumer markets, 136
consumers, 36, 66, 133, 137, 145, 155
consumption, 100, 116, 133, 145, 152, 155, 166
control, 5, 30, 39, 41, 45, 54, 56, 114, 137, 138, 160, 166, 169, 172
conversion, 171
conviction, 51
cooling, 74
corn, 145
corporate governance, 176
corruption, 6, 33, 43, 52, 70, 114, 179
cost saving, 75, 83
costs, 3, 4, 31, 35, 38, 45, 53, 58, 70, 77, 85, 86, 124, 127, 135, 145, 148, 149, 150, 151
cotton, 153
country of origin, 114, 130
covering, 37, 102
credit, 5, 111, 122, 127, 131, 136, 141, 142, 156, 168, 171
credit rating, 168
creep, 178
crime, 113
crops, 139, 153
crowding out, 5
cultivation, 101, 148, 164
currency, 111, 164, 171, 176, 177, 181
current account, 171
customers, 3, 171
cycles, 36

D

dairy industry, 154
data collection, 121, 155
data processing, 23, 110
dating, 71, 147, 172
death, 50, 147
debt, 5, 42, 171, 176
debt service, 171
decision making, 41, 117
decisions, 43, 56, 69, 75, 84, 117, 155, 175, 177, 178
deduction, 68, 69
defense, 2, 47, 113, 167, 179
deficit, 6, 111, 149
definition, 51, 111, 126, 178
delivery, 66, 139
demographics, 123, 131, 133
Department of Agriculture, 121, 139, 153, 155, 156, 158, 159, 160, 161, 162
Department of Commerce, 12, 47, 51, 91, 92, 98, 109, 110, 111, 112, 113, 114, 116, 117, 131
deposits, 41, 177
depreciation, 48
derivatives, 78, 113, 177
detergents, 36
developed countries, 11, 15, 35, 59, 61
developed nations, 61
developing countries, 14, 15, 16, 42, 59, 61, 77, 85, 116, 140
developing nations, 61
development policy, 1
diet, 132
direct investment, viii, 14, 80, 130, 148, 163
direct taxes, 143, 144
directors, 117, 173, 176
disclosure, 86, 178
discrimination, 61
distillation, 100
distribution, 13, 22, 31, 36, 39, 42, 46, 52, 54, 60, 102, 114, 127, 137, 148, 150, 167, 169, 172
diversification, 131, 133, 135, 153, 159
diversity, 2
division, 36, 158
domestic demand, 31, 131, 145
domestic economy, 180
domestic industry, 67, 75, 77, 79, 87
domestic investment, 70, 131
domestic laws, 55, 59
domestic policy, 121, 122
dominance, 177
draft, 52, 153, 174, 175
drawing, 20
drug delivery, 78
drug discovery, 75, 83
drugs, 78, 80, 84, 85, 174
duration, 61
duties, 44, 61, 67, 180
dyes, 174
dynamism, 34, 124

E

earnings, 47, 68, 109, 129, 171, 173, 180
e-commerce, 62, 167
economic activity, 39
economic cooperation, 44, 58
economic crisis, 2
economic development, 37, 42
economic growth, vii, viii, 1, 2, 6, 10, 34, 35, 36, 37, 38, 42, 121, 122, 141
economic integration, 11
economic liberalization, 63
economic policy, 2
economic reform, vii, viii, 1, 2, 163, 175, 177
economic reforms, vii, 1
economic transformation, 7
economies of scale, 68, 70
education, 39, 69, 87, 112, 160, 167
educational system, 33, 39, 40
electricity, 3, 6, 29, 38, 127, 169
electronic systems, 74
emerging markets, 85, 176
emission, 65
employees, 5, 12, 21, 35, 37, 40, 49, 50, 70, 112, 147, 179, 180
employment, 2, 3, 5, 26, 30, 36, 50, 67, 118, 123, 136, 137, 147, 173
employment growth, 30, 136
energy, 1, 2, 21, 28, 42, 100, 102, 110, 112, 149, 164, 165, 179
enthusiasm, 11, 31, 33
environmental regulations, 49
EPC, 90
equity market, 5, 41, 42, 176
evolution, 75, 86, 155
exchange rate, 67, 115, 123, 131, 171
exclusion, 78
exercise, 7, 117, 165, 174
expenditures, 4, 28, 69, 80, 117, 134, 135, 153
expertise, 39, 40, 78, 86, 118
exploitation, 137, 139
explosives, 101, 113, 167
export promotion, 2, 68
exporter, 47
exports, 6, 12, 30, 35, 43, 45, 47, 51, 64, 65, 68, 69, 71, 102, 117, 137, 145, 162, 170, 171, 181

exposure, 133, 176
external financing, 5
extraction, 20, 151
extreme poverty, 3

F

fabrication, 31, 53, 70
failure, 57
family, 116
farmers, viii, 22, 121, 122, 123, 124, 127, 129, 131, 136, 138, 139, 140, 141, 145, 149, 153, 155, 156
farmland, 53, 122, 139, 141, 164
farms, 3, 139
FDA, 85
FDI inflow, 6, 11, 12, 13, 14, 15, 16, 20, 21, 22, 24, 25, 28, 29, 31, 49, 63, 80, 81, 109, 110, 130, 182
federal law, 49
feet, 54
fertilizers, 130, 174
finance, 26, 42, 65, 93, 101, 168, 174
financial crisis, 176
financial institutions, 5, 6, 172, 178
financial sector, 41
financial support, 112
financial system, 5
financing, 39, 42, 70, 102, 151, 181
Finland, 107
firm size, 123
fiscal deficit, 6, 173
fish, 144
fisheries, 148
flexibility, 5, 37, 38, 50, 58, 69, 147
flour, 146
fluctuations, 149, 162
focusing, 62, 152
food industry, 148
food intake, 133
food processing industry, 138, 144, 147
food products, 131, 137, 144, 154
footwear, 2
foreign banks, 41, 100, 165, 177
foreign direct investment, vii, 1, 3, 5, 6, 9, 10, 11, 63, 74, 123, 124, 129, 159, 179
foreign exchange, 12, 47, 68, 129, 168, 171, 173, 180, 181
foreign firms, 10, 13, 15, 16, 24, 35, 39, 41, 42, 44, 47, 48, 53, 59, 74, 79, 80, 81, 109, 112, 148
formal sector, 112
franchise, 169
fraud, 43
free trade, 43, 102, 106, 107, 108
free trade area, 106, 107, 108
freedom, 141
fruits, 85, 144
fuel, 25, 68, 69, 74, 75
full capacity, 71, 73
funding, 39, 41, 43, 44, 110, 154
funds, 38, 48, 130, 136, 156, 164, 170, 171, 176, 177, 178, 179

G

GDP, vii, 1, 2, 3, 4, 5, 6, 12, 67, 111, 124, 125, 126, 127, 131, 132, 162, 182
GDP deflator, 111
General Agreement on Tariffs and Trade, 58
general education, 39
generation, 3, 25, 29, 44, 68, 70, 102, 112, 149, 150, 169
generic drugs, 85
Global Competitiveness Report, 94, 111, 113
global economy, 11, 41
global markets, 122, 145
globalization, 86
GNP, 35
goals, 68, 75, 136
gold, 5, 110, 168
goods and services, 37, 111, 138, 180
governance, 179
government intervention, 136
government policy, 156
government procurement, 43, 179
government revenues, 143
government securities, 176
grades, 155
grading, 122, 139, 149, 155, 156
grains, 155, 156
grants, 42, 47, 69, 114
gross domestic product, 38, 124, 125, 131
groundnut oil, 138
groundwater, 149, 151
groups, 23, 62, 133, 162
growth rate, 5, 63, 162
guidelines, 50, 100, 101, 102, 103, 116, 164, 165, 167, 169, 170, 177, 180, 181

H

hands, 78, 169, 179
harmonization, 114
health, 7, 34, 42, 43, 51, 77, 78, 81, 82, 111, 119
health care, 43, 119
health insurance, 7
health problems, 77

hedging, 156
high school, 39
higher education, 3, 34, 39, 41, 111
highway system, 45
highways, 42, 45, 166
hiring, 5, 147, 173
holding company, 62, 110, 168, 170
hopes, 71
hospitals, 46, 178
hotels, 60, 110, 167, 178
house, 167
household income, 153
households, 3, 132, 133, 149, 150
housing, 5, 30, 45, 46, 47, 53, 164, 166, 167, 168
hub, 40, 62, 71, 75
hybrid, 110, 153
hydrocarbons, 113

I

illiteracy, 4, 6
images, 89, 159
IMF, 93, 108, 110, 113
implementation, 14, 48, 49, 69, 77, 80, 129, 136, 141, 148
import restrictions, 63
import substitution, 1, 136
imports, 1, 2, 6, 35, 45, 63, 114, 116, 123, 129, 159, 162, 170
incentives, vii, 9, 10, 11, 12, 39, 43, 44, 45, 48, 67, 70, 129, 131, 135, 144, 173, 181
income, 27, 36, 44, 48, 61, 62, 66, 68, 116, 122, 123, 131, 132, 133, 143, 145, 159, 171, 177, 181
income tax, 44, 48, 145, 181
increased competition, 41, 67
independence, 76, 111, 137
indigenous, 72, 76
Indonesia, vii, 1, 4, 33, 58, 61, 99, 107, 116
industrial sectors, 44
industrialized countries, 35, 41
inefficiency, 124
infectious disease, 86
inflation, 34, 111, 141
information technology, 12, 41, 42, 46, 109, 147
inheritance, 139
injury, iv, 50, 147
innovation, 34, 78, 79, 111, 148
insecurity, 79
insight, 14
inspections, 44
inspectors, 49
instability, 113
institutions, 7, 34, 68, 111, 149, 166, 175
instruction, 2, 39
instruments, 42, 74, 176
insulin, 84
insurance, 13, 26, 42, 49, 57, 60, 87, 109, 167, 175
integration, 54, 86, 140, 165
intellectual property, 10, 48, 51, 75, 76, 77, 79, 86, 87, 153
intellectual property rights, 51, 79
intentions, 14, 109, 176
interest rates, 41, 65, 67, 141
interference, 57
intermediaries, 177
International Bank for Reconstruction and Development, 42, 93
International Chamber of Commerce, 51, 93
International Development Association (IDA), 42
international financial institutions, 14, 41, 42
international law, 55
International Monetary Fund, 93
international standards, 51, 67, 83, 86, 109, 149, 174, 176
international trade, 1, 6, 7, 35
internet, 25, 52, 54
intervention, 156
interview, 110, 118, 119
intra-regional trade, 61
inventions, 52, 76, 77, 78, 80, 175
investment incentive, 47
iron, 75, 100

J

jobs, 2, 3, 4, 5, 6, 10, 37, 50, 71, 137
joint ventures, 10, 13, 15, 31, 67, 74, 148, 163, 174
journalists, 171
judges, 116
judgment, 55
jurisdiction, 49, 57, 115, 172

L

labeling, 155
labor, 2, 3, 4, 5, 6, 33, 35, 36, 37, 45, 48, 49, 50, 68, 69, 70, 75, 94, 112, 113, 136, 147, 175
labor force, 36, 75
labor markets, 49
labour, 67, 92
lack of confidence, 176
land, 22, 39, 45, 46, 47, 49, 68, 101, 124, 136, 139, 140, 141, 145, 151, 159, 174, 175, 180, 181
land acquisition, 180
land use, 174

landscape, 85
land-use, 49, 175
language, 2, 39
lawyers, 168, 171
layoffs, 37, 50, 180
leadership, 7
legality, 79
legislation, 87, 136, 147, 148, 175, 180, 181
leisure, 20, 30, 31
lending, 41, 42, 60, 142, 176, 177
liberalization, 2, 6, 9, 12, 48, 62, 163
licenses, 10, 48, 60, 76, 77, 113, 138, 163, 178
line, 72
links, 49, 177
liquidity, 156, 176
literacy, 2, 4
literacy rates, 2
litigation, 51, 55
living standards, 34
loans, 5, 41, 42, 53, 109, 117, 177, 178
lobbying, 62
local government, 139, 148
logging, 151
logistics, 13, 30, 54
long distance, 54, 60

M

machinery, 26, 28, 44, 68, 110, 114, 130, 138, 168, 173, 179
magazines, 102, 169
maintenance, 38, 39, 42, 145, 149, 165, 166, 169
major cities, 20, 38, 52
management, 18, 39, 55, 62, 75, 82, 83, 86, 101, 154, 166, 168, 169, 177
manipulation, 176
manpower, 50
manufactured goods, 10
manufacturer, 21, 44, 84, 86, 169
market access, 58, 60, 116, 118
market capitalization, 176, 177
market share, 41, 66, 75, 79
market structure, 139
matrix, 96
measures, 58, 61, 77, 136, 173, 176
meat, 133, 144, 145
media, 62, 90, 102, 161
mediation, 56, 116
membership, 58
merchandise, 45
mergers, 13, 28, 81, 109, 118
metallurgy, 40
metals, 22, 110
middle class, 10, 34, 66
milk, 133, 134, 144
minimum wage, 50, 147
mining, 21, 35, 100, 110, 165, 166, 168, 178
minority, 72
mobile phone, 35
mobile telecommunication, 40
model, 65, 72, 75, 139, 140, 147
models, 71, 72
modernization, 154
money, 58, 78, 179
monopoly, 13
morale, 41
motion, 60, 110
motivation, 85
movement, 39, 62, 87, 124, 136, 137, 156, 172, 178
multinational companies, vii, 9, 48, 76, 78, 83, 85
multinational corporations, 11, 12, 80
multinational firms, 83
music, 52

N

nanotechnology, 53
narcotics, 47
nation, 58, 116, 130
National Institutes of Health, 98
national security, 48, 61
natural gas, 102
natural resources, 21, 42
negotiating, 61
negotiation, 106, 107, 108, 172
novelty, 78

O

objectives, 67, 137
obligation, 57, 77
OECD, 10, 53, 95, 108, 114, 116, 117
Official Development Assistance, 29
oil, 25, 32, 42, 44, 110, 112, 138, 146, 156
oils, 123, 133, 135, 137, 144
oilseed, 145
operator, 54, 60, 115
order, 44, 45, 49, 57, 75, 85, 110, 116, 131, 164, 175, 178
organic chemicals, 30
outsourcing, 4, 12, 17, 65, 70, 74, 89
Overseas Private Investment Corporation, 42, 57, 95, 172, 179
oversight, 45, 137

P

packaging, 155
palm oil, 145, 146
partnership, 30, 115
patents, 51, 52, 75, 76, 77, 78
peer group, vii, 1, 2, 3, 4, 6
per capita income, 34, 132
percentile, 134, 135
perceptions, 34
permit, 61, 77, 123, 148, 156, 159, 174, 177
personal computers, 31
pharmaceuticals, 10, 11, 21, 51, 52, 75, 77, 79, 84, 86, 175
piracy, 51, 90, 174
planning, 45, 48, 53, 54, 62, 71, 117, 150, 164
plants, 37, 53, 70, 71, 72, 73, 149
plasma, 53
plastics, 30
political parties, 180
politics, 41
pollution, 45, 173
polymer, 40, 70
poor, 35, 36, 37, 44, 45, 122, 123, 139, 149, 150
poor performance, 123
population, 2, 3, 11, 34, 35, 40, 44, 62, 66, 123, 132, 133
portfolio, 61, 79, 87, 109, 164, 165, 166, 168, 170
portfolio investment, 61, 109, 164, 165, 170
portfolio management, 168
portfolios, 176
ports, 4, 30, 37, 38, 45, 46, 166, 169
Portugal, 107
positive relation, 127
positive relationship, 127
poultry, 139, 144, 145
poverty, vii, 1, 33, 35, 122, 124, 132
poverty line, 35, 124
poverty reduction, 122, 132
power plants, 169, 174
precedent, 141
preference, 60
premiums, 155
pressure, 127, 139, 145, 159
prevention, 61
price instability, 127
prices, 3, 54, 122, 123, 124, 127, 128, 129, 136, 137, 143, 145, 155, 156, 159, 176
primary school, 4, 39
primary school enrollment, 4
private banks, 5, 165, 177
private firms, 1, 13, 39, 41, 42, 45, 154
private investment, viii, 39, 121, 122, 123, 124, 126, 127, 129, 131, 136, 139, 149, 150, 151, 153, 154, 156, 159
private sector, 1, 29, 37, 38, 39, 42, 100, 139, 152, 153, 155, 166, 172
private sector investment, 39
privatization, 164, 172
producers, 52, 53, 66, 74, 80, 112, 124, 129, 141, 145, 148
production costs, 145
production function, 86
productivity, 5, 50, 66, 122, 123, 127, 152, 159
productivity growth, 127, 152
profit, 50
profitability, 127, 148
profits, 39, 44, 48, 68, 110, 145, 148, 171, 173
program, viii, 12, 36, 38, 83, 163, 164, 172, 175
programming, 25
proliferation, 175
promote innovation, 52
property rights, 111
prosperity, 6
public expenditures, 126
public health, 77
public investment, 126, 127, 131, 151, 153, 156
public policy, 85
public sector, 45, 49, 60, 102, 112, 124, 141, 152, 168, 176, 177
pulse, 137
pumps, 74, 149, 151
purchasing power, 34

Q

quality improvement, 65
quality standards, 137
quotas, 58

R

radar, 89
radio, 100, 110
range, vii, 9, 20, 36, 41, 74, 82, 116, 131, 136, 139, 155, 180
raw materials, 145, 173, 181
real estate, 30, 44, 53, 110, 148, 164, 171, 174, 178
real terms, 123, 129, 141, 143, 153
real wage, 7
reason, 30, 43, 78, 85
recognition, 12, 56
recollection, 54
reconstruction, 100

recovery, 55, 149
recruiting, 4
redistribution, 36
refining, 102, 130, 168, 178
reforms, vii, viii, 1, 2, 41, 48, 111, 121, 122, 123, 124, 127, 129, 131, 136, 139, 140, 150
region, 20, 21, 30, 42, 48, 62, 66, 82, 110, 157
regional manufacturing, 115
regulation, 5, 10, 41, 48, 49, 100, 136, 147, 152, 160
regulators, 49, 74, 114, 175
regulatory framework, 148, 172
rehabilitation, 181
reinsurance, 60
reintroduction, 180
relationship, 12, 83, 86, 127
reliability, 54
relief, 51, 62
remittances, 171
repair, 70, 165
reputation, 66
resale, 53
research funding, 154
resentment, viii, 163
reserves, 168, 171, 177
resistance, 124
resolution, 49, 51, 55, 57, 77, 116, 172
resources, 43, 51, 52, 77, 78, 90, 149, 177
restaurants, 110
retail, 13, 21, 53, 54, 69, 71, 117, 123, 143, 144, 156, 159, 167, 169, 176
retirement, 37, 49, 50, 147, 180
returns, 122, 124, 153
revenue, 25, 80, 142, 144
rice, 123, 127, 137, 138, 151, 156
rings, 74
risk, 42, 57, 79, 122, 136, 137, 139, 141, 155, 156
risk factors, 156
risk management, 122, 156
rolling, 72, 169
royalty, 76, 114, 171
rubber, 30, 100, 168
rural areas, 21, 35, 36, 38
rural population, 38, 139

S

safety, 51, 67, 113
sales, 10, 26, 36, 38, 41, 51, 63, 65, 66, 71, 79, 80, 82, 117, 141, 143, 144, 145, 170, 171, 173, 176, 181
salinity, 151
satellite, 165
savings, 5, 49, 50, 111
savings rate, 111
scaling, 70
school, 37, 39
search, 25
secondary data, 123
securities, 49, 60, 175, 176
security, 50, 54, 75, 83, 86, 102, 136, 164, 170, 173
security services, 164
seed, 140, 164
seizure, 97, 98
semiconductor, 26, 31, 53, 115, 175
semiconductors, 31, 110
sensitivity, 136
separation, 147, 165
service provider, 79
service quality, 54
sewage, 45
shape, 131
shaping, 136
shares, 11, 12, 20, 22, 24, 28, 31, 32, 33, 48, 109, 129, 164, 171, 176, 178
sharing, 52, 168
shortage, 149, 155
signals, 52, 136
signs, 124
silver, 168
Singapore, 7, 13, 14, 18, 22, 23, 31, 62, 79, 81, 88, 91, 97, 108, 112, 115, 117, 182
skills, 3, 12, 40, 85
small firms, 2, 5, 80
socialism, 7
software, 2, 6, 12, 17, 18, 21, 25, 37, 40, 43, 52, 110, 167, 175, 178, 181
solar cells, 53
soybean, 146, 156
space, 44, 54
spectrum, 44, 178
speed, 38, 49
sports, 173
stability, 156
staffing, 153
standards, 65, 67, 79, 80, 86, 110, 148, 155, 175
state laws, 37
state-owned banks, 41, 165, 177
state-owned enterprises, 172
statistics, 14, 15, 22, 23, 24, 25, 91, 108, 109, 110, 119, 160
statutes, 83
steel, 21, 75, 92, 100
steel industry, 75
stock, 6, 13, 28, 30, 41, 137, 155, 164, 168, 169, 170, 171, 176, 177, 178
stock exchange, 13, 41, 170, 177

stock markets, 171, 176, 177
storage, 25, 46, 53, 123, 124, 125, 127, 136, 137, 139, 154, 155, 156, 167
strategies, 75, 164
strength, 13, 85, 111
students, 2, 39
subscribers, 54
subsidy, 127, 131, 154
subsistence, 3
Sudan, 108
sugar, 137, 138
Sun, 84, 109
supervision, 49
suppliers, 60, 65, 67, 70, 74, 79, 138
supply chain, 123, 137, 143, 148, 152, 156
support services, 56
Supreme Court, 115, 116
surplus, 111, 152
sustainability, 124
switching, 40
systemic risk, 176

T

takeover, 178
talent, 66
targets, 68, 75, 141
tariff, 2, 6, 43, 44, 45, 47, 68, 70, 136, 145, 149, 150, 180
tariff rates, 6, 44
tax deduction, 48
tax incentive, 10, 47, 144, 168
tax rates, 113, 143, 144, 173
tax system, 143
taxation, 11, 39, 62, 90, 116, 124, 130, 136, 143, 144, 156, 179
teacher instruction, 41
technical assistance, 42
technology transfer, 69, 171
telecommunications, 1, 10, 12, 13, 21, 23, 25, 28, 29, 31, 49, 53, 60, 110, 130, 173, 175, 177, 179
telecommunications services, 23
telephone, 23, 41, 60, 110
television, 52
tenants, 141
tenure, 139
terminals, 155
territory, 45, 56, 59, 110, 180
test data, 77
textiles, 30, 168
theft, 113, 149
threats, 79
threshold, 50, 115, 180
timber, 130
tobacco, 2, 47, 113, 166
tolls, 39
total factor productivity, 152
total revenue, 142
tourism, 10, 20, 30, 31, 60
toys, 2, 173
trade agreement, vii, 9, 61, 62, 63
trade liberalization, 37, 61, 62
trade policy, 58, 102, 121, 124
trademarks, 51, 52, 171, 175
trading, 4, 41, 43, 58, 97, 98, 102, 123, 130, 137, 138, 148, 155, 156, 159, 169, 170, 174, 176, 177
traffic, 30, 38, 39, 150
training, 34, 52, 70, 111, 165
traits, 11
transaction costs, 155, 176
transaction value, 14
transactions, 13, 14, 15, 16, 110, 139, 144, 171, 174, 176, 177, 181
transition, 2, 5, 59, 67, 76, 77
transition period, 59, 76, 77
transmission, 54, 60, 102, 149, 150, 169
transparency, 139, 173, 179
transport, 29, 30, 31, 38, 42, 100, 122, 123, 130, 148, 150, 151, 154, 156, 166, 170
transportation, 1, 4, 6, 10, 12, 21, 26, 28, 29, 31, 38, 42, 44, 45, 63, 70, 75
transportation infrastructure, 70, 75
treaties, 52, 56, 58, 62, 116, 174
trial, 55, 77, 82, 83
triggers, 175, 178
trust, 86
turnover, 33, 37, 177

U

uncertainty, 75, 80, 85, 156, 173
unemployment, 69
UNESCO, 174
uniform, 32, 164
unions, 175, 180
universities, 2, 37, 39, 41, 112, 152
urban areas, 36, 38, 133
urban population, 36
urban settlement, 173
urbanization, 123, 131, 133

V

value added tax, 144
variables, 155

VAT, 143, 144
vegetable oil, 133, 145
vegetables, 101, 133, 135, 144, 146, 148, 164
vehicles, 63, 64, 65, 66, 67, 68, 70, 71, 117, 118
venture capital, 72, 168, 170
venue, 56, 58
vertical integration, 145
village, 155
vision, 65, 67
voice, 102, 115, 170
voting, viii, 163, 164, 165, 178

W

wage level, 34, 50
wage rate, 11
wages, 10, 12, 33, 35, 49, 50, 111, 147, 180
wall painting, 36
war, 4
waste management, 42
water resources, 151, 159
water supplies, 149, 151
weapons, 47
wells, 151
wheat, 123, 127, 137, 138, 145, 151, 156
wholesale, 13, 26, 28, 54, 123, 148, 155, 159, 170
wind, 149
withdrawal, 79
women, 36, 147
workers, 2, 3, 4, 5, 6, 7, 12, 26, 35, 37, 39, 49, 50, 69, 111, 112, 147, 173, 180
working conditions, 49
working hours, 69
World Trade Organization, 58, 76, 98, 116, 145
writing, 83